hello,
COOKIE DOUGH

hello,
COOKIE DOUGH

110 DOUGHLICIOUS CONFECTIONS
to eat, bake & share

KRISTEN TOMLAN
Founder & CEO of

WITH MANDY NAGLICH
PHOTOGRAPHY BY EVAN SUNG

GRAND
CENTRAL
PUBLISHING
NEW YORK BOSTON

Copyright © 2019 by Kristen Tomlan.

Photography by Evan Sung.

Cover design by Laura Palese.

Print book interior design by Laura Palese.

Cover copyright © 2019 by Hachette Book Group, Inc.

Hachette Book Group supports the right to free expression and the value of copyright. The purpose of copyright is to encourage writers and artists to produce the creative works that enrich our culture.

The scanning, uploading, and distribution of this book without permission is a theft of the author's intellectual property. If you would like permission to use material from the book (other than for review purposes), please contact permissions@hbgusa.com. Thank you for your support of the author's rights.

Grand Central Publishing
Hachette Book Group
1290 Avenue of the Americas
New York, NY 10104

grandcentralpublishing.com
twitter.com/grandcentralpub

First Edition: October 2019

Grand Central Publishing is a division of Hachette Book Group, Inc. The Grand Central Publishing name and logo is a trademark of Hachette Book Group, Inc.

The publisher is not responsible for websites (or their content) that are not owned by the publisher.

The Hachette Speakers Bureau provides a wide range of authors for speaking events. To find out more, go to www.hachettespeakersbureau.com or call (866) 376-6591.

Names: Tomlan, Kristen, author.

Title: Hello, cookie dough / Kristen Tomlan, Founder and CEO of DŌ Cookie Dough Confections.

Description: First edition. | New York: Grand Central Publishing [2019] |

Includes index.

Identifiers: LCCN 2019009318|
ISBN 9781538748886 (hardcover) |
ISBN 9781538748862 (ebook)

Subjects: LCSH: Cookies. | LCGFT: Cookbooks.

Classification: LCC TX772 .T66 2019 |
DDC 641.86/54—dc23

LC record available at https://lccn.loc.gov/2019009318

ISBNs: 978-1-5387-4888-6 (hardcover);
978-1-5387-4886-2 (ebook)

Printed in the United States of America

LSC-W

10 9 8 7 6 5 4 3 2 1

To all the rule
breakers out there:
Follow your dreams.
If I can dough it,
so can you.

Contents

Confections

Celebrate

Badge Key

Think of these badges as your toolkit to help identify recipes with special features.

PLAN *Ahead*

These recipes may take a bit, but they're worth the wait!

GREAT MADE GF

An easy flour substitution for a gluten-free treat.

NATURALLY GF

Gluten-free-ers rejoice! No substitution needed.

SHOP *Special*

Inspired by the famous confections served at the DŌ flagship.

EASY TO MAKE *Vegan*

With the simple adjustments on pages 36–37, they're vegan!

SUPER *Quick*

Only have 30 minutes? Make one of these!

KRISTEN'S *Fav*

The recipes I make (and crave) again and again.

kids LOVE

Make these with (or for!) kids—they're a hit every time.

CUSTOMIZE *Me*

Use any cookie dough in this book to personalize these recipes.

hello,
COOKIE DOUGH

———

We've always known cookie dough as our frenemy. Something so tempting, but ultimately bad, even dangerous. All the happy memories of baking up delectable cookies are tinged with tiny moments of guilt. "I shouldn't have let my daughter lick the spoon," or "I'm feeling a little sick—is it because I couldn't resist the cookie dough?"

I used to have those guilty days too, and I hated them! So I started on a mission: to make cookie dough all about joy—the feeling of bliss when you get that little sugar rush after a few spoonfuls from the mixing bowl. As you'll see, the journey wasn't always easy, but with a goal so simple and sweet, I knew I could do it! And now...

I'm happy to tell you the time has come to meet a whole new side of cookie dough. To go from "No, no" to "HELLO!!!!!" No more sneaking around the mixing bowl—dive right in and say "Bonjour," "Howdy," "Hey, there" to your newest, sweetest friend in the kitchen. Pure, real cookie dough that you can eat AND bake.

This book will teach you not only *how* to make cookie dough safe to eat but also all of the best ways to enjoy it—from unbaked on the couch with craveable mix-ins to topping gorgeous cakes as the centerpiece of your next party.

So, without further ado, let me introduce you to my business partner, my lifelong crush, my dedicated BFF, Cookie Dough!

MY STORY

It might seem like an overnight sensation, but DŌ wasn't built in a day. I'm from the suburbs of St. Louis, Missouri, where I grew up in a rambunctious family of six. My mom, Karen, is the captain of the ship, the ultimate multitasker keeping it all together. She's very much the boss of the clan, and my dad, the World's Nicest & Most Loving Creature to Walk the Planet™ is very much along for the ride.

I'm the second of the four kids, or "number two piece of poo," as my siblings still like to call me. And how can you blame them? I'm not the first, the model child—my older sister, Lauren, gets that title. And I'm not the only boy, the prince of the family—that's my brother, Trey. And I'm not the baby of the family, the "best surprise ever"—talking about you, Maddie. I'm the typical second child—the conflict resolution queen, the most likely to get picked on (and also the most likely to be forgotten), the people pleaser, and the troublemaker of the bunch.

When I was young, our home was always buzzing with a million activities, with fights, and friends, and laughter; and mostly it was overflowing with lots and lots of love. I was an awkward kid (don't believe me, see photo 6), trying to get good grades, play on the soccer team, and maybe kiss a boy, but I didn't feel like I totally fit in anywhere. Well, anywhere other than my kitchen. There, in front of my mixing bowl, I was totally myself.

The kitchen was my escape from the world of homework and sibling rivalry, a place where I could experiment and be creative...and get all my mom's attention. I followed my mom's every move as she gracefully prepared everything from a quick casserole for a family dinner to an elaborate, multicourse meal when she was entertaining. She's a physical-therapist-turned-stay-at-home-mom-turned-cookbook-author-and-chef-turned-back-to-physical-therapist. A woman of many talents. She taught cooking classes all over St. Louis—from private kitchens to educational workshops. But her most eager student was waiting at home: me, Kristen—Kris for short.

I took everything she taught me and ran with it. I checked out every cookbook from the library. I signed myself up for summer school because it meant I could take cooking class. I tried to weasel my way into the adults-only cooking school at Dierbergs, my local grocery store. After wearing out multiple Easy-Bake Ovens, I left them in the dust for the grown-up version; I was a real baker.

Showing off my baking skills by sharing my creations with the people I loved was my favorite pastime. I whipped up nightly desserts, cakes for friends' birthdays, and cookies for absolutely no reason at all—they were my specialty. As a human Cookie Monster (swap the blue fur for bright blonde hair), I loved all cookies, but my favorites were homemade by me, so I could sneak some cookie dough straight from the bowl.

Cookie dough has always been my true love, and I have my dad to ~~blame~~ thank for that. Whenever I baked, I always made at least a double batch of dough: half to bake into chewy delicious cookies and the other half to save for my dad and me to chow down on, unbaked. He'd come home from work, get a whiff of fresh-baked cookies, and head straight to the fridge to find his secret stash, marked "DAD'S—DO NOT EAT"—an attempt to keep my siblings' dirty paws off it. It was our special ritual.

Baking was my thing, but it was just a sweet hobby. I never considered a career in the food industry. Instead, I harnessed all of my creative energy and went to design school. I chose to major in interior design at the world-renowned College of Design, Architecture, Art, and Planning (DAAP) at the University of Cincinnati.

The first inkling of what would grow to be DŌ came to me in January 2012. I had graduated college and was living in New York when a few girlfriends and I decided to take a trip to Philadelphia to visit my college roommate, Caroline. We ate our way through the city, including a stop in a local bakery. While deciding what to order, I spotted a freezer stocked with cookie dough. The purpose was to take the dough to go and make fresh, bakery-quality cookies at home...but I had a different idea.

I quietly turned to my friends and asked if they wanted to ditch the cookies and split this cookie dough with me. The answer was an enthusiastic "YES!" But, as much as I wanted to sit down in that adorable shop and dig in to the cookie dough with my friends, it wasn't exactly socially acceptable (yet!). We headed to the car with our forbidden treat, where we passed around the tub, pulling chunks of cookie dough out with our fingers until it was empty.

1. *Age four . . . and always wearing pink!* 2. *My fifth birthday party—a baking class!* 3. *Shooting a cooking show pilot with my mom.* 4. *My Easy-Bake Oven obsession was REAL.* 5. *The whole family during our summer vacation on Hilton Head Island.* 6. *First Day of fourth grade for me (on the left...yes, that's me. LOL!).*

1. *Chris and me :)* **2.** *Recipe-testing vegan options at my old office, Lippincott!* **3.** *Where it all began...my tiny 450-square-foot apartment.* **4.** *I was always surrounded by family when I was in the burn ICU with SJS/TENS at NewYork–Presbyterian Hospital.* **5.** *My wedding day: July 5, 2014.*

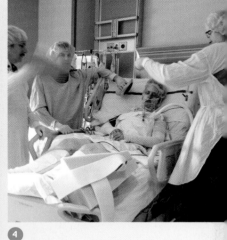

That's when the idea hit me: If we all loved cookie dough so much, why did we have to hide it? Had I ever met someone who didn't like cookie dough? Why wasn't there a place where you could sit and enjoy it? Why hadn't anyone made it totally safe to eat? Why couldn't you have cookie dough exactly as you craved it—in a bunch of flavors? With ice cream? Baked? Unbaked? Half-baked? Is that a thing? Oh my god...I could make it a thing.

I realized there was an entirely untapped market of cookie dough lovers in the world waiting for me to make something just for them! The girls and I left the trip with fun memories and lots of laughs, but I left with a little something extra: the idea for a business. I came home and all I could talk about was my concept for this crazy thing—and it already had a name: DŌ.

For a couple more years, my cookie dough idea stayed just that—an idea. I was consumed with life, with wedding planning, and with my busy career at Lippincott, a global brand strategy and design consultancy. I was creating innovative retail experiences for clients including BMW, Kiehl's, Delta, Walmart, Samsung, and Cracker Barrel. I enjoyed my job. It was challenging and inspiring, and I was working with some of the smartest, most talented people in the biz. Over the course of five years I honed my expertise in customer experience, retail design, marketing, branding, and more. Though I didn't know it at the time, I was refining the skills and building the confidence I needed to embark on my own business venture.

My friends and family sometimes asked me about how that "dough" idea was going. I'd have to answer, "Oh, I haven't done anything with that, yet." Eventually, I realized I was guilty of committing one of my biggest pet peeves—talking about doing something but not actually doing anything about it. I sure as hell wasn't going to be that person any longer. In January 2014, during a lull in the wedding planning process, I decided it was time for some action.

So we rolled up our sleeves. Chris (my then-fiancé, now-husband) and I dedicated all of our free time to working on the DŌ business plan. We didn't actually know how to go about opening a business, so we just started with what we knew. I began with baking and branding. Chris, who (very conveniently) has an architecture and business background, started guesstimating the numbers and putting them down on paper. For everything else, we asked our dear friend Google. Together, the three of us made a good team.

The most immediate challenge I faced was making cookie dough that was safe to eat. The easy answer was to remove the eggs to eliminate the risk of salmonella, but I was not interested in making something that was *like* cookie dough. No way. I would be serving 100 percent *real* cookie dough—the kind you could eat AND bake, the kind I'd been enjoying all these years.

I spent months researching, experimenting, taste-testing, and trying every egg substitute under the sun. Still, no egg-free egg-wannabes were as good as the real deal. Eventually, I found a safe-to-eat genuine real egg (more about that on pages 29–30). One problem down. But egg wasn't the only tricky ingredient. During my research, I discovered raw flour also can contain harmful bacteria (what?!?). So my quest for safe-to-eat flour began (more about that on page 31). After many months, I cracked the safe-to-eat-cookie-dough code, swapping risky family recipes with my new ready-to-eat creations.

By May 2014, Chris and I were almost done with the business plan. We decided to hold off on the final investment and money conversation until after our wedding and honeymoon. And just when you think you've got it all figured out, like they say, God laughs, right? Yup.

I got sick. In my typical all-or-nothing fashion, it wasn't just sick, but suddenly and very dramatically life-threateningly ill. I went from going a million miles a minute to being admitted to the ICU. An allergic reaction to an antibiotic I was prescribed developed into a rare and serious condition called Stevens-Johnson syndrome (SJS). Mine progressed to toxic epidermal necrolysis syndrome (TENS), a diagnosis with a terrifying 30 percent mortality rate. The

result was essentially chemical burns covering my body, occurring from the inside out. My skin, my largest organ, was literally falling off. And my seemingly perfect life began to fall apart with it.

My condition quickly deteriorated. I was placed in a medically induced coma because I could no longer breathe without the help of machines, and I was likely going to lose my eyesight. Doctors suggested that my parents and soon-to-be husband stop discussing wedding plans and start talking about funeral plans instead.

I spent three weeks in the Burn ICU at NewYork-Presbyterian Weill Cornell, one of the best burn trauma centers in the world. Thanks to a lot of prayers, support from my family and friends, an incredible medical team, and my fierce determination, I had a miraculous recovery.

I was released from the hospital four weeks before my wedding. At the age of twenty-six, I had to move back in with my parents in St. Louis to recover. Despite my near-death experience, Chris and I were married (mostly) as planned on July 5, 2014.

After the wedding, it was back to New York to visit my doctors and continue my recovery. All I wanted was the clearance to go back to my career and resume my normal life. When I was finally able to return to work full-time a couple months later, I found that my "normal" was not all I hoped it would be. After everything I'd been through, my day-to-day just didn't seem as fulfilling as I remembered. I felt like I was running through the motions but working without a purpose. I was haunted by this nagging question "What would make me happy?" So, I did what felt most natural. I dusted off my mixer.

Getting back in the kitchen was my own personal therapy, the only thing that blocked out the pain of my arduous recovery. It was the only time I was able to feel like my "old self" who I was attempting (and failing) to mourn. Baking made it all go away. I had discovered an answer to that nagging question and a "new me" with a mission.

I knew I had nothing to lose. I mean, c'mon, I'd almost died! Life is short and there's no time to waste when it comes to chasing after what

you want. And I wanted to pick up my business plan, right where I'd left off.

My illness brought me more clarity than I'd ever had before. Even more than that, it showed me that I was strong, brave, and I had enough fight in me to accomplish whatever I put my mind to.

So, I did it. Well, we did it. Chris and I.

In December of 2014, on the six-month anniversary of being released from the hospital, I opened the virtual doors to my dream come true, DŌ, Cookie Dough Confections, my gourmet, edible and bakeable cookie dough brand.

1. *Opening Day of the shop: January 25, 2017! I could not have been MORE excited (or nervous)!!!* **2.** *Our custom "it's dōlicious" step as you walk into the shop. It's one of my favorite details!*

THE DŌ STORY

I had always imagined DŌ as a shop—a physical retail *experience* where people could visit to enjoy cookie dough. But following my illness, after practical and thoughtful consideration, I chose to launch my brand online, running the business entirely out of my Brooklyn apartment. Looking back now, it was the best decision I could have made. I was still working as a full-time consultant—and when I say full-time, I mean a New Yorker's full-time. I worked late nights and long weekends to meet deadlines on top of being expected to travel at a moment's notice.

In the back of my mind, I knew that I would have to commit to just one career. But as excited as I was about this passion project (my side hustle, if you will), I wasn't sure I wanted to quit my day job. I was nervous to leave my comfortable bubble and the career I'd worked so hard to create to jump into the unknown. And besides, I felt like I owed it to my company to stick it out. After taking almost four months off when I was sick, I didn't want to leave them hanging. I ended up staying on for a few more months, working a flexible part-time schedule (thanks, Lippincott).

Though it was exhausting to work two jobs, launching online had perks: It gave me time to adjust as I transitioned industries; it gave me space to wrap my head around the challenges of running a business; and it allowed me to share my love of cookie dough with a national audience. Social media and articles from *Glamour* magazine and Refinery29 helped things take off quickly. My business almost immediately exceeded all of my expectations.

Chris and I would come home from work and stay up into the early (and then late) hours of the morning to keep up with the dozens of orders we received each day. Our not-so-spacious freezer wasn't cutting it, so two commercial deep freezers moved into our one-bedroom, 450-square-foot apartment. It came at the expense of pretty much every other belonging we owned—including all my beautiful, shiny new wedding gifts, which were temporarily relocated to my in-laws' in Ohio.

The fantastic response to DŌ took a toll, and not just on my apartment. I was exhausted. I always give 100 percent of my energy to the things I take on in life, so while working two jobs I was maxed out at an unbearable 200 percent. Every "free" moment was spent tackling website maintenance, customer service, order fulfillment, and production, which left no time for sleep. Work-life balance didn't exist because I was busting my ass just to have work-work balance, on top of the still-constant doctors' appointments and therapy sessions necessary to continue my recovery. In one month I traveled to Cape Town, South Africa, twice for my day job and came straight back to NYC for a series of eye surgeries attempting to reverse some of the damage done by SJS/TENS. When I returned home from the hospital, a giant stack of containers needing labels stared back at me and my glamorous new accessory: an eye patch. With no time for "downtime," it was clear that the life I was living was neither sustainable nor healthy.

Ultimately, I followed my heart. I quit my day job and dedicated myself full-time to DŌ.

My first move as a full-time DŌ Pro was moving the business out of my apartment. In April 2015, with my first hire, Brianna, DŌ opened a commercial kitchen space in Midtown Manhattan. Bri, fresh out of pastry school, was a gift from the almighty dessert gods. She's the only person I've ever met who loves baking and sugar more than I do, and she caught on to the brand's mission right away. She's a rock star, the ultimate Hardbody (thanks, Christina Tosi, for that enlightening term), and I'm convinced that she has cookie dough running through her veins. She is still my Executive Pastry Chef today.

The new commercial space was intended to help increase my capacity to fulfill online orders. A real kitchen meant that we could produce more dough and store more materials, so I could ship more packages around the country. What I didn't expect was the amount of walk-in traffic we would get now that we had a physical address.

Once word got out that we had a space in the city, fans skipped online ordering altogether and came in person to see what flavors they could get scooped fresh from our mixing bowls. The problem was, we didn't have anything for them to buy. Our production was ONLY for existing orders—we had no extra dough lying around. But who was I to leave a cookie dough craving unfilled?! I couldn't tell these people no. So, we increased our batch sizes and started keeping "extras" on hand to sell to walk-in

customers. The policy was simple: We had what we had, and when we were out, we were out. Pretty soon, we had "regulars" we knew by both name and flavor preference.

I was always impressed by those early customers' persistence. Since it was not meant to be customer facing, visiting our kitchen was not glamorous or easy. The space was hidden on the second story of a 2nd Avenue walk-up that looked like an apartment building, sandwiched between a smoke shop and a questionable psychic. When new customers visited for the first time, they always said the same thing: "I wasn't sure if I was in the right place! Walking up was pretty sketchy, but this is sooo cute," pointing to the polka-dot wallpaper and colorful mixers. Needless to say, it wasn't exactly the experience I had in my mind for my customers or for my brand. DŌ needed a traditional, all-cute, non-"sketchy" storefront, so I turned my attention to creating the cookie dough shop I'd always dreamed of.

The process started with location scouting. No two New York City neighborhoods are the same. What if I picked the wrong one and my business went under? Where do you even start in a city like New York? I explored my options, looking at storefronts in as many neighborhoods as possible. After an unsuccessful eight-month roller coaster, I nearly gave up. Then, a location in Greenwich Village took me by surprise.

The space wasn't what I thought I was looking for (in fact, it was double our budget and double the size). It was a run-down, rat-infested former sandwich shop. It needed a lot of work—as in ripping out every surface, wall, and floor. But it was on the ideal tree-lined two-way street, and through all the scum, I could see it had good bones. When I closed my eyes, I saw marble countertops, bright white subway tile, colorful walls, and a neon DŌ logo. Redoing the shop would be a challenge, but I'd never let a challenge

stop me before. I signed a lease for the space. Then the demo began.

Chris's construction management expertise, coupled with my background in design, meant the two of us were largely able to plan, demo, and act as our own general contractors for the remodel. The shop would capture the true spirit of the brand and be an experience in itself, complementary to the cookie dough served there. Instagram loves the food industry and the food industry loves Instagram, so I designed the most photo-friendly shop possible. The color scheme popped on camera, the wallpaper created natural backgrounds, and the special lightbulbs (5000 Kelvins) provided ideal picture-taking conditions.

I've always wanted DŌ to feel approachable, so I installed a huge window that divided the kitchen and the customers, allowing them to watch cookie dough being made. I decorated the space with hand-painted KitchenAid mixing bowls and my grandfather's

1. *The original kitchen on 2nd Avenue with a crew of awesome ladies!* 2. *Behind the counter at our scoop shop: "What can I get you?"* 3. *Our flagship shop in Greenwich Village, New York.* 4. *The day I died and went to heaven meeting Chrissy Teigen (ahhhhh!).*

custom-made whisk light fixtures, little details to make the shop feel like the home kitchen of your dreams.

On January 25, 2017, after lots of sweat, tears, late nights, and spending nearly every dollar we had, we opened our flagship shop—the first cookie dough scoop shop the world had ever seen. It was the beginning of the lines, the beginning of the press frenzy, and the beginning of the cookie dough craze.

Today, DŌ is known for specializing and innovating all things cookie dough. At the flagship shop, we serve up to two thousand pounds (A LITERAL TON) of cookie dough a day by the scoop, blended into milkshakes, stacked onto sundaes, baked and half-baked into a variety of confections, and more!

We bring our unique cookie dough sweetness to weddings, bachelorette parties, bar and bat mitzvahs, and corporate events through our catering and events business. Our ever-growing wholesale program allows us to reach fans outside of our neighborhood through brands and establishments that we love. And our exciting partnership program gives me the creative outlet to develop fresh and innovative cookie dough concepts that pop up all over the US. With every new order and every happy customer, DŌ gets sweeter and sweeter. And yes, it's extra sweet that some of the happy customers I've met are Bethenny Frankel, Ryan Seacrest, Usher, Karlie Kloss, Chrissy Teigen, and John Legend.

When I stop to think about where DŌ is today, I can hardly believe any of this. I still have days when I pinch myself to make sure I'm not dreaming. Like the time I saw myself in *People* magazine, the first time I heard "four-hour-long line," the day I demoed my cookie bomb (page 214) on *The Chew*, or the morning I woke up to watch Al Roker and crew eating DŌ for breakfast on the *TODAY Show*. All of this because of something as simple as cookie dough.

Now I'm ready to introduce it in a whole new way: Everyone, say HELLO to cookie dough!

This cookbook is the first time I'm sharing exactly how to make the recipes that took cookie dough from "No, no" to "Hello!" There aren't any impossible-to-find ingredients or techniques that only a pastry chef can master. We're starting this new relationship off simple and sweet with easy-to-follow recipes to fulfill any craving. When I introduce you to my lifelong friend, Miss Cookie Dough, don't forget it's a two-way street. Sure, I'll show you how it's done, but we're breaking new ground here and the making and baking are up to you! It's finally safe to eat, totally customizable, and ready to take center stage on your dessert table. Say it with me:

Hello, Cookie Dough!

Kristen Tomlan

Show me how you
say hello to cookie dough!

TAG ME
@kristentomlan

DON'T FORGET
#hellocookiedough

CHECK OUT
@cookiedonyc

1. *Teaching a baking class at our Cookie AcaDŌmy!* 2. *The infamous line (that we had to move across the street). At its longest it was 4.5 hours!* 3. *Holding my little sister, Maddie, and rocking the ultimate bowl cut (see Cookie Bowls, page 290).* 4. *Our old kitchen. The polka-dot wall has been a staple in our space since the very beginning!* 5. *DŌ on the go!* 6. *My family saving the day on opening weekend!* 7. *My "I DŌ"-themed belated bachelorette party on Hilton Head Island, South Carolina.*

8. *Opening the doors on day one to a line down the block!* **9.** *Always an excuse to eat cake—especially on my third birthday!* **10.** *Eating Stacy-Approved Peanut Butter Snickerdoodle with THE Stacy London!* **11.** *Snow day cookie dough: one of our most-liked Instagram photos to-date!*

Meet Cookie Dough:

ALL THE DOs -&-

Don'ts

COOKIE DOUGH 101

We've all heard it:

DO NOT EAT
RAW
COOKIE DOUGH

WARNING:
BAKE
BEFORE
CONSUMING

DO NOT
CONSUME
UNBAKED

STOP!
BAKE ME FIRST!

Maybe it came from your mom, your grandma, an article online, or even the side of a package. However it was worded and however it was delivered, the message was loud and clear: Raw cookie dough can make you sick.

Maybe that's what makes cookie dough sooo delicious? It's like the forbidden fruit you know you shouldn't have but just can't resist. Even though "everyone does it," there actually are a couple of common culprits in traditional cookie dough (aka not mine) that have been known to get people sick.

Lucky for you, I've never backed down from a challenge! Safe-to-eat cookie dough can be yours by adhering to the few simple steps that follow. I've done the work for you, and it's easier than you think. Finally, you can indulge in your favorite treat, homemade, in the comfort of your kitchen, and without the risk! Hello, Cookie Dough!

I hope you enjoy my not-so-secret and no-longer-forbidden obsession.

WARNING

STOP:
DO NOT SKIP THIS SECTION!

!

REMEMBER:
The processes described here are exact. At-home bakers need to follow them precisely and do so at their own risk.

ELIMINATE THE RISK

My love for cookie dough is strong, and I'm not going to let a few pesky ingredients get in the way of eating it straight from the mixing bowl. The good news is that it's so easy to whip your eggs and flour into safe, ready-to-eat shape at home! You'll need these tips for ALL of the recipes in the book, so don't skip this section.

From Egg to Egg-ceptional

OK, I get it. Eating raw eggs can make you sick. Mom, you were right, as usual. Eggs are the black sheep of the cookie dough world. In the US, they have a reputation for being dangerous salmonella carriers, and they're to blame for the general conception that raw cookie dough is a no-no. Truth is, only about one in twenty thousand eggs carries salmonella. While the likelihood of getting sick from a single egg is low, recipes often call for multiple eggs, and it takes only one bad egg to infect a whole batch (so please don't take your chances!!). But never fear, my dough lovers, pasteurization is the key. And it is easy to find pasteurized eggs in stores or to pasteurize eggs at home all by yourself!

What does **pasteurized** even mean, you ask? That's an egg-cellent question. Pasteurization is a heat process that kills any potentially harmful bacteria or pathogens that might be present in a raw ingredient. When pasteurizing eggs, they are slowly heated to a specific temperature high enough to kill the pesky contaminants (like salmonella), but not so high (or for so long) that they begin to cook. They are then cooled back down to a stable temperature to use in our recipes. Pasteurized eggs retain the same properties as regular eggs, but they are safe to eat raw or cooked.

OPTION 1
The supereasy and super-foolproof way. Get egg-cited!

News flash! You can buy pasteurized eggs in your local grocery store! Take a look in the dairy section (near the regular eggs) for packaged liquid egg whites. They often come in cardboard cartons with a resealable opening, and you can check the side panel of the package to ensure the liquid is **fully pasteurized**. Make sure to read the ingredients to confirm the only ingredient is 100 percent egg whites. A great brand to look for is AllWhites. Products like Egg Beaters, on the other hand, often add artificial coloring and sometimes even spices like onion powder and garlic, which would be great in scrambled eggs, but are NOT recommended in cookie dough. So double-check those labels.

What about the egg yolk? you might ask. You won't miss it—I promise! We made up for it with the other ingredients in our dough recipes. And what to do with the rest of the carton? Make yourself an egg white omelet, pour some in your smoothie for extra protein (you'll never taste it), or make more cookie dough!

OPTION 2
The egg-stra special at-home way.

To pasteurize your own eggs, all you need is a saucepan, water, eggs (in-shell and at room temperature), a timer, and an instant-read thermometer. Because this can be a bit of a process, I recommend doing a handful of eggs at a time to keep on hand for future uses. And, if you don't end up with any immediate cookie dough needs, you can still use those eggs for anything you would normally use eggs for! Just remember to mark the eggs you treat so you know which ones are safe to use in your cookie dough. Grab a Sharpie and mark a "P" on the shell...or a star, or a smiley face. ☺

Directions:

1 Find a saucepan that will fit the number of eggs you are treating in a single layer. Fill the saucepan with enough water to cover the eggs by about ½ inch, but don't put the eggs in yet! You'll need to estimate how much water it will take, so go ahead and overestimate to avoid having to add more water later.

2 Attach the thermometer to the side of the saucepan. The end of the thermometer should be right in the middle of the water—don't let it touch the bottom of the pan, or you'll get a false reading. Heat the water very

slowly by turning the burner on low. We're aiming for a strict 140°F. The water should not rise above 142°F, so once it gets close to temperature, you'll have to stick by the stovetop and adjust the heat as needed to ensure that you don't accidentally end up with hard-boiled eggs.

3 Once the water reaches 140°F, keep it there for 2 full minutes before very carefully placing the eggs in the water. Using a plastic ladle helps, because it holds an egg perfectly, keeps your hands dry, and will help avoid splashing hot water everywhere.

4 After adding the eggs, the water temperature will lower a bit. Adjust the heat to bring the temperature back up to 140°F and hold it there for exactly 5 minutes. Watch the heat and adjust as necessary to avoid going over 142°F. Egg whites begin cooking at 144°F, and we don't want that. After 5 minutes, remove the eggs using a ladle or slotted spoon, or gently pour the saucepan contents into a strainer. Rinse your pasteurized eggs with cold water. Voilà, you did it! You pasteurized your own eggs at home!

5 In addition to cookie dough, you can use the eggs to make homemade mayonnaise, hollandaise sauce, Caesar dressing, eggnog, or any recipe calling for raw egg.

6 If you use this method at home, feel free to use the whole egg, yolk and all, in your recipes. For every ¼ cup of pasteurized egg white, substitute 1 egg. Use this chart as a guide:

Egg White to Shell Egg Conversion

Pasteurized egg whites	=	Pasteurized shell eggs
¼ cup	=	1 whole egg
⅓ cup	=	1 whole egg + 1 egg yolk
½ cup	=	2 whole eggs

Flour Power

If kitchens had WANTED posters, raw eggs would be the culprit printed on them. We can easily identify that villain. But raw flour is the sneaky one, the bad guy that somehow dodged the cameras. He's making people sick without anyone noticing. Everyone automatically blames the crimes on eggs, when maybe it really was the flour making them ill all along.

The Centers for Disease Control refers to flour as a "field product," meaning it comes straight from the field to the consumer without undergoing a treatment process. If you think about it, the wheat is grown in large fields with birds flying overhead and critters scampering here and there. Unfortunately, there isn't a "kill step" during the milling process that gets rid of anything those creatures may have left behind (yuck!). As a result, flour is a known carrier of Shiga toxin–producing *E. coli. E. coli* definitely is not a bacteria you want to mess with, especially with young children, the elderly, pregnant women, or anyone with a weakened immune system.

Once the flour makes the journey from the field to your counter, it camps out there for months, giving any bacteria that may be present ample time to grow in your flour.

You typically aren't at risk when it comes to eating flour in traditional recipes, because you perform the "kill step" when you cook or bake it. BUT what if you're not cooking the flour? What if you're eating raw cookie dough? Licking the spatula? Sneaking some brownie or cake batter? It's not safe to do any of the above until the flour is heat-treated to eliminate potential bacteria. And, actually, it's not just flour that you should be heat-treating before consuming it raw. You should also heat-treat any grains

that are considered raw agricultural products, like oats, cake mix (it has flour in it), and even your gluten-free flour blend (page 36).

Fortunately, it's easy to heat-treat all-purpose (AP) flour and other grains at home. Phew! *E. coli* is killed at 160°F, so you'll want all of your flour to hit a temperature of 165°F to make certain it's safe to eat. You've got a few options...

OPTION 1
The Kristen method (aka make your life easy and just buy it online).

We sell our custom-blended heat-treated flour both online and in-store. So, if you're too busy, too impatient, or just don't want to deal...then buy it from us. I'll ship it right to your door. You're welcome.

OPTION 2
The piece-of-cake microwave method (minus the actual cake).

1. For this, you'll need a microwave-safe bowl, AP flour (or any grain), an instant-read thermometer, and a spatula. You can choose to either heat your entire bag of flour (why not?), or just treat what you need for a single recipe. If you are heating just enough for the recipe, add an extra cup in there to be sure you'll have enough!

2. Place the flour in the bowl and microwave on high for 30 seconds at a time, stirring between each interval. Stir well to make sure none of the ingredient burns (microwaves have those tricky hot spots). Use an instant-read thermometer to test the grain in several places to make sure it has reached 165°F throughout. If you get a lower reading in one area, just stir and heat for an additional 30 seconds until it's all ready!

OPTION 3
The easy, peasy oven method.

1. Preheat the oven to 300°F. Spread more flour than the recipe calls for onto a baking pan (like a 9"x13" or an 8"x8"—something with sides). Then follow a process similar to the microwave method by stirring the flour and checking the temp at 2-minute intervals. Make sure to check a few different spots in the pan to confirm you're safe.

2. If flour sticks to the bottom or sides of the pan, that's OK! Leave it there... you heated more than you need for the recipe, anyway. Don't scrape stuck-on flour into your measuring cup for dough or cookies, as it creates small clumps that will add an unpleasant texture. Remember, soft, fluffy flour = rich, creamy dough.

3. Flour needs to cool completely before use. It will take about 30 minutes (patience is TOUGH!). You can place the pan in the fridge and let it cool there if you're in a rush.

4. If your flour is really clumpy, your oven might be too hot or your microwave might have hot spots. Don't worry—you can break it up with your fingers, vigorously whisk it in a bowl, or sift the flour and discard chunks if necessary.

5. Voilà, heat-treated flour ready to use in any dough!

Now, on to the rest of the ingredients.

THE GOODS TO MAKE THE GOODS

Maybe you're Martha Stewart or maybe you're not even sure which room in the house is the kitchen. Either way, welcome! This section summarizes all the little things about ingredients that I always wondered, that I took for granted, that my mom has taught me, and that I learned over the many years of baking (and not baking). Happy making!

Butter

Everything is better with butter. We exclusively use **unsalted butter** at DŌ. (Vegans, don't you worry...we'll get to you on page 37.) Unsalted butter has a higher fat content and less moisture (water), which means more DŌlicious baked (and unbaked) goods!

I'm not a big fan of cooking with artificial ingredients, added trans fats, or imitation anything when I don't have to. So, forget about butter-flavored wanna-bes, put away the oil, leave shortening behind, and don't touch the margarine. Go for good old-fashioned butter—the fresher and better quality, the richer your cookie dough will be.

/////////// *Kristen's Tip* ///////////

These recipes have been tested with American-style, sweet cream butter, which is very easy to find in grocery stores.

//

Flour

In this book, "flour" is always **all-purpose (AP) flour**. For cookie dough that stays unbaked, I'll specifically call for **heat-treated all-purpose flour** (see the heat-treating methods on page 31). There are other instances when you can use regular AP flour in baked goods, but I'll let you know when that's the case.

In the shop, we use a completely customized "Queen of AP" flours that we blend ourselves (and you can buy in our shop!). Part of the blend is made from hard winter wheat (also known as bread flour), which is planted in the fall, survives the winter, and is harvested in the spring. The extended time between planting and harvesting allows the wheat to create more gluten-forming protein, a substance that builds structure and "stretchiness" in baked goods. The other part of my customized flour blend is soft flour. It's made of softer wheat with more carbohydrates and less protein. This softer variety is best used for cakes and delicate pastries. By blending the two, we get our own AP flour that is just perfect for our creamy cookie doughs and gooey-but-still-chewy cookies.

/////////// *Kristen's Tip* ///////////

I'm a big fan of King Arthur Unbleached All-Purpose, but other unbleached, bleached, or enriched flours will work as well, if that's what you have in your cabinet. (I can't say the same for whole wheat flours—I don't bake with them!)

//

Eggs

When the dough, frosting, or filling is going to remain unbaked in a recipe, I specify using a **pasteurized egg white**. (Go back to pages 29–30 to find out about purchasing or pasteurizing eggs at home.) The other egg we will use in this book is a **whole shell egg**. When I just say "whole egg," I mean a normal large egg.

/////////// *Kristen's Tip* ///////////

Don't skip the eggs! The safe-to-eat pasteurized eggs are super important to your dough recipes—they are the main binding agent, they allow us to bake the dough, and they add flavor!

//

Sugar

You'll see "sugar" printed on many (well, most!) of the pages in this book. When it just says "sugar" in the recipe, I'm talking **granulated white sugar**. It's a common ingredient on your grocery store shelves, so it may not seem all that glamorous, but granulated sugar is the super multitasker workhorse of cookie making. Sweetness! Structure! Texture! Aeration!

Substituting organic or coarser sugars will affect the texture of your cookie dough and, as a result, your baked cookies as well.

Brown Sugar

Brown sugar is granulated sugar with added molasses, which gives baked goods a deep caramel flavor and a moist, soft-baked texture. In this book, brown sugar always refers to **light brown sugar**. Dark brown sugar will still work; just expect a stronger molasses flavor and a slightly darker hue to your dough...still delicious! Remember to store your brown sugar in an airtight container, because it will harden if exposed to air.

Confectioners' Sugar

This is the same thing as **powdered sugar**. It's sugar that's been ground superfine, so it is perfect for whipping up into buttercreams and icings.

Leaveners

Every time you bake, you're creating a mini act of science. Tiny reactions happen every time a batch of cookies hits the oven. I'll spare you the high school science lesson—here's the CliffsNotes version: Cookies go from cold, dough-y balls to warm, gooey treats when heat reacts with liquid and leavener(s) in the dough to release steam and carbon dioxide. Stick with me, OK? We mostly use **baking soda**, a base that reacts with acidic ingredients (brown sugar, cocoa powder, lemon, etc.). **Baking powder** is a fancy "double-acting" leavener—it's a base and an acid in one. It first reacts with liquid and then again when it meets the heat. **Cream of tartar** (tartaric acid) is my favorite because it's a by-product of wine-making—the residue left at the bottom of the wine barrel, to be exact. Who knew wine's long-lost cousin was to thank for pillow-y soft cookies like my snickerdoodles (page 68)?! Since these leaveners create tiny dessert miracles, you can't substitute/omit/change them! End of science lesson.

//////// *Kristen's Tip* ////////

Leaveners lose potency over time. Check to make sure they are still active every six months. Active baking powder will bubble in water, and active baking soda will have a strong reaction with vinegar (think volcano science experiment stuff).

Cornstarch

My recipes call for **cornstarch** to make each cookie extra thick, soft, and chewy because it is both a leavener and a binding agent. It works like magic but can be temperamental. The superfine texture sticks to everything (hint: you don't want to spill it), including itself, which causes clumping in dough. Always thoroughly whisk cornstarch together with your other dry ingredients first!

Salt

Salt is used to bring out the natural flavors of whatever you're making. It activates your taste buds and is a necessary ingredient to give sweetness an extra pop! Different recipes call for different amounts, but every recipe has at least a pinch of salt in it. We use **fine sea salt** in the shop, and I do the same at home. It dissolves easily, is less refined, and has some mineral qualities, which I love.

Vanilla

You will find vanilla extract in almost all of my recipes! Good-quality vanilla is worth the splurge—it will go a long way, as you use only a small amount in each recipe. I use Nielsen-Massey Madagascar Bourbon Vanilla for home baking, which you can find at Williams Sonoma, specialty groceries, or craft stores. I recommend avoiding imitation vanillas—they just won't cut it here.

Some of my recipes call for a **whole vanilla bean**. Vanilla beans have a more potent and fresh vanilla flavor, plus, their seeds add tiny black specks that you expect from "French vanilla"–flavored ice cream. If you don't have a vanilla bean, you can substitute 2 teaspoons vanilla extract.

//////// *Kristen's Tip* ////////

Beanilla.com is an excellent website that ships high-quality vanilla beans and extracts nationwide.

Chocolate

We use only the highest quality at our shop—Callebaut or Valrhona. While I use **milk**, **white**, and **dark** in recipes, I myself am a **semisweet chocolate** girl. It's an optimal balance of chocolate flavor and sweetness. If you're a dark lover, or a classic milk kinda guy, *you dough you*; go ahead and make the substitution. It won't taste exactly like the creations in my shop, but it will taste how YOU want it, and that's what I'm all about!

Cocoa Powder

Natural? Dutched? Sweetened? Unsweetened? Isn't it all the same thing ground up? It kinda is, and it kinda isn't! I typically use **unsweetened, Dutch-process**, but you can use whatever you have in your pantry. There won't be a huge difference in these recipes.

Cinnamon

Cinnamon doesn't just add spice, it also makes chocolate taste more cocoa-y and rich and balances sugar. No need to go for the expensive stuff here; **ground cinnamon** from the baking section of your grocery store will work perfectly. Save your cash for your vanilla fund.

/////////// *Kristen's Tip* ///////////

As a rule of thumb for all spices, check the expiration date and replace every six to twelve months. Freshness = flavor.

Sprinkles

Sprinkles bring the party. If I'm about to enjoy some sweatpants time on the couch with a bowl of dough, all I have to do is throw a handful of sprinkles in the mix and now it's a ~party~ for one!

/////////// *Kristen's Tip* ///////////

My favorite sprinkles are from Sweetapolita.com (Seriously, go check out Rosie's sprinkles!), but I also show you how to make your own sprinkles on page 289 if you're feeling extra Pinterest-y.

Jimmies

These are oblong cylinders we know and love from our childhood ice cream parlors. Jimmies hold on to their color, so I love to dump them in cupcake batters, cookie doughs, and frostings. Too many jimmies can give treats a chalky flavor, so use just enough for a pop of color.

Nonpareils

These are tiny, round sprinkles. They are called "hundreds and thousands" in the UK, which I think is just the cutest name ever; so let's call them that. Use them to adorn the outside of layered cakes, coat truffles, or top candies. Be warned: These shouldn't be mixed into cookie dough—the colors bleed and you'll end up with gray cookie dough and crunchy white balls. Also, the wax on the outside of the spheres melts right off at high temperatures, so be careful when using them in the oven.

Sequins

Any non-tube or sphere-shaped sprinkle is considered a **sequin**. Cute heart sprinkles, tiny Christmas trees, itty-bitty flowers…you get the point. Pastry chefs often call them "quin sprinkles" or "quins," so use that lingo if you want to sound official! Sequins got their name because they were originally just those flat disk-style sprinkles. As cutting technology improved, tiny shaped sprinkles (like hearts and stars) emerged. These shaped sprinkles were made of the same material as all the old disk sprinkles, so the name stuck. Now quins are all over the place—I saw some shaped like dinosaurs the other day. Dinosaurs! Look how far sprinkle technology has come.

Sanding Sugar

Sometimes called **sugar sprinkles**, this is very coarse sugar dyed bright colors. If you're using it on cookies, top them before they go in the oven, and if you're sprinkling this bad boy on top of anything with icing, do so when the icing is fresh so the sanding sugar sticks! The only thing it *isn't* good for is mixing into dough or icing. The color can bleed and you'll be left with gray, grainy dough. No thanks!

Food Coloring

We use **gel food coloring** at the shop. It's better than liquid food coloring, because the dye is more concentrated, which means recipes require fewer drops. Less liquid makes for a thicker, more scoopable dough.

/////////// *Kristen's Tip* ///////////

AmeriColor brand (my personal fav) is easy to find and perfect for your most colorful creations. On Amazon it comes in a multipack of twelve different vibrant hues to give you all the colors of the rainbow, plus, it guarantees that you'll have food coloring for days!

Oats

When we use oats, we are using **quick-cooking oats**. Since we will (usually) be consuming the cookie dough unbaked, we like to pulse our oats in the blender or food processor to transform them into a coarse flour. This technique will give you good, hearty oat flavor, without the feeling that you're eating chunks of uncooked oats! If you're gluten-free, make sure you are getting the certified GF kind.

/////////// *Kristen's Tip* ///////////

*Keep in mind, oats are a grain and should be **heat-treated** just like flour (see page 31).*

Caramel Bits

I love love love caramel, and I was floored when customers seemed perplexed by the caramel bits on our topping bar at DŌ. I mean, yes, they kind of look like mini chickpeas, which would be a really gross addition to cookie dough. They are little chewy drops of heaven that melt into luxurious caramel in your mouth or in the oven! Now that I've told you about caramel bits, you'll notice them in the baking section of your local grocery store.

Caramel Sauce

We have the world's best **Homemade Salted Caramel Sauce** (recipe on page 70). You really should try it. If you're in a pinch, or if making your own caramel isn't in the cards, go for a high-quality jar of salted caramel sauce—NOT the liquid-y syrup that comes in a squirt bottle.

/////////// *Kristen's Tip* ///////////

My favorite store-bought caramel is Coop's Caramel, but you can look for the Williams Sonoma or Stonewall Kitchen brands as backup.

Peanut Butter

The recipes in this book were tested using **Skippy Creamy Peanut Butter**. I'm a Skippy girl at heart, but, unfortunately...I married a Jif man. The journey to peace in our household was a long one that started with a war of the peanut butters. Occasionally, we kept both in the pantry, but when I did the shopping you know I was coming home with only my Skippy. In the darkest days, I would go to the pantry mid-recipe to find the only peanut butter was Jif. Ugh! It was only after my husband, Chris, realized that no Skippy meant no peanut butter treats that he caved and we became a full-on Skippy house. Naturally, this is a full-on Skippy cookbook, but of course, feel free to use your favorite brand.

There are times we use **natural peanut butter** (don't worry, I'll tell you), but go for the no-stir kind. That extra oil on top can be a problem if it's not properly mixed.

Candies and Mix-Ins

You'll find only **brand-name candies** in cookie doughs at the shop (M&M's vs. chocolate candy drops / Reese's Peanut Butter Cups vs. chocolate-coated peanut butter cups). You get the point. Feel free to use whatever you like best and is most accessible for you.

Marshmallow

For mini marshmallows, we recommend Kraft Mini Marshmallows. If you need a vegan or kosher version, go for the type we use at the shop, Dandies, which can be found at Whole Foods. The Trader Joe's brand is great too.

When I say Marshmallow Fluff, I mean Marshmallow Fluff. You can't substitute marshmallows. Fluff all the way! Sorry!

Other Dairy

If a recipe calls for dairy (sour cream, cream cheese, etc.), go for the **full-fat version**. When it comes to milk and cream, we'll specify what type to use. If you plan on substituting a nondairy alternative, the results may vary.

Gluten-Free, Flavor-Full

I dreamed up DŌ as a place that anyone could come to fall in love (or back in love!) with cookie dough. I wanted to be sensitive to dietary restrictions and allergies, to tiny cravings and big indulgences. There are four gluten-free and two vegan flavors on the shop's permanent menu, and we're constantly experimenting with new recipes to add to the mix!

In truth, this book wouldn't be complete without a way to make (almost) every recipe gluten-free, because I went gluten-free in 2013! Hold up. Say what? A pastry chef and cookbook author who is gluten-free? Is that like the chef who can't be trusted because he/she is skinny?

No, no, it's not like that. Let me explain.

During my last years of college and my first years in New York, I was in and out of doctors' offices constantly.

I had a chronic sinus infection that lasted several years, a mild addiction to Excedrin Migraine to keep my everyday headaches somewhat manageable, eczema and acne that refused to clear up, and insomnia that drove me insane. I was told I had upper GI issues, no, lower GI...I had so many diagnoses and prescriptions, yet none of it seemed to help. Then a friend gave me *Wheat Belly* by William Davis, MD. The stories in that book had me saying, "Wait, that's me!!" I figured if this book was anywhere close to being true, I should at least try living the gluten-free life. Within two weeks, I was feeling so much better. All of these unrelated issues completely went away. I was able to get off all of the medication, and I haven't looked back since. (OK, maybe every time I can't eat from the bread basket at a restaurant, I look back, but other than that, NEVER!)

Lucky for YOU, I developed all of my original cookie dough recipes before I went gluten-free. And I have the best team ever that tests every recipe, gluten-full and gluten-free. Each new recipe has to pass both tests.

Today, store shelves are covered in gluten-free flour options: almond, rice, coconut, and whatever trendy flour is "of the moment." (I heard next it's going to be cricket, *ew*, but who knows!) For baking, no gluten-free flour on its own can substitute for all-purpose flour. To replace all of the structure and texture-creating elements of AP, you need to blend gluten-free flours.

Skip the extra step of blending your own by buying a gluten-free blend at your grocery store. Brands I like: Cup4Cup™ Multipurpose Flour, King Arthur Gluten-Free Measure for Measure Flour, and Namaste Perfect Flour Blend.

Because I'm gluten-free, I was set

on making the flour blend that would bake into the ideal cookie. That gooey center, chewy edges, dreamy softness I've been telling you about. We've done a lot of testing at the shop, and this is our favorite blend for fluffy dough and chewy cookies. See the recipe at right.

This blend is inspired by America's Test Kitchen's all-purpose gluten-free blend. The soy milk powder works as a dairy-free binder, so you can use this blend in vegan cookies too! You can use this flour in all of the recipes in this book, including the more complicated confections like homemade DŌnuts and our stunning layer cake.

If you don't have these ingredients at your local grocery store (look for Bob's Red Mill), you can order them all online very easily.

Vegans Love Cookie Dough Too!

I've professed my love for butter, and I've told you how important eggs are... but, vegans, don't you worry. I have tricks up my sleeve for you too. After a lot of testing, tweaking, and throwing-it-all-in-the-trash-ing, these flavors are perfect.

We have two vegan flavors that are always available in the shop, which you also can make at home—Stacy-Approved Peanut Butter Snickerdoodle (page 180) and Chocolate Chip with a Vegan Twist (page 174).

In order to make most cookie dough recipes vegan, both eggs and butter need replacing (and many of the chocolates and mix-ins too). For the egg substitute, I've had the most success mixing soy milk with cornstarch to re-create the liquid and binding properties of the egg. Simply swap out the pasteurized egg measurement for soy milk. (Example: ¼ cup pasteurized egg white = ¼ cup soy milk). For every ¼ cup of soy milk, add 2 tablespoons of cornstarch. I'm confident you can do the math.

Add the mixture at the same time, in the same way, that the recipe directs you to add eggs. While we use soy milk at the shop because we are sensitive to nut allergies, any dairy-free milk will work in this situation; almond, cashew, and oat are all great!

On to the butter replacing! I use a blend here too, vegan butter (I like Earth Balance Vegan Buttery Sticks, which can be found at most grocery or natural foods stores and come in regular or soy-free options) and coconut oil. For every stick of butter in the original recipe, substitute 5 tablespoons of vegan butter and 3 tablespoons of coconut oil. These ingredients should be room temperature, just as the recipe directs for butter. When mixing, add the vegan butter in first and cream until smooth before adding the coconut oil.

As with any substitution, results may vary. Butter and egg add essential characteristics to cookies, mainly binding and structure. These ingredients do a good job replacing those qualities, but your results will not be exactly identical to our original recipe.

BEYOND GLUTEN-FREE AND VEGAN

I've tried to accommodate a number of lifestyle and dietary choices in this book. There's no way I can cover the allergies and nutritional needs of every single person on the planet (I wish I could!), but I've tried my best. Feel free to modify the recipes with your favorite flours, fats, and mix-ins. I can't guarantee the success, but I love hearing about your kitchen experiments! Let me know what works for you.

//

DŌLICIOUS GLUTEN-FREE FLOUR BLEND

4⅓ cups plus 1 tablespoon white rice flour

1½ cups brown rice flour

1¼ cups potato starch

⅔ cup tapioca starch

3 tablespoons soy milk powder

// Combine all the ingredients in a large bowl, whisking after each addition. Once well combined, transfer to an airtight container. For best results, store in the refrigerator for up to 3 months. Remember, if you're using this for cookie dough and don't plan on baking it, make sure you heat-treat it according to the instructions on page 31.

ALL THE THINGS TO MAKE ALL THE THINGS

Just like opening a bottle of wine without a corkscrew can end in disaster, you can't make foolproof cookies without the right gear. You need to be equipped—and familiar—with all the things you'll need to make all the things in this book. Don't worry, you don't have to go spend a fortune buying all of Crate & Barrel, although wouldn't it be nice to have a fortune to go blow at Crate & Barrel?

Stand Mixer

I love a good arm workout, but when it comes to baking, I'm not exactly looking for exercise. Cookie dough is thick stuff, so you'll need a motor to do the mixing! I suggest using a stand mixer (like our colorful KitchenAid ones in the shop). Besides giving you freedom to work hands-free while mixing dough, stand mixers also get more air into confections for the fluffiest cookies and lightest buttercreams. If you don't have a stand mixer, a hand mixer will work just fine—you'll just need to beat your dough for slightly longer than the recipe specifies to fully incorporate the ingredients.

Measuring Tools

Measuring is an essential part of baking. Every ingredient has a specific purpose and needs to be used in the correct amount to make your treat heavenly soft or devilishly gooey. I'll let you in on some of my secrets on page 44.

Make sure you have measuring cups for dry ingredients (I like to use stainless steel), a glass liquid measuring cup or two, and a set of good measuring spoons!

//////// *Kristen's Tip* ////////

If you bake a lot, I highly recommend purchasing a digital kitchen scale. There are fewer dishes to wash, it speeds up the process, and ensures accuracy every single time!

Rubber Spatula

Getting every last bit of cookie dough out of a bowl is a must. Fingers work well, but I find you still can do a final scrape with a rubber spatula and get one last mouthful. *Ahhh*, sweet victory!

Rubber spatulas also are used to fold delicate ingredients into dough, spread chocolate or toffee, frost desserts, and stir sugar while it caramelizes. But bowl scraping...bowl scraping is where they really shine.

Finding the right rubber spatula can be tricky. So tricky that even after trying dozens of options, I couldn't find one to stock in the shop. So I had to make my very own spatula with a heat-resistant head and a tapered wooden handle. It's sturdy but light, and every time I get that one last scrape out of the bowl, it is with the total pleasure of using my own creation. We sell the spatula I designed in the shop and online.

Cookie Dough Confections
New York, New York

dō

Volume to Weight Conversions

Here's a quick chart for all the ingredients in our most-used recipe, **Signature Chocolate Chip** (page 60):

Ingredient	Volume Measure	Weight Conversion
All-purpose flour	1 cup	125 grams
Granulated sugar	1 cup	200 grams
Brown sugar	1 cup	220 grams
Pasteurized egg white	1 cup	400 grams
Butter	1 stick (8 tablespoons)	113 grams
Cornstarch	1 tablespoon	8 grams
Baking soda	1 tablespoon	15 grams
Sea salt	1 tablespoon	9 grams
Vanilla extract	1 tablespoon	13 grams
Chocolate chips	1 cup	170 grams

rimmed
baking sheet

cookie scoop

Cookie Scoops

You know that feeling when you pull a batch of cookies out of the oven and they are all perfect? Like, so perfect you can't pick out the best ones for the 'gram? If you do, you're probably using a cookie scoop. Portioning each cookie perfectly helps the whole batch cook evenly, which means you get the most beautiful versions of your cookies possible.

Kristen's Tip

For at-home baking I use an OXO #40 scoop (it's a 1½-tablespoon portion), and that's what these recipes were tested with. If you want your cookies to look exactly like ours at the shop, go for the blue-handled #16 NSF cookie scoop, which is 2¾ ounces.

Baking Sheets

I used to swear by rimless cookie sheets because it's easy to slide the cookies right off. However, since founding DŌ, I'm a fan of baking sheets with rims. Full sheets, half sheets, and quarter sheets—whatever fits! The rims make it so much easier to grab, rotate, and take the sheets out of the oven.

Kristen's Tip

Go for baking sheets that are lighter in color—darker baking sheets could leave you with overdone cookie bottoms. Yuck!

Cooling Rack

A wire rack will give you the ideal air circulation around your cookies, allowing them to cool evenly and, more important, quickly! If you don't have a wire rack, that's OK! You can let your cookies cool completely on the baking sheets—just know they will continue baking a bit from the residual heat of the pan.

Instant-Read Thermometer

You absolutely must have an instant-read thermometer if you plan on heat-treating your own flour or grains or pasteurizing your own eggs. Since you need a thermometer for that task, you might as well get a good one—there are many other important duties it will perform. It's important for making candy, checking the temperature of water baths, and heating frying oil. Oh, yes—we're frying donuts...check out page 201.

Oven Thermometer

If there is one thing I've learned, it's never trust an oven! You can get an oven thermometer for less than $10, and it will keep you from over- and underbaking everything you make, not just desserts!

Heavy-Bottomed Pan

Many recipes in this book (like my Homemade Salted Caramel Sauce on page 70) can be tricky without a pan that applies even heat. Look for pans with some weight to them to avoid scorching sauces and reductions.

Microwave

This magical machine performs all types of kitchen tasks quickly, efficiently, and, sometimes, without needing to dirty an extra bowl or pan. I use the microwave to melt butter and chocolate, soften cream cheese and ice cream, and even to boil water, because it takes forever on the stovetop. I'm such a big fan of the microwave that I use it to cook an entire mug cookie (page 233). Each microwave is slightly different, so use the heating times in this book as guidelines.

Cupcake Tins

Why do you need cupcake tins for a cookie dough book? I have four words for you: cookie dough IN cupcakes (page 210). Picking your tins is more important than you might think—to reduce the risk of overdone bottoms, look for tins that are lighter in color and aren't too heavy.

Offset Spatula

This kitchen tool is best known for making the task of frosting anything a hell of a lot easier. And it makes other things easier too! It can slide under a sheet of toffee for easy lifting, help lower the top tier of a cake, transfer cookies from baking sheet to cooling rack in a pinch, stir things, scrape things...do anything to things!

Piping Bag

Piping bags make decorating cookies and frosting cupcakes a breeze! Go for the disposable ones (the reusable ones are a pain to clean), and if you don't have a piping bag, a supersturdy ziplock bag will suffice!

Food Processor

Food processors will pulverize anything, make the ultimate animal cookie butter (page 103), grind caramel popcorn into flour (page 114), and chop nuts evenly!

Kristen's Tip

A food processor is one of my absolute favorite wedding gifts ever! I use it for all things sweet and savory. It's definitely worth the investment, plus, they go on sale often!

PICTURE-PERFECT
Parchment Paper

Getting baked bars or frozen treats out of a square pan is not only a pain in the ass, it's also ugly. Why put in the work on a dessert only to dent the topping or crumble the corners when removing it from the pan?! Crumble no more! With this lining method, confections will come out of the pan picture-perfect. The added bonus? No more stuck-on gunk to soak and scrub when you're cleaning up.

1 Lay the roll of parchment next to the longest side of the pan. Cut a piece that is 6 inches longer than the pan (you'll have 3 extra inches on each side).

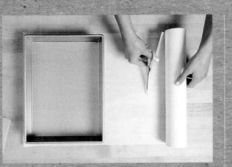

2 Repeat using the width of the pan, to cut another piece.

3 Fold the longer piece of parchment lengthwise to fit perfectly between the two walls of the pan.

4 Fold the ends of the parchment at 90-degree angles so the piece fits snugly in the bottom of the pan. The parchment should touch all four pan walls and none of the bottom of the pan should be visible.

5 Repeat the folding method with the other piece of parchment and lay it perpendicular on top of the first.

6 You will have four "tabs" of parchment sticking straight up. These make perfect handles for removing cakes, crusts, and other treats from square pans.

7 After baking, chilling, or freezing, just pull up on the exposed parchment tabs to remove your treat. Voilà! Perfection.

Parchment Paper

Parchment paper makes for easy cleanup, cookies that don't stick, and less of a chance of too-brown bottoms. You can purchase parchment paper in a roll, but I love the pre-cut sheets that fit right in my pans...no more struggling with the blade on the side of the box that NEVER works.

A great alternative is a silicone baking mat (Silpat is our go-to brand) because they are reusable and easy to clean. If you're an avid baker, I suggest investing in one.

Kristen's Tip

Step away from the foil! I know it works for your roasted vegetables (my favorite way to clean up after dinner; I feel you!), but foil conducts heat, and you want to keep that away from cookie bottoms. And waxed paper? Please don't put that in the oven... the wax will melt and you'll basically have a layer of crayon stuck to your cookie.

Baking Pans

My recipes call for both 8"x8" pans and 9"x13" pans. My favorite baking pans have corners that are exact 90-degree angles (OCD much?). When you want that bakery-style edge on your Ice Cream SanDŌ (page 239), or if you're doin' it for the 'gram and you want that perfect corner on your brownie, you've got to get a pan from Chicago Metallic or USA Pan.

Rolling Pin

You'll need a rolling pin if you plan to make cut-out cookies or our Play Dough (page 108). If you're in a pinch (and an adult), a bottle of wine will do!

Refrigerator and Freezer

One of the hardest parts about baking is the "wait until the thing I really want to eat is room temperature" step. I'm staring at the most delicious brownie I've ever seen, and I have to just...wait?! The freezer and refrigerator are your BFFs when it comes to easing this pain.

After cooling for 5 minutes on the counter in their pan, cookies, blondies, caramel sauce, and other treats can cool in the refrigerator or freezer—just don't forget about them or they will dry out. The one major exception to this rule is anything that is made with a true cake batter (like Molten Cookie Dough Cupcakes; page 210). Cakes have more air circulating through their delicate structure than a gooey brownie does. Cold air inside a freshly baked cake is a recipe for unwanted crumbles.

When chilling warm sauces or compotes in the freezer, stir them every few minutes so they chill evenly and you'll be good to go!

If I ask for a pan that you don't have in your collection, don't worry! These **pan substitutes** will work in a pinch, but keep in mind that the baking time may change slightly.

Baking Pan Conversions

I don't have a . . .	Use a . . .
8"x8" pan	9" round cake pan or 9"x5" loaf pan
9"x13" pan	two 9" round cake pans or three 8" round cake pans
10" Bundt or 9" tube pan	10" round cake pan, two 9"x5" loaf pans, or 7"x11" pan

DOUGH MAKING FUNDŌMENTALS

Almost every dough in this book is made with the same technique. It's the way I learned to make cookies and the method most at-home bakers will be familiar with: the method for American drop cookies. When I was having sweet dreams about DŌ, they were about the dough people are most nostalgic for—that back-of-the-chocolate-chip-bag classic flavor. Many of the steps in my recipes will look familiar, but each instruction has a purpose. With these tips, you'll be mixing up cookie dough like a DŌ Pro in no time!

PICTURE-PERFECT MEASUREMENTS

Precise measurement is the first step in every recipe. Unlike savory cooking, in which you can toss in a little of this and adjust with a little more of that, baking is a much more precise practice. A small thing like too much sugar in a cookie will cause it to go flat and crunchy when you wanted soft and chewy.

To avoid mishaps, I recommend *mise en place*-ing your recipe, which, in French, means "everything in its place." I like to measure out my ingredients before I mix a single thing. That way I'm never rushed when measuring, I never forget something, and I make sure I actually HAVE all the ingredients before I get three quarters of the way in and realize I need to run to the grocery store.

Flour and other powdery ingredients are the biggest problem children when it comes to mismeasuring. You'll need to fluff the flour to aerate it by using a spoon to scoop flour into a dry measuring cup. The scooping motion lets in enough air for an accurate measurement, without the work of sifting. (I'll let you know when you absolutely must sift.) Add spoonfuls to the measuring cup until it is heaping. Then use the back of a knife or offset spatula to level the flour.

Unlike flour, which you should never scoop with the measuring cup, **granulated sugar** is for the scooping. Dip your cup directly into sugar, then level the cup. Easy!

Brown sugar should be spooned into a measuring cup like flour and then lightly packed with the back of the spoon to make sure there are no air pockets or lumps.

My cookies call for many sticky (and tasty!) ingredients like **peanut butter, maple syrup, and honey**. These ingredients sit on the line between liquid and dry, causing a mini measuring dilemma. The trick here is to use a dry measuring cup and, before adding the sticky ingredient, spray the cup with nonstick cooking spray, like PAM.

For liquids like **milk, water, and egg whites,** use a glass liquid measuring cup, then get down at eye level to make sure your measurement is spot-on. You might remember this from high school science: the "meniscus" (aka the middle of the liquid's slight arch) should hit the measurement line. Be careful! The edges of the liquid will appear slightly higher, which can result in a mismeasurement.

THE BUTTER TEST

Bakers love butter. It's true. It's our golden goddess. Butter does best when it's soft and room temperature, so it's able to spread easily among ingredients during mixing. Plus, room-temperature butter retains more air during creaming, which is what makes those soft chewy cookies we're shooting for.

But how do you know butter is just the right temperature? Go ahead and poke it.

Put your finger on top of your stick of butter and lightly press down. It should feel slightly cool to the touch without being greasy, and your finger should leave an imprint without changing the shape of the stick. The best way to soften butter and other dairy is to leave it out on the counter for an hour before you start baking. If you're in a pinch, slowly bring it to room temperature in the microwave at 50% power, 10 seconds at a time.

WHIP IT REAL GOOD

"Cream the butter and sugar." It's like you see this step and think, "OK, stir the butter and sugar together." HOLD UP! Creaming is so much more than mixing together fat and sugar. During this step you are adding a third— superimportant—ingredient: air!

As your mixer beats the butter and sugar against the walls of the bowl, tiny pockets of air form between the sugar crystals and the butter. You should see a noticeable lightening in color of the contents of your mixing bowl. The more air you add, the lighter the color and the fluffier your dough becomes— same for your cookies…if you make it that far. Take the time to fluff up your recipe in this step—you won't regret it.

EXPERT ADDITIONS OF EGGS AND EXTRACTS

When egg whites and extracts are added to the mixer, it can cause some splashing, so take it *slowww*. Set your mixer to low while you're pouring the ingredients in to avoid an unnecessary egg facial.

Egg is the binder ingredient in these recipes—the ingredient that really marries the butter-sugar bond you're forming. You want to mix the cookie dough until it is light and fluffy like a cloud. You'll know you've got it when your mixture almost doubles in size and looks completely smooth and creamy.

FINALLY FLOUR

OK, I know you see it on sooo many recipes: "Mix just until combined," and you're like, "Uhhh…I think I know what that means?"

Don't worry, here I am to clarify! "Mix just until combined" means mix on low speed until you can't see the ingredient anymore. With flour, mix just until it's not all white and powdery. Every grain doesn't need to disappear—DŌn't overdo it!

When cookies are overmixed, they become gummy and tough from overproduction of gluten. Gluten is what gives baked goods like cookies their structure. But as you may guess, too much structure isn't a good thing. Your cookies will become tough hockey pucks, not the buttery, chewy, extra-soft cookies we're going for.

CAREFUL NOW

You've given so much tender lovin' care to your dough so far, but we have one more step—a last delicate move to make sure you don't ruin all of your hard work while stirring in the delicious mix-in flavors and ingredients. Remove the bowl of cookie dough from the mixer! Do not put your chips and mix-ins right in. This is where the arm workout comes in…you need to fold them in with love (and your spatula).

Grab a rubber spatula and carefully fold in any remaining ingredients. To do this while keeping the integrity of your fluffy dough, pour about half of the mix-ins on top of the dough.

Then get your spatula under the dough and scoop up and over the mix-ins. Basically, you fold the dough in half, which is where we get the term "folding." Dump the rest of your mix-ins on the freshly folded dough, and now place your spatula under the dough again so you can fold it in half the other way. Fold your dough like this three or four more times, alternating fold sides each time, and you're set!

If you're adding in a sauce like caramel or Nutella, add it last and resist the urge to fully mix. Two or three turns will do. You want to get a ribbon effect, with beautiful bands of the sauce contrasting with the cookie dough.

KEEP IT COOL

OK, I'm not here to call myself a health guru, but I'm so not into artificial crap in my desserts. That means: no preservatives and only the highest-quality ingredients we can get.

What this means for you is that your dough should stay cold. Natural ingredients will start to break down after several hours without refrigeration. For a full list of my storage tips, see My Go-To Baking & Storage DŌrections on page 48.

Plus, chilled or frozen dough is always good to keep on hand, ready to eat or be made into warm cookies at a moment's notice.

DOUGH BAKING FUNDŌMENTALS

OK, so you've measured out the ingredients and mixed your dough to perfection. Your job—if you're a cookie dough purist—is done. Go grab a spoon. If you happen to be a champion of self-control and plan on baking your cookie dough into full-on cookies, you've got a few more steps to go!

When you make textbook drop cookies, they'll have a chewy outside (I call this the cookie crust) and a soft,

gooey inside. I like my cookies thick, super soft, and even a little underbaked in the center. I love to break off pieces of the crust and finish by popping the middle into my mouth for a super-indulgent bite, but there's no wrong way to eat a cookie.

These are my baking tips to keep cookies coming out just right, time and time again!

CHILL OUT

For the absolute best cookie, chill the dough for 24 hours before baking. It may seem like a long wait, but the extra time in the refrigerator allows the sugar crystals to soak into the fat, it lets the butter and room temperature ingredients re-solidify, and the vanilla and brown sugar flavors have more time to really develop. Cold dough also ensures that the cookies spread slowly

in the oven, leaving you with thicker, chewier, perfect cookies.

If you can't bear to wait for a baked treat, then chill the dough in the freezer as long as you can stand to wait! Come on, you can make it an hour. You'll set yourself up for award-winning indulgences instead of just OK cookies.

BRING THE HEAT

When I ask you to preheat your oven, I'm not just asking you to turn it on to the correct temperature and toss your cookies in whenever you're ready. Please, let your oven signal that it's arrived at temperature and then wait **an additional 15 minutes** before you throw your cookies in there. Patience, people!

Cookies are in the oven for such a short amount of time, you really want them to hit that high heat as soon as they get inside. An under-temp oven equals thin, hard cookies, and you're not asking for that, are you?! When your oven signals that it is heated, that means it has JUST hit the right temperature, so the minute you open that door—boom!—hot air out, cold air in, and you'll have a flat, crunchy future.

TOP ME OFF!

People always say you eat with your eyes. I don't know about you, but that is SO true for me. That's why I like to make each DŌssert look like a masterpiece. My cookies are so Insta-worthy because I top them before I put them in the oven. No chocolate chips hiding in the bottom of the cookie, no sprinkle-less patches, just beautiful, even toppings.

After using a cookie scoop to portion your dough, press some of your desired toppings into the top of each scoop. Don't press hard enough to dent your cookie, just enough so the toppings stick.

KEEP YOUR COOL

What most people don't realize is that the cookie baking process doesn't end when you take them out of the oven. The final step is cooling. Just as heating dough in the oven is important, so is bringing those ingredients back to room temperature—it allows cookies to solidify their shape and texture, plus you won't burn your mouth on the hot chocolate. Cookies need 3 to 5 minutes to cool in order to hold their structure so they won't break when lifting them off the sheet.

Baking & Storage DŌrections

My cookie dough recipes are all formulated for easy baking! If you want to make any dough in this book into a delicious cookie, just follow these steps. Soft, gooey, warm cookies are only a few minutes away...

Baking

1 First, transfer your cookie dough to an airtight container or press a piece of plastic wrap onto the top of the cookie dough. Place in the refrigerator to chill for 24 hours. If you can't stand to wait, place in the freezer for at least 2 hours. (This step helps your cookies hold their shape and gives you that nice gooey cookie center, so don't skip it!)

2 Once the dough is chilled, preheat the oven to 350°F.

3 Line rimmed baking sheets with parchment paper or silicone baking mats. Use a cookie scoop to portion cold dough onto the baking sheets, leaving about 3 inches between scoops. For soft-baked, gooey cookies, bake for 9 to 11 minutes, until the edges are lightly golden and the centers are just set. Check halfway through baking to ensure your cookies are cooking evenly. Rotate the baking sheet if needed. For crispier cookies, keep them in the oven for an additional 2 to 3 minutes, until the edges are golden brown.

4 Remove from the oven and let cool on the baking sheets for 5 minutes. Enjoy warm or transfer to a wire rack to cool completely.

Kristen's Tip

Bake time will vary based on the size of your cookies, the strength of your oven, the mix-ins used in the recipes, the temperature of your dough, and a number of other factors. So, turn on your oven light and resist the urge to walk away. Don't abandon your cookies!

Storage

DOUGH IN THE REFRIGERATOR

When you're not eating cookie dough, keep it in the fridge. All dough recipes are good for **1 week** in the fridge unless otherwise noted in the recipe. To keep the very best flavor, press plastic wrap onto the top of the dough and store it in a container with an airtight lid.

DOUGH IN THE FREEZER

Use the same method as above for freezer storage. The doughs in this book can be stored in the freezer for up to **1 month**. To thaw, place in the refrigerator for 6 hours for best results. If you want to speed it up, leave it on the counter for about 1 hour. If you're in a real hurry, heat frozen dough in the microwave on 50% power in 10-second intervals. Check after each interval to ensure no mix-ins or toppings have melted.

PRE-SCOOPED DOUGH

Use your cookie scoop to portion your dough onto a baking sheet lined with parchment. Freeze for at least 30 minutes. Store frozen scoops stacked in an airtight container or a freezer-grade ziplock bag.

FRESH COOKIES

Cookies should be stored in an airtight container at room temperature. Yes, you have that cookie jar for a reason. Unless otherwise specified in the recipe, cookies are best enjoyed within **3 days**.

FROZEN COOKIES

If you want to hold on to your cookies for more than just a few days, freeze them! Cookies can be frozen for up to 3 months. To bring them back to life after freezing, pop them in a preheated 275°F oven and check them every 5 minutes. You also can let them thaw on the countertop—just make sure they are out of their container so they don't get soggy from condensation.

COOKIE TROUBLESHOOTING

Baking the perfect cookie can be TOUGH. I get it. Even after giving your dough major TLC, you can end up with a cookie fail. Let me guess—you followed the recipe, just as it said. You did your very best, but they're still not flawless. These are the troubleshooting lessons I've learned from baking thousands of batches of cookies at home and in the DŌ kitchen.

THEY ARE CAKEY!

Are your cookies less gooey and more gummy? They have too much egg, which throws off the cookie's balance because of all the extra moisture. Make sure your pasteurized egg whites are fully at room temperature and measured correctly before adding them.

THEY ARE TOUGH AND CRUMBLY!

Remember, spoon your flour into the measuring cup—if you don't, you'll end up with too much in your cup. Cookies that remind you of a biscuit have too much flour.

THEY ARE FLAT AS A PANCAKE!

Did you notice a bit of crunchy "brittle" on the edges? You used too much sugar. Make sure you are leveling your measuring cup as described on page 44 to avoid crispy cookies.

THEY ARE DARK ON THE BOTTOM!

Did you use a dark baking sheet? Try a lighter one and line it with parchment paper. Also, try moving your cookie rack so it isn't as close to the bottom of the oven.

THEY ARE PALE AND BARELY PUFFED!

Do your cookies look...blah? Check to see if your leaveners are expired or old. Be honest, did you forget them altogether? Sad cookies are a sign of no leavener.

THEY ARE PERFECT!

They're round and thick, fudgy in the center with melty chocolate throughout and just enough crunch on the edges. Way to GO! You're a DŌ Pro!

Still having trouble?

HELP! MY COOKIES ARE STILL FLAT!

- Chill your cookie dough! The colder the dough starts out, the thicker the cookies will end up.

- Never use hot baking sheets. Your cookie dough will start to spread the second it hits the pan.

- Heavy-handed on the butter? I know, it's good, but make sure your measurements are precise. Cookies with too much fat can't hold structure.

- Temp too low? If your oven *says* it's 350°F but it's lying and it's *actually* 300°F, your cookies will slllooowly spread instead of quickly bake.

- Put down the PAM! Use parchment paper or a silicone baking mat to keep your cookies from sticking. Cooking spray can be absorbed into cookies, causing them to loosen and spread.

I'M STILL GETTING GUMMY, TOUGH COOKIES!

- Did you overmix? You may have developed too much gluten with that extra mixing. Remember, "mix *just* until combined."

- Maybe they're overbaked? Check your oven temp and time. Pull cookies out when they are beautifully barely golden!

THEY DIDN'T BAKE EVENLY AT ALL!

- Rotate, rotate, rotate! Most home ovens bake unevenly. Try rotating the sheet 180 degrees halfway through the bake time. If you're baking two sheets at once, rotate their rack placement too—move the bottom to the top and vice versa.

- Use a cookie scoop. When cookies are different sizes, they have no chance at baking evenly. Come on, your hands can handle the workout!

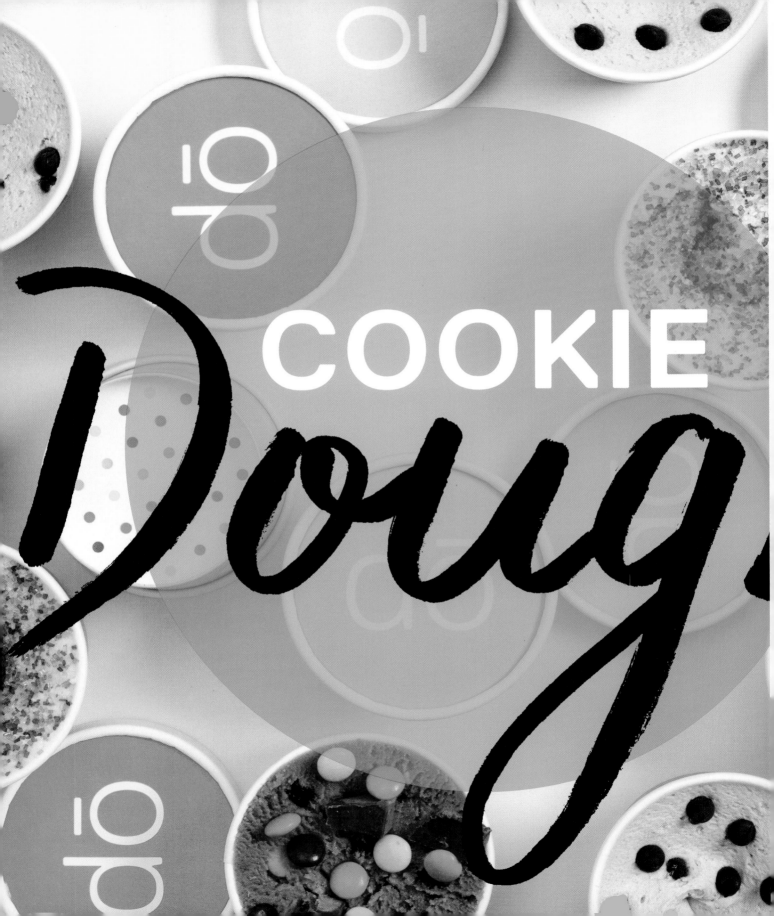

COOKIE

Dough

Classics and Signature Combos

The week before we opened, my husband, Chris, asked, "What are we going to do if no one comes? We aren't going to make payroll." I responded, "The real question is…what are we going to do when we run out of cookie dough?" //

The grand opening of DŌ was January 25, 2017, a cold winter day in NYC, but I was sweating in places I didn't know a person could sweat. I didn't have enough staff (I didn't know that yet), I really didn't have enough dough (which I definitely didn't know yet), and I had never thought about how to manage a line in my shop let alone down the block (again, not even on my radar). What I did have was unbridled enthusiasm, a heart full of hope, and sugar coursing through my veins.

A line of anxious customers stretched all the way down the street and as soon as I opened the door my little shop was packed to capacity. A constant stream of people excitedly ordered their big scoops of dough with even bigger smiles, just as I'd hoped they would. The most amazing part was the nostalgia that filled the shop, the cookie dough–tinged memories customers shared of their moms and grandmas as they waited in line.

By 8 p.m., we'd sold out of everything, and I hadn't had a minute to take a breath. Even with my staff furiously mixing away in the kitchen, we couldn't keep up, and we had to close early. But we didn't go home; we stayed up all night mixing, baking, and cleaning to get ready for day two.

Luckily my family was scheduled to visit to celebrate opening weekend with me. I called to let them know they should cancel any plans. This would be a "working celebration."

As soon as they arrived, they jumped right in. My dad, my brother, Trey, and sister Maddie were on dough-scooping duty. My sister Lauren and my mom were in the kitchen. My poor brother-in-law, James, washed dishes for twelve hours straight, and Chris, my saint of a husband, was out in the cold attempting to manage the FOUR(!!!)-hour line. Cookie dough was disappearing so quickly that we served it right out of the mixing bowl. We powered through, no time for breaks.

Halfway into day four, we didn't run out of just cookie dough, we ran out of everything. Every last bag of sugar and chocolate chips had been used up. I was "couldn't-possibly-make-one-more-scoop" cleaned out. I had no choice but to close for two whole days and wait for ingredients to arrive.

I needed more—more staff, more ingredients, more napkins, more mixers, more refrigerators, more everything! I doubled all my orders, and then I doubled them again. If people seemed qualified and were available to start immediately, I hired them on the spot. It took two months and a contract with a production facility in the Bronx before I got the hang of things. Ah, the good old days. ///

/// Our signature combinations are family recipes transformed into the flavors that are the core of DŌ. They're the favorite scoops at the shop, and I hope they become your household favorites too.

THE EIGHT CLASSIC BASES

When I was first getting DŌ up and running, I had so many flavor ideas. I wanted to re-create every great cookie I'd ever eaten, every childhood memory, and every bake sale. Soon I had so many recipes floating around that it was hard to keep them straight, and even harder to have a productive day in the kitchen making them. I decided to get organized. Narrowing down my favorite types of cookie dough was hard, but I ended up with six bases that cover all my favorite flavors and textures. The secret is out—these are the recipes we sell daily in our shops and ship across the country. I'll show you the trick to transforming these six bases into our most popular combos by mixing, swirling, and adding more flavors!

Signature

This is the base that tastes just like those chocolate cookies you made growing up. Plenty of brown sugar gives this base a depth of flavor that is warm and cozy. It's what most people expect when they dream about cookie dough!

Brownie Batter

Of course I have a base for chocolate lovers! Instead of using only cocoa powder like most chocolate cookies do, I use real melted chocolate in this base to make it extra rich and luxurious.

Sugar Cookie

Sugar cookie dough is made with 100 percent white sugar, which gives it a light texture and a simple, sweet flavor. Because it's a little more basic than the other bases, it's the ideal canvas for indulgent mix-ins like Nutella or pieces of pecan pie (page 166).

Peanut Butter

Smooth, creamy peanut butter used in this base gives the dough a silky consistency. The peanut butter also helps this dough bake into decadent cookies with moist centers.

Oatmeal

We lightly chop the oats in this base, giving them an uneven look in the dough and a rustic texture. The hint of cinnamon helps enhance the flavors of the mix-ins like carrots (see Kick Ass Carrot Cake on page 159) and even chocolate!

Cake Batter

Real cake mix gives this base a flavor reminiscent of those cupcakes you used to take to school on your birthday. That artificial-but-in-the-best-way flavor is now captured in cookie dough form.

KEEP READING FOR ALL OF OUR SIGNATURE COMBOS!

58 \ THE EIGHT
CLASSIC BASES

\ MAKES
32 scoops

\ TIME 'TIL DOUGH
15 minutes

\ TIME 'TIL COOKIES
2 hours 30 minutes

Signature

It's official; I'm a full-fledged adult (sad, I know). As much as I miss being a kid with no responsibilities or bills to pay, being an adult has perks. Like making my own decisions—eating cookies for breakfast, covering everything I eat in rainbow sprinkles, and mixing whatever I'm craving into cookie dough. Which is how some of my most popular flavors came to be! You can't go wrong mixing your favorite things into this base, or hell, forget the mix-ins altogether. Signature in its pure, unadulterated birthday suit (aka CommanDŌ) is pretty freaking perfect.

2¼ cups heat-treated all-purpose flour (instructions on page 31)

2¼ teaspoons cornstarch

1 teaspoon baking soda

¾ teaspoon salt

1½ sticks (12 tablespoons) unsalted butter, at room temperature

¼ cup granulated sugar

1 cup brown sugar

⅓ cup pasteurized egg whites, at room temperature

1 tablespoon vanilla extract

// In a medium bowl, whisk together the heat-treated flour, cornstarch, baking soda, and salt. Set aside.

// In the bowl of a stand mixer fitted with the paddle attachment, beat the butter on medium speed until smooth and creamy, about 2 minutes. Add the granulated and brown sugars and mix on medium until light and fluffy; about 4 minutes will do the trick. Use a rubber spatula to scrape the bowl. Add the egg whites and vanilla and mix until fully incorporated, about 2 minutes.

// Add half of the flour mixture and mix on low speed just until the powdery texture of the flour disappears, about 15 seconds. Immediately add the rest of the flour mixture and mix until combined. Scrape the bowl and mix a final 15 seconds.

// Remove the bowl from the mixer and steal a lick right from the bowl. To make our Signature Combos, use a rubber spatula to gently fold in the "fold" ingredients first. Then, if it calls for it, drop "swirl" mix-ins in tablespoon-size scoops in four different locations in the bowl. Use a rubber spatula to gently swirl until you see thick ribbons of that mix-in. Last, sprinkle on "top" mix-ins and you're done!

// Look at you—already a cookie dough pro! Bravo!

If you happen to have some dough left over, see My Go-To Baking & Storage DŌrections on page 48.

Signature Combos:

1 CONFETTI

A party in a bowl! Use your favorite colorful sprinkles.

FOLD:

½ cup rainbow sprinkles

½ cup semisweet chocolate chips

½ cup white chocolate chips

2 GIMME S'MORE

Classic campfire flavors will have you saying "Gimme s'more!"

FOLD:

4 graham crackers, roughly chopped

⅓ cup toasted mini marshmallows

2 (1.55-ounce) bars milk chocolate, roughly chopped (I use Hershey's)

3 LATE-NIGHT MUNCHIE MADNESS

Crunchy, salty, chocolate-y, made for sneaking out of the fridge.

FOLD:

Chocolate-Covered Potato Chips (instructions follow)

½ cup M&M's

SWIRL:

½ cup Marshmallow Fluff (toasting optional)

Chocolate-Covered Potato Chips

1 cup semisweet chocolate chips

1 tablespoon coconut oil

10 to 20 potato chips

// In a small microwave-safe bowl, heat the semisweet chips with the coconut oil in the microwave on 50% power in 30-second increments. Stir well between each increment. Repeat just until melted. Let the chocolate cool slightly, then dip the chips into the chocolate one by one and lay on waxed paper to cool.

// Measure 1 cup of the cooled chocolate-covered potato chips. Press the chips into the measuring cup. It's OK if they break. Save the rest of the chips for munching on later.

Kristen's
TIP

The easiest way to toast marshmallows is to use a hand torch or broiler. If you don't have either of those, dig out the random kebab sticks you have hanging out in the back of your drawer and pretend you're by the fire as you roast marshmallows over your gas burner. To toast Marshmallow Fluff, you definitely need a hand torch.

Signature Chocolate Chip

True love. It happened to me at a very young age. I certainly was one of the lucky ones—no dating apps or awkward first dates. Some people never experience true love, or it may take them their entire lives to find it. I was young—actually, just four or five years old when I first fell hard. And, of all places, I found love in my parents' kitchen. My significant other? Chocolate chip cookie dough. Forget first crushes, high school sweethearts, and college flings—chocolate chip cookie dough and I are actual forever soul mates. We're truly, madly, deeply in love.

No question about it—this recipe is the OG. The best-seller. The ultimate nostalgic dessert. The one you and I crave most when it comes to cookie dough. Now it's your turn to fall head over heels.

2¼ cups heat-treated all-purpose flour (instructions on page 31)

2¼ teaspoons cornstarch

1 teaspoon baking soda

¾ teaspoon salt

1½ sticks (12 tablespoons) unsalted butter, at room temperature

¼ cup granulated sugar

1 cup brown sugar

⅓ cup pasteurized egg whites, at room temperature

1 tablespoon vanilla extract

1 cup semisweet chocolate chips

// In a medium bowl, whisk together the heat-treated flour, cornstarch, baking soda, and salt. Set aside.

// In the bowl of a stand mixer fitted with the paddle attachment, beat the butter on medium speed until smooth and creamy, about 2 minutes. Add the granulated and brown sugars and mix on medium until light and fluffy; about 4 minutes will do the trick. Use a rubber spatula to scrape the bowl. Add the egg whites and vanilla and mix until fully incorporated, about 2 minutes.

// Add half of the flour mixture and mix on low just until the powdery texture of the flour disappears, about 15 seconds. Immediately add the rest of the flour mixture and mix until combined. Scrape the bowl and mix a final 15 seconds.

// Remove the bowl from the mixer and use a rubber spatula to fold in the chocolate chips.

// Ready to fall in love? Dig in!

If you have more willpower than I do and find yourself with extra, see My Go-To Baking & Storage D̄Orections on page 48.

Signature Chocolate Chip Batch Conversions

ingredient	half batch	single batch	double batch
heat-treated all-purpose flour (instructions on page 31)	1 cup + 2 tablespoons	2¼ cups	4½ cups
cornstarch	1 teaspoon	2¼ teaspoons	1 tablespoon + 1 teaspoon
baking soda	½ teaspoon	1 teaspoon	2 teaspoons
salt	½ teaspoon	¾ teaspoon	1½ teaspoons
unsalted butter, at room temperature	¾ stick (6 tablespoons)	1½ sticks (12 tablespoons)	3 sticks (24 tablespoons)
granulated sugar	2 tablespoons	¼ cup	½ cup
brown sugar	½ cup	1 cup	2 cups
pasteurized egg whites, at room temperature	2½ tablespoons	⅓ cup	⅔ cup
vanilla extract	1½ teaspoons	1 tablespoon	2 tablespoons
semisweet chocolate chips	½ cup	1 cup	2 cups

Brownie Batter

My love for unbaked sweets doesn't stop at cookie dough. I know, I know, I feel like I'm cheating (sorry, cookie dough). But there is just something about chocolate-y, smooth brownie batter that I can't resist.

When I was in high school in St. Louis, babysitting was one of my many jobs. There was this family that lived up the street with five kids (ages two through eleven), a dog, and a bird. Every single time I went over there, it was absolute madness—in the best way possible! One of my go-to tricks to pass the time, and to get the kids to stop fighting for a few seconds, was to bake with them. I always made two boxes of brownies—one to eat (I left out the egg—no one knew back then about the flour risk) and one to bake, so I had something to show off when the parents came home. I divvied up the unbaked batter into six bowls, and we would dive right in, spoonful after spoonful.

2 cups semisweet chocolate chips (divided)

¾ stick (6 tablespoons) unsalted butter, at room temperature

1 cup plus 2 tablespoons heat-treated all-purpose flour (instructions on page 31)

¼ cup cocoa powder

1½ teaspoons cornstarch

1 teaspoon baking powder

½ teaspoon salt

¼ cup granulated sugar

1 cup brown sugar

½ cup pasteurized egg whites, at room temperature

2 teaspoons vanilla extract

// In a small microwave-safe bowl, heat 1 cup of the chocolate chips with the butter in the microwave on 50% power in 30-second increments. Stir well between each increment. Repeat just until the chocolate is melted. Set aside.

// In a medium bowl, whisk together the heat-treated flour, cocoa powder, cornstarch, baking powder, and salt until well combined. Set aside.

// Pour the melted chocolate mixture into the bowl of a stand mixer fitted with the paddle attachment. Add the granulated and brown sugars and mix on medium until well combined, about 2 minutes. Use a rubber spatula to scrape the bowl. Add the egg whites and vanilla and mix just until well incorporated, about 2 minutes. The mixture will be very runny.

// Add the flour mixture and mix on low just until the powdery texture of the flour disappears, about 30 seconds. Scrape the bowl and mix a final 15 seconds.

// Remove the bowl from the mixer and use a rubber spatula to fold in the remaining 1 cup chocolate chips.

// Enjoy as is, or try one of our Signature Combos. Use a rubber spatula to gently fold in the "fold" ingredients first. Next, sprinkle on "top" mix-ins and you're done!

// Batter's up! Dig in now for that classic brownie batter experience.

// For a cookie dough–like consistency, press plastic wrap onto the batter and chill the whole bowl in the refrigerator for at least 15 minutes before you get after it with a spoon!

If you're planning on finishing this later, see My Go-To Baking & Storage DŌrections on page 48.

Signature Combos:

① CHOCOLATE DREAM

Brownie batter meets milk's favorite cookie.

FOLD:

¼ cup semisweet chocolate chips

8 roughly chopped Oreos

② CARAMEL CHOCOLATE PRETZEL

Bringing a little salty crunch to this chocolate party!

FOLD:

⅓ cup pretzels, roughly chopped

⅓ cup caramel bits

⅓ cup chocolate chips

TOP:

Flaky sea salt, like Maldon

1

2

Kristen's TIP

Because the consistency of this dough is more like brownie batter, mix it extra carefully to keep your countertops— and apron—clean.

66 \ THE EIGHT
CLASSIC BASES

\ MAKES
32 scoops

\ TIME 'TIL DOUGH
35 minutes

\ TIME 'TIL COOKIES
2 hours 55 minutes

Brookie Dough

I can categorize my life into two time periods: BB (Before Brookie) and AB (After Brookie). BB was a good time, don't get me wrong, but AB was like upgrading my flip phone to an iPhone or trying Nutella for the first time. I never, ever want to go back to BB.

And DŌ fans agree; they're the reason this flavor is still on our shop menu. We introduced it as a seasonal flavor inspired by our Brookie Bar (see page 207), because we wanted to mix the best of both worlds—a **BRO**wnie and a co**OKIE**. The first day we had this dough on our menu, we sold almost 500 pounds of it and we could *barely* keep up with the demand! It quickly became our second-best-selling dough. When its time as a seasonal flavor was up, we ran a poll on social media to see if we should keep it around. In a landslide vote, Brookie won a spot on the regular menu. Do me a favor, after you have your first bite of this one, DM me (@kristentomlan)—I want to hear about your life AB. I know it will never be the same.

½ **batch** Brownie Batter dough (page 64)

½ **batch** Signature Chocolate Chip dough (page 60)

// Make the Brownie Batter dough. Chill in the refrigerator for about 15 minutes, until it no longer runs off the back of a spoon.

// Meanwhile, make the Signature Chocolate Chip dough. Set aside.

// In a large bowl, add half of the Brownie Batter dough and half of the Signature Chocolate Chip dough. Use a rubber spatula to gently mix together. Continue to stir until the doughs combine but swirls of the two separate doughs are still visible.

// Add the rest of the Signature Chocolate Chip dough. Stir with the rubber spatula just to incorporate. Finally, add the rest of the Brownie Batter and give the dough just a few stirs.

// This ever-popular, best of both worlds dough is ready to eat. Hello, AB.

If you didn't eat it all in one sitting, see My Go-To Baking & Storage DŌrections on page 48.

/////////// *Kristen's Tip* ///////////

This flavor is a huge hit because of the distinct swirls of Brownie Batter and Signature Chocolate Chip dough. Less is more when it comes to mixing the two— and hey, your stirring arm will thank you!

//

Sugar Cookie

I'd found it: The dream location for my flagship shop. It was a complete mess, a real fixer-upper in Greenwich Village, but I knew it was the one.

We enthusiastically submitted our paperwork but were crushed to find out that there was already an offer on the space. Our broker said he would follow up with the landlord when he was back from surgery.

"From surgery??" I had an idea... what's a better get-well-soon gift than cookie dough? We had Sugar Cookie, my favorite base, in the mixing bowl, and I figured it might be the ticket to tip the scales in my favor.

I did serious research until I found the landlord's full name, and eventually, the crème de la crème: his office address. I sent colorful containers of Sugar Cookie flavors adorned with a bow and a handwritten note that may have mentioned that if he had a change of heart on the lease for the LaGuardia Place space to please let us know . . . and maybe there was a business card with my contact info, just for good measure. Off it went, my "last hope" in package form.

The next day, my phone rang. It was the landlord, thanking me for the thoughtful gift.

"My wife thinks it's so cute and my boys won't stop eating it," he said, laughing. Score! He had given the other company his word, with only a week to sign the documents. He said, "If they don't sign by Monday, it's yours."

Monday, at 2 p.m., the phone rang again. This time, with the best news ever.

2½ cups heat-treated all-purpose flour (instructions on page 31)

1 tablespoon cornstarch

1½ teaspoons cream of tartar

¾ teaspoon baking powder

¾ teaspoon baking soda

¾ teaspoon salt

1½ sticks (12 tablespoons) unsalted butter, at room temperature

1 cup plus 2 tablespoons sugar

⅓ cup pasteurized egg whites, at room temperature

1½ teaspoons vanilla extract

// In a medium bowl, whisk together the flour, cornstarch, cream of tartar, baking powder, baking soda, and salt. Set aside.

// In the bowl of a stand mixer fitted with the paddle attachment, beat the butter on medium speed until smooth and creamy, about 2 minutes. Add the sugar and mix on medium until light and fluffy; about 4 minutes will do the trick. Use a rubber spatula to scrape the bowl. Add the egg whites and vanilla and mix until fully incorporated, about 2 minutes.

// Add half of the flour mixture and mix on low just until the powdery texture of the flour disappears, about 15 seconds. Immediately add the rest of the flour mixture and mix until combined. Scrape the bowl and mix a final 15 seconds.

// Remove the bowl from the mixer and steal a lick right from the bowl. To make our Signature Combos, use a rubber spatula to gently fold in the "fold" ingredients first. Then, if it calls for it, drop "swirl" mix-ins in tablespoon-size scoops

in four different locations in the bowl. Use the rubber spatula to gently swirl until you see thick ribbons of that mix-in. Last, sprinkle on "top" mix-ins and you're done!

// Your masterpiece is ready! Suga suga, how you get so fly?

Craving some cookies? Have extra cookie dough? See My Go-To Baking & Storage DŌrections on page 48.

Signature Combos:

1 SUGAR COOKIE

Add a hint of rainbow sparkle.

TOP:

½ cup rainbow sugar

2 SNICKERDOODLE

A supersoft version of the classic cookie.

FOLD:

¼ cup cinnamon sugar (3 tablespoons sugar mixed with 1 tablespoon cinnamon)

3 HEAVENLY

It's named Heavenly for a reason.

FOLD:

½ cup semisweet chocolate chips

½ cup caramel bits

SWIRL:

¼ cup Nutella

TOP:

Flaky sea salt, like Maldon

CONTINUES →

I've fallen in love with every recipe at DŌ, so picking a favorite flavor is like picking a favorite child—nearly impossible. But, if my parents had it in them to pick me as their favorite (shhh! don't tell my three siblings), then surely I can pick one! If you twisted my arm, if you made me, if I had to pick one...it would be Heavenly. No surprise that customers agree—it's one of the most popular flavors of all time!

4 **SALTY AND SWEET**

Sweet caramel and a crunch of sea salt
are a match made in heaven!

FOLD:

½ cup dark chocolate chips

SWIRL:

½ cup Homemade Salted Caramel Sauce
(recipe at right)

TOP:

Flaky sea salt, like Maldon

HOMEMADE SALTED CARAMEL SAUCE

NATURALLY
GF

Makes *about 2 cups sauce*
Active time: *15 minutes*
Time 'til caramel sauce: *1 hour 15 minutes*

Now this bit of perfection is to. die.
for. I'm talking in your cookie dough, on
your ice cream—or eat it straight out
of the jar with a spoon—to die for. One
batch is enough for your dough...and a
tiny bit extra just for you.

⅓ cup water

1¼ cups sugar

1 stick (8 tablespoons) unsalted butter, at
room temperature

⅔ cup heavy cream, at room temperature

2 teaspoons sea salt

// Measure all of your ingredients and
have them within arm's reach—this
recipe moves fast!

// Use a heavy-bottomed saucepan and
turn your burner to medium heat. Add the
water and sugar to the pan and stir just
until the sugar is evenly distributed. Once
the mixture comes to a boil, stop stirring
while the liquid boils off. If you stir, it will
promote crystallization, which will result
in grainy caramel.

// Boil over medium heat for 8 to
10 minutes, watching very closely. Resist
the urge to walk away! Give the pan
a few swirls to make sure the sugar is
getting evenly heated. Once you notice
the sugar turning amber in color, watch
very closely because the sugar can burn
easily, and burned sugar is super bitter!
If you notice the sugar getting dark too
quickly, reduce the heat slightly or pull the
pan away from the heat.

// Once the mixture gets to a nice
medium caramel color, add the butter and
whisk vigorously until completely melted.
The mixture will bubble aggressively, but
just keep stirring.

// Once the butter is mixed and the
foaming settles, remove the pan from
the heat. Continue to whisk while slowly
adding the cream. This also will cause
bubbling and foaming, but don't stop
whisking! Once the sauce is mixed and
the foaming has settled, whisk in the salt.

// Let cool completely—at least
1 hour—before using it or pouring the
sauce into a jar. To speed cooling, stir the
caramel every 15 minutes in the fridge.
Resist the urge to taste until it is cooled
completely—hot sugar can be very
dangerous!

// The sauce can be stored in an airtight
container in the refrigerator for up to
2 weeks. Stir before using or heat up
in the microwave at 50% power for
30-second intervals if you want your
caramel sauce warm!

Peanut Butter

Snicker away. I'll say it all day: I'm nuts for some freakin' nuts. PEAnuts, that is.

One day when I was young I decided, or rather, in typical little-Kristen fashion, I stubbornly insisted on making my own peanut butter. I was only seven, but you better believe I was I-N-D-E-P-E-N-D-E-N-T (thanks, early 2000s pop radio, for teaching me to spell) and I didn't want help. Adorable, right?

I started with what I thought I knew: peanuts. OK, check. They need to get crushed, so the potato masher... naturally. Maybe some water? Gotta make it creamy, so yeah, add some water. Well, that didn't work, so there must be flour in it; everything that I put flour into got thick and smooth, so I mixed in some flour. Guess how it turned out...

...Like pure shit. A big ol' bowl of wet peanuts covered in a nasty flour paste. Even though she kept offering, I wouldn't accept my mom's help (independent, remember?). I finally gave up, declaring that I hadn't even wanted peanut butter in the first place... obviously. These days, I stick to Skippy.

1¼ cups heat-treated all-purpose flour (instructions on page 31)

2 teaspoons cornstarch

½ teaspoon baking soda

½ teaspoon salt

1 stick (8 tablespoons) unsalted butter, at room temperature

¾ cup peanut butter

¼ cup granulated sugar

½ cup plus 1 tablespoon brown sugar

¼ cup pasteurized egg whites, at room temperature

1½ teaspoons vanilla extract

// In a medium bowl, whisk together the flour, cornstarch, baking soda, and salt. Set aside.

// In the bowl of a stand mixer fitted with the paddle attachment, beat the butter and peanut butter on medium speed until smooth and creamy, about 2 minutes. Add the granulated and brown sugars and mix on medium until light and fluffy; about 4 minutes will do the trick. Use a rubber spatula to scrape the bowl. Add the egg whites and vanilla and mix until fully incorporated, about 2 minutes.

// Add half of the flour mixture and mix on low just until the powdery texture of the flour disappears, about 15 seconds. Immediately add the rest of the flour mixture and mix until combined. Scrape the bowl and mix a final 15 seconds.

// Remove the bowl from the mixer and steal a lick right from the bowl. Make one of our signature combos. Use a rubber spatula to gently fold in the "fold" ingredients first. Then, if it calls for it, drop "swirl" mix-ins in tablespoon-size scoops in four different locations in the bowl. Use the rubber spatula to gently swirl until you see thick ribbons of that mix-in.

// OK, peanut butter nuts, your dough is ready!

If you happen to have some dough left over, see My Go-To Baking & Storage DŌrections on page 48.

Signature Combos:

1 FLUFFERNUTTER

The genius of Marshmallow Fluff meets perfect peanut butter dough.

FOLD:

¾ cup dark chocolate chips

¾ cup Marshmallow Fluff

2 NUTS FOR NUTS

If you're crazy for Reese's, you'll go nuts for this.

FOLD:

½ cup Reese's Pieces, chopped

9 Reese's Peanut Butter Cups

3 PACK ME A PB&J

Lunch box, meet dessert bowl.

FOLD:

⅓ cup chopped peanuts

SWIRL:

½ cup seedless raspberry jelly (or your favorite J option out there)

////////////////////////

Kristen's
TIP

////////////////////////

If you're a classic peanut butter cookie lover, leave out all the mix-ins. Before baking, roll in white sugar and use a fork to press them down on a lined baking sheet to create that classic crisscross pattern.

74 \ THE EIGHT
CLASSIC BASES

\ MAKES
30 scoops

\ TIME 'TIL DOUGH
16 minutes

\ TIME 'TIL COOKIES
2 hours 30 minutes

Oatmeal

SHOP *Special*

There is nothing worse than biting into an oatmeal cookie expecting sweet chocolate chips, but instead getting a mouthful of unwanted shriveled raisins. It's probably the number one reason I have trust issues.

I'm not sure if I even need to explicitly mention this, but I'm 100 percent team chocolate and 100 percent NOT team raisin. If you happen to be a fan of those sad, dried grapes in your cookies (and cookie dough), feel free to sub out my amazing, decadent, creamy chocolate to give your dough a little less sweet and a little more chew. I will judge you, but I'll do my best to keep it to myself. Raisin lovers, slide into my DMs on Instagram (@kristentomlan) so we can have a candid conversation about your questionable life choices.

1½ cups oats

1 cup heat-treated all-purpose flour (instructions on page 31)

1 teaspoon cornstarch

½ teaspoon baking soda

½ teaspoon ground cinnamon

½ teaspoon salt

1 stick (8 tablespoons) unsalted butter, at room temperature

¼ cup granulated sugar

1 cup brown sugar

¼ cup pasteurized egg whites, at room temperature

1 tablespoon vanilla extract

// In a food processor or blender, pulse the oats 3 or 4 times, until they have a roughly chopped consistency. The oats shouldn't be as fine as flour but definitely should be more powdery than whole oats.

// Heat-treat the oats according to the instructions on page 31.

// Once the oats are cooled completely, in a medium bowl, whisk together the oats, flour, cornstarch, baking soda, cinnamon, and salt. Set aside.

// In the bowl of a stand mixer fitted with the paddle attachment, beat the butter on medium speed until smooth and creamy, about 2 minutes. Add the granulated and brown sugars and mix on medium until light and fluffy; about 4 minutes will do the trick. Use a rubber spatula to scrape the bowl. Add the egg whites and vanilla and mix until fully incorporated, about 2 minutes.

// Add half of the flour mixture and mix on low just until the powdery texture of the flour disappears, about 15 seconds. Immediately add the rest of the flour mixture and mix until combined. Scrape the bowl and mix a final 15 seconds.

// Remove the bowl from the mixer and steal a lick right from the bowl. Make one of our Signature Combos. Use a rubber spatula to gently fold in the mix-ins.

// Regardless of what team you picked, DIG IN to some oatmeal dough!

If fresh-baked cookies are more your thing, see My Go-To Baking & Storage DŌrections on page 48.

Signature Combos:

1 **OATMEAL M&M**

Team chocolate...all the way!

FOLD:

¾ cup M&M's

½ cup semisweet chocolate chips

2 **WHITE CHOCOLATE CRANBERRY**

Cranberry and oats—that's healthy, right?

FOLD:

½ cup dried cranberries

¾ cup white chocolate chips

3 **OATMEAL RAISIN**

OK, fine, raisin lovers...this one's for you.

FOLD:

1 cup raisins

76 \ THE EIGHT
CLASSIC BASES

\ MAKES
36 scoops

\ TIME 'TIL DOUGH
25 minutes

\ TIME 'TIL COOKIES
2 hours 45 minutes

Cake Batter

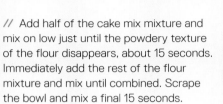

SHOP
Special

What are the things in your life that you celebrate? Birthdays? Yes! You got a promotion at work? Good for you! Parked in that prime spot at the grocery store? Killing it! Did you get out of bed after snoozing your alarm only four times? You DŌserve this! I think you should celebrate anything and everything that makes you feel good. When I think of celebrating, I think of two things: cake (because, duh) and cookie dough (because, well, me). Lightbulb moment: Cake Batter cookie dough. Genius, I know. It's everything light and sweet that you love about cake and everything rich and creamy that you love about cookie dough. Plus some sprinkles.

We use a white vanilla cake mix, but if you really want to get wild, grab the Funfetti, yellow cake, devil's food, or straight-up chocolate. It's your party, you can try what you want to!

1½ cups cake mix (½ box)

1⅓ cups heat-treated all-purpose flour (instructions on page 31)

2½ tablespoons cornstarch

½ teaspoon baking soda

½ teaspoon salt

1½ sticks (12 tablespoons) unsalted butter, at room temperature

½ cup granulated sugar

½ cup brown sugar

¼ cup pasteurized egg whites, at room temperature

2 teaspoons vanilla extract

⅓ cup sprinkles (we typically use jimmies)

½ cup semisweet chocolate chips

½ cup white chocolate chips

// Heat-treat the cake mix according to the instructions on page 31.

// Once the cake mix has cooled completely, in a medium bowl, whisk together the cake mix, flour, cornstarch, baking soda, and salt. Set aside.

// In the bowl of a stand mixer fitted with the paddle attachment, beat the butter on medium speed until smooth and creamy, about 2 minutes. Add the granulated and brown sugars and mix on medium until light and fluffy; about 4 minutes will do the trick. Use a rubber spatula to scrape the bowl. Add the egg whites and vanilla and mix until fully incorporated, about 2 minutes.

// Add half of the cake mix mixture and mix on low just until the powdery texture of the flour disappears, about 15 seconds. Immediately add the rest of the flour mixture and mix until combined. Scrape the bowl and mix a final 15 seconds.

// Remove the bowl from the mixer and use a rubber spatula to fold in the sprinkles, semisweet chips, and white chips.

// Like cake, but even batter! Your dough is ready to eat.

Trust me, you'll want to bake this dough too! See My Go-To Baking & Storage DŌrections on page 48.

/////////// *Kristen's Tip* ///////////

This is the way we serve cake batter in the shop. The flavor stays the same, but the sprinkles are ever changing! You can use the cutest ones you can find, or if you're a true DIY-er, make your own (see page 289).

///

WHAT TYPE OF
cookie dough lover are you?

THE NOSTALGIC ONE

I see you, dragging your finger across the spatula and licking the beaters. You eat it straight from the bowl...and always will, just like you did growing up. That smooth, velvety texture is undeniably tempting. Guess what? I'm right there with you.

THE PURIST

You're looking for the quickest way to get cookie dough in your mouth. You grab some from the fridge, maybe get a sturdy spoon—or just use your fingers—and start eating right away. You enjoy bite after bite until it's totally gone, unless you have some willpower to save a bit for later!

THE SNEAKY ONE

We know what you're hiding behind the frozen peas and that box of ice pops— your secret stash of cookie dough. In fact, go ahead and just hide behind the freezer door and eat it right there—you even keep the spoon in the container so no one hears that noisy utensil drawer open!

THE TOPPER

You know EVERYTHING tastes better with DŌ on top. You've experimented with endless combinations: adding it to your ice cream, your toast, your brownies, your...just about anything. It's cool—you dough you.

THE PROFESSIONAL

This isn't your first cookie dough rodeo. You know heating DŌ in the microwave for *just* a few seconds creates a texture that's like a fresh baked cookie center. Melty mix-ins, ooey gooey dough, and all around soft and warm is how you like it.

THE BAKER

Kudos to you for keeping your DŌ around long enough to make it to the oven! You live a baked, chewy cookie way of life. They are crispy and lightly golden on the outside, steamy and sweet on the inside, and give you a sense of accomplishment. I mean, look at you, you *baked* something today.

THE PLANNER

Whoa there, type A—I like your style. You have pre-scooped cookies hiding in your freezer ready to pop in the oven the moment a surprise guest drops by. Just like Martha Stewart, you'll have effortless, fresh-baked cookies in under 15 minutes. Bravo!

THE IMPROVISERS

Yeah, you know it says use a cookie scoop, but you don't have one of those... or can't find it (not surprising). That's OK...you're pretty good at guesstimating. You plop random shapes of cookie dough right on the sheet. They still bake up super yummy!

When You Feel Like Dessert for Breakfast

///

Growing up in the craziness of a big family teaches you to be self-sufficient at an early age. Mom made us start packing our own lunches as soon as we were able to see over the countertop. Breakfast at our house was a "fend-for-yourself" meal. It was impossible to make something fancy and be ready for carpool by 7 a.m. I was totally content with a few handfuls of dry cereal. As I got older, and lazier, I'd grab a pack of Nutter Butter cookies and wash them down with a Diet Coke on the way out the door. I wasn't exactly the pinnacle of health in high school—thank God for an adolescent metabolism.

These days, running the business means plenty of late nights, so I'm not wasting a single second of sleep waking up early to make breakfast. Most mornings I run straight from bed, out the front door, and off to work (mobile-ordering a Starbucks espresso along the way, of course). If I'm lucky, I'll grab a fresh-baked cookie at the shop as soon as I get there. Peanut butter is protein, right? Maybe I haven't come all that far from my teenage Nutter Butter and Diet Coke days.

/// If you're like me, and you prefer your breakfast to taste a lot more like dessert, then these recipes are for you.

Cereal Bowl

kids
LOVE

Even though bowls of cereal were never really my thing, ziplock *bags* of cereal were definitely my jam. I loved taking a bag of dry cereal along with me to snack on throughout the day. On my long list of favorites were Fruit Loops, Cap'n Crunch, Fruity Pebbles, Honey Nut Cheerios, Cinnamon Toast Crunch, and, of course, Cookie Crisp. (Try to tell me you didn't read that as CooOOoOookie Crisp—it's impossible not to.)

The beauty of this recipe is that you can use any breakfast cereal you want! (Although I wouldn't recommend bran cereal—unless you've got some other issues you're hoping to take care of.) Throw in a handful of yogurt chips to stand in for the milk (yogurt > milk, always), and finally we've got a bowl of cereal I actually want to eat.

2 cups your favorite sweet cereal (divided)

1½ cups heat-treated all-purpose flour (instructions on page 31)

1 tablespoon cornstarch

1½ teaspoons cream of tartar

¾ teaspoon baking powder

¾ teaspoon baking soda

¾ teaspoon salt

1½ sticks (12 tablespoons) unsalted butter, at room temperature

1 cup plus 2 tablespoons sugar

⅓ cup pasteurized egg whites, at room temperature

1½ teaspoons vanilla

½ cup yogurt chips (I order these from nuts.com)

// In a food processor or blender, pulse 1½ cups of the cereal until it has the texture of flour. You may need to open the food processor once or twice and stir between pulses to make sure you have an even consistency. Measure 1 cup of the "cereal flour" and discard the rest.

// In a medium bowl, whisk together the "cereal flour," heat-treated flour, cornstarch, cream of tartar, baking powder, baking soda, and salt. Set aside.

// In the bowl of a stand mixer fitted with the paddle attachment, beat the butter on medium speed until smooth and creamy, about 2 minutes. Add the sugar and mix on medium until light and fluffy; about 4 minutes will do the trick. Use a rubber spatula to scrape the bowl. Add the egg whites and vanilla and mix until fully incorporated, about 2 minutes.

// Add half of the flour mixture and mix on low just until the powdery texture of the flour disappears, about 15 seconds. Immediately add the rest of the flour mixture and mix until combined. Scrape the bowl and mix a final 15 seconds.

// Remove the bowl from the mixer and use a rubber spatula to fold in the remaining ½ cup cereal and the yogurt chips.

// It's time to fill your cereal bowl with cookie dough!

Craving some cookies? Have extra cookie dough? See My Go-To Baking & Storage DŌrections on page 48.

Cinnamon Roll Outta Bed

GREAT MADE GF   **KRISTEN'S Fav**

There are only two smells that will get me out of bed in the morning: bacon and freshly baked cinnamon rolls. The cinnamon rolls that really get me moving are the extra-gooey ones. I like them oozing cinnamon sugar syrup, still dough-y on the inside, and slathered in sweet vanilla frosting...with some bacon on the side.

When I served this at the shop, it was Sugar Cookie (page 68) with chunks of chopped-up baked cinnamon rolls folded in, and it was wildly popular. Today Cinnamon Roll Outta Bed has evolved into an even more DŌlectable treat with a base speckled with cinnamon and a huge helping of frosting shards. The best part? There's no need for an oven! You can go straight from bed to some cinnamon roll heaven, no baking time required.

1¾ cups Bedhead Cinnamon Bark (recipe follows)

2½ cups heat-treated all-purpose flour (instructions on page 31)

1 tablespoon cornstarch

1½ teaspoons cream of tartar

1 teaspoon ground cinnamon

¾ teaspoon baking powder

¾ teaspoon baking soda

¾ teaspoon salt

1½ sticks (12 tablespoons) unsalted butter, at room temperature

1 cup plus 2 tablespoons sugar

⅓ cup pasteurized egg whites, at room temperature

1½ teaspoons vanilla extract

// Make the Bedhead Cinnamon Bark. Roughly chop it until you have ½-inch pieces. Set aside.

// In a medium bowl, whisk together the heat-treated flour, cornstarch, cream of tartar, cinnamon, baking powder, baking soda, and salt. Set aside.

// In the bowl of a stand mixer fitted with the paddle attachment, beat the butter on medium speed until smooth and creamy, about 2 minutes. Add the sugar and mix on medium until light and fluffy; about 4 minutes will do the trick. Use a rubber spatula to scrape the bowl. Add the egg whites and vanilla and mix until fully incorporated, about 2 minutes.

// Add half of the flour mixture and mix on low just until the powdery texture of the flour disappears, about 15 seconds. Immediately add the rest of the flour mixture and mix until combined. Scrape the bowl and mix a final 15 seconds.

// Remove the bowl from the mixer and use a rubber spatula to fold in the cinnamon bark pieces with a rubber spatula.

// If dough is for breakfast, it's time to start your day off right!

If you're planning to save some for dessert too, see My Go-To Baking & Storage DŌrections on page 48.

*Eat with your eyes? Find
inspiration on the next page.*

BEDHEAD
CINNAMON BARK

Makes *16 servings*
Active time: *10 minutes*
Time 'til bark: *30 minutes*

½ stick (4 tablespoons) unsalted butter

¼ cup brown sugar

1 tablespoon ground cinnamon

2 cups white chocolate chips

// Line a rimmed baking sheet, at least
18"x13" (the size of a standard baking
sheet) with waxed paper or a silicone
baking mat.

// In a medium microwave-safe bowl,
heat the butter and brown sugar in the
microwave on 50% power in 30-second
increments. Stir well between each
increment. Repeat just until melted.
Whisk the cinnamon into the melted
butter mixture and set aside.

// Place the white chocolate chips in
a separate microwave-safe bowl. Heat
in the microwave on 50% power in
30-second increments. Stir well between
each increment. Repeat just until the
chocolate is melted. Pour the melted
white chocolate into the center of the
lined baking sheet. Use a rubber or offset
spatula to spread into an even layer, a
little less than ¼ inch thick. It will nearly
fill the baking sheet.

// Give the butter mixture a stir; it
should be thicker than when you added
the cinnamon. Drizzle the butter mixture
over the white chocolate in horizontal
lines. Use a rubber or offset spatula to
make vertical lines in the white chocolate,
dragging the cinnamon syrup to create a
crosshatch pattern.

// Place the baking sheet in the freezer,
uncovered, for 15 to 20 minutes, until the
bark is solid.

// Remove from the freezer and break or
cut to serve, mix into dough, or store in
an airtight container in the refrigerator for
up to 5 days.

Cinnamon Roll Outta Bed, page 84

A Cinnamon Roll Worth Fighting Over, page 195

Disappearing Poppy Seed Pound Cake, page 88

Cookie Dough Packed Crêpes, page 200

DŌnuts, page 201

Disappearing Poppy Seed Pound Cake

KRISTEN'S
Fav

My mom has always made these incredible lemon poppy seed muffins. They are light, fluffy, lemon-y, and topped with a simple sugary glaze. And they're bite-size—so you can eat triple the amount!

One morning my mom baked a fresh batch of her famous muffins for my dad to take to work. As they were cooling, she told my then five-year-old brother, Trey, to have some for breakfast. When she came back to the kitchen, the whole batch had disappeared! She asked Trey what happened, and he matter-of-factly said, "You told me to have some, so I did." I'd always teased him about being dropped off on our front doorstep, but this was the first time I had to admit my brother definitely was related to me.

My mom's muffins really are eat-a-whole-batch good. And this is the cookie dough version, plus blueberries. If you decide to bake them, I recommend dipping them into the glaze and hiding them from friends, family, and five-year-olds.

FOR THE DOUGH

1 (16-ounce) box pound cake mix (divided)

1 cup fresh blueberries

½ cup heat-treated all-purpose flour (instructions on page 31)

2 tablespoons cornstarch

½ teaspoon baking soda

½ teaspoon salt

1 stick (8 tablespoons) unsalted butter, at room temperature

½ cup brown sugar

¼ cup pasteurized egg whites, at room temperature

¼ cup sour cream

1 teaspoon lemon extract

1 teaspoon vanilla extract

1 teaspoon lemon zest

1 teaspoon poppy seeds

FOR THE LEMON GLAZE (IF BAKING)

¼ cup lemon juice

2 cups confectioners' sugar

1 tablespoon lemon zest

// Heat-treat the pound cake mix according to the instructions on page 31. Let the cake mix cool completely.

// In a small bowl, combine 1 tablespoon of the heat-treated cake mix and the blueberries. Toss to coat and set aside.

// In a medium bowl, whisk together the remaining heat-treated cake mix, the heat-treated flour, cornstarch, baking soda, and salt. Set aside.

// In the bowl of a stand mixer fitted with the paddle attachment, beat the butter on medium speed until smooth and creamy, about 2 minutes. Add the brown sugar and mix on medium until light and fluffy; about 4 minutes will do the trick. Use a rubber spatula to scrape the bowl. Add the egg whites, sour cream, lemon extract, and vanilla and mix until fully incorporated, about 2 minutes. Add the lemon zest and poppy seeds and mix an additional 30 seconds.

// Add half of the flour mixture and mix on low just until the powdery texture of the flour disappears, about 15 seconds. Immediately add the rest of the flour mixture and mix until combined. Scrape the bowl and mix a final 15 seconds.

// Remove the bowl from the mixer and use a rubber spatula to fold in the coated blueberries.

// Lemon blueberry dough is ready to disappear!

Trust me, you'll want to bake this dough! See My Go-To Baking & Storage DŌrections on page 48.

Don't forget the glaze!

// While the cookies cool, make the glaze: In a large bowl, slowly mix the lemon juice into the confectioners' sugar with a whisk. Once the glaze is thick enough to coat the back of a spoon, stir in the lemon zest.

// Dip the tops of the cooled cookies into the glaze. Place the cookies on a wire rack while the glaze sets. (I won't tell if you eat a few cookies before the glaze sets—they're hard to resist!)

Eat with your eyes? Find inspiration on pages 86–87.

I'm Bananas for Nutella®

My feelings for Nutella are passionate and unwavering. That heavenly chocolate hazelnut spread never, ever disappoints. It knows exactly how to put a pep in my step, never talks back, and like any good relationship, has always been there for me.

Bananas, on the other hand, I'm not a *huge* fan of. You'll never find me just eating a plain banana (forget the taste, watching someone eat a whole banana is painfully awkward), digging into banana pudding (I'll save that for my husband, Chris), or cutting up a banana for my toast (give me all the butter instead). I even pick around all the fake banana-flavored candies—no banana Runts, no banana Laffy Taffy, and never a banana Now and Later. Yuck.

But, I get it—people dig banana—so this recipe was for you, banana lovers...at least at first. What I learned while testing it was that I'll eat a banana ANYTIME if it's paired with Nutella and mashed up into some cookie dough.

½ cup ripe banana (about 1 large banana)

2¼ cups heat-treated all-purpose flour (instructions on page 31)

2¼ teaspoons cornstarch

1 teaspoon baking soda

¾ teaspoon salt

1½ sticks (12 tablespoons) unsalted butter, at room temperature

¼ cup granulated sugar

1 cup brown sugar

1 tablespoon vanilla extract

⅓ cup Nutella

// Using a fork, mash the banana in a small bowl and set aside.

// In a medium bowl, whisk together the heat-treated flour, cornstarch, baking soda, and salt. Set aside.

// In the bowl of a stand mixer fitted with the paddle attachment, beat the butter on medium speed until smooth and creamy, about 2 minutes. Add the granulated and brown sugars and mix on medium until light and fluffy; about 4 minutes will do the trick. Use a rubber spatula to scrape the bowl. Add the banana and vanilla and mix until fully incorporated, about 2 minutes.

// Add half of the flour mixture and mix on low just until the powdery texture of the flour disappears, about 15 seconds. Immediately add the rest of the flour mixture and mix until combined. Scrape the bowl and mix a final 15 seconds.

// Remove the bowl from the mixer. Drop the Nutella in 1½ tablespoon–size scoops in four different locations in the bowl. Use a rubber spatula to gently swirl until you see thick ribbons of Nutella. Don't overmix—you're finished!

// If you're going bananas, go ahead and dig in!

If you didn't eat it all in one sitting, see My Go-To Baking & Storage DŌrections on page 48.

Kristen's
TIP

Waffle croutons are a GAME
CHANGER on salad. They're the
ultimate crunchy topping that adds
a sweet pop to lunch! Make a double
batch next time and try it.

Waffle-y Sweet Morning

My definitive ranking of traditionally sweet breakfast foods:

3RD PLACE: French Toast
2ND PLACE: Pancakes
1ST PLACE: Waffles

If you don't agree with me, let me explain why you're wrong. Waffles have built-in butter and maple syrup holders. They're made to ensure those two best parts of any carb-based breakfast make it into your mouth, no syrupy stickiness dripping off your bite or butter melting onto the plate. And by syrupy stickiness, in this case, I mean the good ol' Aunt Jemima stuff. As much as I love all-natural maple syrup straight from Vermont, this recipe really needs that buttery sweetness that Aunt Jemima does better than anyone else.

Do you agree with me now? Is there anything better than a waffle? Well…maybe waffle croutons. I invented this method to make Eggos keep their crunch, even when they're drowning in cookie dough.

FOR THE WAFFLE CROUTONS

4 frozen waffles, like Eggo

⅜ stick (3 tablespoons) unsalted butter

2 tablespoons pancake syrup, like Aunt Jemima

FOR THE DOUGH

2½ cups heat-treated all-purpose flour (instructions on page 31)

1 tablespoon cornstarch

1½ teaspoons cream of tartar

¾ teaspoon baking powder

¾ teaspoon baking soda

¾ teaspoon salt

1½ sticks (12 tablespoons) unsalted butter, at room temperature

1¼ cups sugar

⅓ cup pasteurized egg whites, at room temperature

⅓ cup pancake syrup, like Aunt Jemima

// **Make the waffle croutons:** Use a sharp knife to cut the frozen waffles into 1-inch pieces. In a large skillet over medium heat, melt the butter. Once melted, stir in the syrup. Add the waffles to the skillet and coat with the syrup and butter mixture. Once coated, arrange them in a single layer in the skillet. Allow them to toast until golden brown, then flip to repeat on the other side. Continue until all sides are toasty. Transfer the toasted croutons in a single layer to a plate lined with waxed paper and set aside to cool.

// **Make the dough:** In a medium bowl, whisk together the heat-treated flour, cornstarch, cream of tartar, baking powder, baking soda, and salt. Set aside.

// In the bowl of a stand mixer fitted with the paddle attachment, beat the butter on medium speed until smooth and creamy, about 2 minutes. Add the sugar and mix on medium until light and fluffy; about 4 minutes will do the trick. Use a rubber spatula to scrape the bowl. Add the egg whites and syrup and mix until fully incorporated, about 2 minutes.

// Add half of the flour mixture and mix on low just until the powdery texture of the flour disappears, about 15 seconds. Immediately add the rest of the flour mixture and mix until combined. Scrape the bowl and mix a final 15 seconds.

// Remove the bowl from the mixer and use a rubber spatula to fold in the waffle croutons.

// Waffle-y sweet dough is done! Utensils are optional.

If you have more willpower than I do and find yourself with extra, see My Go-To Baking & Storage DŌrections on page 48.

94

WHEN YOU FEEL LIKE
DESSERT FOR BREAKFAST

MAKES
35 scoops

TIME 'TIL DOUGH
3 hours

TIME 'TIL COOKIES
2 hours 45 minutes

Coffee Toffee

I wasn't always addicted to coffee. Somehow I got through college, design studio, and countless all-nighters without coffee—I absolutely hated the taste. Instead, I drank a ton of iced tea (still love iced tea) and Diet Coke (these days I try my hardest to not drink soda). It wasn't until I understood real sleep deprivation, the starting-your-own-business-and-also-working-full-time-without-any-end-in-sight sleep deprivation, that I turned to coffee. Today, my coffee addiction is REAL—as in five shots of espresso, extra ice, a tiny splash of almond milk, and half a packet of raw sugar real. Every. Single. Morning. I know most people don't take their coffee that seriously—or that potent. I'll keep my thick-and-dark-as-gasoline order all to myself and give you this sweeter version of a coffee favorite: Coffee Toffee.

1 cup But First, Toffee (recipe at right)

2¼ cups heat-treated all-purpose flour (instructions on page 31)

2 tablespoons instant espresso

2¼ teaspoons cornstarch

1 teaspoon baking soda

¾ teaspoon salt

1½ sticks (12 tablespoons) unsalted butter, at room temperature

¼ cup granulated sugar

1 cup brown sugar

⅓ cup pasteurized egg whites, at room temperature

1 tablespoon vanilla extract

// Make the But First, Toffee. Once cooled, roughly chop until you have ¼-inch pieces. Measure 1 cup and set aside.

// In a medium bowl, whisk together the heat-treated flour, instant espresso, cornstarch, baking soda, and salt. Set aside.

// In the bowl of a stand mixer fitted with the paddle attachment, beat the butter on medium speed until smooth and creamy, about 2 minutes. Add the granulated and brown sugars and mix on medium until light and fluffy; about 4 minutes will do the trick. Use a rubber spatula to scrape the bowl. Add the egg whites and vanilla and mix until fully incorporated, about 2 minutes.

// Add half of the flour mixture and mix on low just until the powdery texture of the flour disappears, about 15 seconds. Immediately add the rest of the flour mixture and mix until combined. Scrape the bowl and mix a final 15 seconds.

// Remove the bowl from the mixer and use a rubber spatula to fold in the chopped toffee.

// Your caffeine fix in cookie dough form is ready to eat!

If fresh-baked cookies are more your thing, see My Go-To Baking & Storage DŌrections on page 48.

//

BUT FIRST, TOFFEE

Serves *12 to 16*
Active time: *15 minutes*
Time 'til toffee: *2 hours 15 minutes*

2 sticks (16 tablespoons) unsalted butter

½ cup granulated sugar

½ cup brown sugar

1 teaspoon molasses

½ teaspoon salt

1 tablespoon instant espresso powder

1 cup dark chocolate chips

Flaky sea salt, like Maldon, for topping

// Line a baking sheet with parchment paper or a silicone baking mat. Set aside.

// In a heavy-bottomed saucepan with a candy thermometer clipped to the side, heat the butter over low heat, stirring occasionally until it is completely melted.

// Add the granulated and brown sugars, the molasses, and salt and stir until the sugar dissolves completely. Turn the heat up to medium, stirring constantly as the mixture bubbles and watching closely so the mixture doesn't burn. Continue to stir for 8 to 10 minutes, watching the candy thermometer. When the mixture reaches 290°F, remove from the heat. Immediately stir in the espresso powder.

// Pour the mixture onto the lined baking sheet and use a rubber spatula to spread it into an even layer, about ¼ inch thick. Let stand for 1 minute.

// Sprinkle the chocolate chips over the toffee in a single layer and let stand for 1 to 2 minutes as the chips soften. Once the chips are glossy, use the back of a spoon or an offset spatula to spread the chocolate evenly over the toffee. Sprinkle with flaky salt.

// Chill in the refrigerator until hardened, about 2 hours. Slice and serve!

// Store the toffee in an airtight container in the refrigerator for up to 1 month.

Kristen's
TIP

If making your own toffee is too intimidating or if you're on a time crunch, this recipe tastes great with crushed Heath Bars or other store-bought alternatives.

When You're Over the Whole Adulting Thing

When I started DŌ at the age of twenty-five, I wasn't always taken seriously. I heard a lot of "how cute" and "oh, that's fun" when I explained my idea to friends and family.

And while many of the most important people in my life supported me following my dream, they didn't totally get it. Why would I leave my successful, and very adult, corporate job to go chase a "childish" thing like cookie dough? But the two people I spent the most time with: my soon-to-be husband, Chris, and my former boss, Randall. They got it.

It seemed counterintuitive. Why would my boss encourage me to dedicate my time and energy to a different job? But he did. Randall is a design and customer experience genius—a big-picture creative thinker with extensive expertise in consumer behavior and trends. I first told him about DŌ after a client meeting when he mentioned he needed "to discover a new dessert craze...what's the next cupcake?" I told him I already had it. It was cookie dough, exactly the way you crave it! He could see it too. From that moment on he constantly sent me cookie dough–related articles and regularly checked in with me about how "that dough thing" was progressing. I always laughed it off and said, "Stop giving me so much work, and I'll actually have time for it."

What I took away from Randall's encouragement was the idea that being an adult didn't mean conforming. Rather, growing up means having the freedom to make your own choices—even if those choices feel a bit childlike sometimes.

/// The recipes that follow are for the days when the most adult thing to do is grab a spoon, embrace your inner child, and stop worrying about what anyone else thinks.

DunkaDŌo

My childhood home was known as the "snack house." I'm talking the totally terrible-for-you '90s snacks you craved like Gushers, Fruit Roll-Ups, frosted brownies, fruit snacks, oatmeal cream pies, Nutter Butters, and more. Friends, babysitters, even my parents' friends couldn't wait to get their hands on a few treats. My all-time, hands-down favorite was Dunkaroos—a pack of cute kangaroo-shaped graham cookies made for dipping one at a time in vanilla frosting.

Sadly, Dunkaroos are extinct (RIP). Once I finish writing this book and have some extra time on my hands, I will officially champion the BBTDP (Bring Back the Dunkaroos Petition) and notify you when it's ready to sign. Since you can't buy Dunkaroos anymore (except on Amazon, where you can get them from Canada— Canadians know what's up), I give you the next best thing: DunkaDŌo!

¼ cup rainbow jimmies

2½ cups heat-treated all-purpose flour (instructions on page 31)

1 tablespoon cornstarch

1½ teaspoons cream of tartar

¾ teaspoon baking powder

¾ teaspoon baking soda

¾ teaspoon salt

1½ sticks (12 tablespoons) unsalted butter, at room temperature

1 cup plus 2 tablespoons sugar

⅓ cup pasteurized egg whites, at room temperature

1½ teaspoons vanilla extract

1 cup Teddy Grahams

½ cup store-bought vanilla frosting (just pick your favorite!)

// In a food processor or blender, pulse the jimmies 3 to 5 times, until you have evenly crushed sprinkle crumbs.

// In a medium bowl, whisk together the heat-treated flour, cornstarch, cream of tartar, baking powder, baking soda, and salt. Set aside.

// In the bowl of a stand mixer fitted with the paddle attachment, beat the butter on medium speed until smooth and creamy, about 2 minutes. Add the sugar and mix on medium until light and fluffy; about 4 minutes will do the trick. Use a rubber spatula to scrape the bowl. Add the egg whites and vanilla and mix until fully incorporated, about 2 minutes.

// Add half of the flour mixture and mix on low just until the powdery texture of the flour disappears, about 15 seconds. Immediately add the rest of the flour mixture and mix until combined. Scrape the bowl and mix a final 15 seconds.

// Remove the bowl from the mixer and use a rubber spatula to fold in the sprinkle crumbs and Teddy Grahams.

// Drop the frosting in tablespoon-size scoops in four different locations in the bowl. Use a rubber spatula to gently swirl until you see thick ribbons of frosting. Don't overmix—you're finished!

// Time to get dunking, this DunkaDŌo is done!

If you didn't eat it all in one sitting, see My Go-To Baking & Storage DŌrections on page 48.

/////////// **Kristen's Tip** ///////////

You might be tempted to do it all from scratch, but for this recipe the only thing that will give you that real Dunkaroo flavor is store-bought frosting. There is something about the sweet, artificial, canned flavor that will make your brain scream NOSTALGIA—trust me!

//

100 \ WHEN YOU'RE OVER THE
WHOLE ADULTING THING

\ MAKES
35 scoops

\ TIME 'TIL DOUGH
18 minutes

\ TIME 'TIL COOKIES
2 hours 40 minutes

Me Want Cookie

DŌ doesn't have a mascot, but if it did, he'd be hanging out on Sesame Street chowing down on his favorite snack. I'm talking about the om-nom-nom aficionado himself, Cookie Monster. It's a natural fit when you think about it. Cookie Monster and I both live for cookies, eat more of them than you might think humanly possible, and, despite our best efforts to be good role models for the kids in our lives, we pretty much end up getting them addicted to sugar (specifically my nieces and nephews #badaunt).

I like to think that Cookie Monster would love cookie dough even more than cookies if he ever had the chance to try it. With this cookie dough I'm doubling down on the nostalgia, tripling up on the cookie, and coloring it blue in honor of you-know-who.

1½ cups chocolate chip cookie pieces (your favorite chocolate chip cookie—boxed or homemade will work!)

8 Oreo cookies

2¼ cups heat-treated all-purpose flour (instructions on page 31)

2¼ teaspoons cornstarch

1 teaspoon baking soda

¾ teaspoon salt

1½ sticks (12 tablespoons) unsalted butter, at room temperature

¼ cup granulated sugar

1 cup brown sugar

⅓ cup pasteurized egg whites, at room temperature

1 tablespoon vanilla extract

5 drops blue food coloring

¼ cup mini semisweet chocolate chips

// Roughly chop the chocolate chip cookie pieces and Oreos. Set aside.

// In a medium bowl, whisk together the heat-treated flour, cornstarch, baking soda, and salt. Set aside.

// In the bowl of a stand mixer fitted with the paddle attachment, beat the butter on medium speed until smooth and creamy, about 2 minutes. Add the granulated and brown sugars and mix on medium until light and fluffy; about 4 minutes will do the trick. Use a rubber spatula to scrape the bowl. Add the egg whites, vanilla, and food coloring and mix until fully incorporated, about 2 minutes.

// Add half of the flour mixture and mix on low just until the powdery texture of the flour disappears, about 15 seconds. Immediately add the rest of the flour mixture and mix until combined. Scrape the bowl and mix a final 15 seconds.

// Remove the bowl from the mixer and use a rubber spatula to fold in the chopped cookies and semisweet chips.

// ME WANT COOKIE (dough)—good thing it's ready!

If you're planning on finishing this later, see My Go-To Baking & Storage DŌrections on page 48.

/////////// *Kristen's Tip* ///////////

If you want Cookie Monster–colored cookies, add an extra 2 to 3 drops of food coloring to the dough before adding the cookie pieces. Cookies always bake up lighter than their dough. For a true-to-monster blue cookie, you'll need to start with dough that is darker in color.

//

The Frosted Fork

One unexpected perk of founding DŌ has been forming relationships with so many brands, influencers, chefs, and people in the food biz. It's a guaranteed good time when creative minds get together to dream up new, exciting, surprising, and creative cookie-dough-inspired ideas!

The Frosted Fork is a flavor born out of a partnership with some notable New York foodie influencers—the girls of @New_Fork_City. After a marathon taste-tasting session, they decided they wanted to use pink and white frosted Circus Animal cookies (a favorite after-school snack of mine) because they're nostalgic, crazy yummy, and who doesn't love all things pink!? But we didn't just chop them up and throw them into the cookie dough. We pureed them (sorry, little animals) to create the best cookie butter swirl of all time.

FOR THE ANIMAL COOKIE BUTTER

1 cup frosted Circus Animal cookies (about 25)

2 tablespoons neutral oil, like canola

FOR THE DOUGH

2½ cups heat-treated all-purpose flour (instructions on page 31)

1 tablespoon cornstarch

1½ teaspoons cream of tartar

¾ teaspoon baking soda

¾ teaspoon baking powder

¾ teaspoon salt

1½ sticks (12 tablespoons) unsalted butter, at room temperature

1 cup plus 2 tablespoons sugar

⅓ cup pasteurized egg whites, at room temperature

1½ teaspoons vanilla extract

½ cup white chocolate chips

// **Make the animal cookie butter:** Place the cookies in a food processor. Pulse until you achieve uniform crumbs. You may need to remove the lid and stir a few times to make sure the cookies crumble evenly. Turn the processor on low and slowly add the oil until the mixture has a spreadable consistency, like peanut butter. Pulse a few additional times. Use a rubber spatula to scrape the cookie butter from the food processor into an airtight container. Set aside.

// **Make the dough:** In a medium bowl, whisk together the heat-treated flour, cornstarch, cream of tartar, baking soda, baking powder, and salt. Set aside.

// In the bowl of a stand mixer fitted with the paddle attachment, beat the butter on medium speed until smooth and creamy, about 2 minutes. Add the sugar and mix on medium until light and fluffy; about 4 minutes will do the trick. Use a rubber spatula to scrape the bowl. Add the egg whites and vanilla and mix until fully incorporated, about 2 minutes.

// Add half of the flour mixture and mix on low just until the powdery texture of the flour disappears, about 15 seconds. Immediately add the rest of the flour mixture and mix until combined. Scrape the bowl and mix a final 15 seconds.

// Remove the bowl from the mixer and use a rubber spatula to fold in the white chips. Drop the animal cookie butter in tablespoon-size scoops in four different locations in the bowl. Use the rubber spatula to gently swirl until you see thick ribbons of animal cookie butter. Don't overmix—you're finished!

// Your dough is forking ready!

If you have more willpower than I do and find yourself with extra, see My Go-To Baking & Storage DŌrections on page 48.

You Are a Goddamn Magical Unicorn

Imagine a world where unicorns actually did exist. There would be these glittery, rainbow-pooping creatures galloping around, making the world a better, more beautiful place. While this unicorn-a-verse may exist only in my dreams, the next best thing is to make cookie dough that is sparkly, beautiful, dazzling, and fancier than every other cookie dough out there. And here it is! It's swirled with jewel tones and special sprinkles; not to mention, it tastes like pure magic. No wonder people were enchanted with this when it was a seasonal flavor the summer we first opened the shop. Everyone could use a little glittery goodness in their life!

2½ cups heat-treated all-purpose flour (instructions on page 31)

1 tablespoon cornstarch

1½ teaspoons cream of tartar

¾ teaspoon baking powder

¾ teaspoon baking soda

¾ teaspoon salt

1½ sticks (12 tablespoons) unsalted butter, at room temperature

1 cup plus 2 tablespoons sugar

⅓ cup pasteurized egg whites, at room temperature

1½ teaspoons vanilla extract

½ cup sprinkles (the fancier the better—I highly recommend Sweetapolita's Unicorn Mix)

3 drops each of purple, blue, and pink food coloring

// In a medium bowl, whisk together the heat-treated flour, cornstarch, cream of tartar, baking powder, baking soda, and salt. Set aside.

// In the bowl of a stand mixer fitted with the paddle attachment, beat the butter on medium speed until smooth and creamy, about 2 minutes. Add the sugar and mix on medium until light and fluffy; about 4 minutes will do the trick. Use a rubber spatula to scrape the bowl. Add the egg whites and vanilla and mix until fully incorporated, about 2 minutes.

// Add half of the flour mixture and mix on low just until the powdery texture of the flour disappears, about 15 seconds. Immediately add the rest of the flour mixture and mix until combined. Scrape the bowl and mix a final 15 seconds.

// Remove the bowl from the mixer and use a rubber spatula to fold in the sprinkles.

// Once the sprinkles are well combined, make 3 small indentations in different places in the dough. I use my finger, but you can also use the back of a rubber spatula. Drop the food coloring in these indentations, one color per indentation.

// Use a rubber spatula to swirl the food coloring into the dough. It should take only a few stirs to do this—too much stirring can make the dough gray. (Gray dough won't give you the magical moment you're looking for!)

// And like magic, you have dough that's ready to eat!

If you magically have some dough left over, see My Go-To Baking & Storage DŌrections on page 48.

Speculoos Snack Attack

Y or N: The best thing about flying is free snacks? I vote yes! When it comes to my plane snacks, the flight attendants can hold the peanuts and the pretzels, I'll take allll the speculoos cookies. You know, those crisp, spiced shortbread cookies that come pre-packed in pairs? Cookie butter is usually made from those guys.

We could have stopped there and made a dough that went cookie butter crazy, but that's not how we roll at DŌ. Ever heard of puppy chow? Maybe you call it muddy buddies, or maybe you've been missing out your whole life, but puppy chow is one of my old-school snacks of choice. We reimagined puppy chow by making it with speculoos cookie butter instead of peanut butter. BAM. Someone call Delta and let them know about this invention (and tell them to give me the royalties)— passengers will be lining up for a one-way trip to speculoos heaven.

FOR THE PUPPY CHOW

4½ cups Rice Chex cereal

½ cup semisweet chocolate chips

¼ cup speculoos cookie butter (Biscoff and Trader Joe's are my favorites)

⅛ stick (1 tablespoon) unsalted butter

½ teaspoon vanilla extract

¾ cup confectioners' sugar

FOR THE DOUGH

1¼ cups heat-treated all-purpose flour (instructions on page 31)

2 teaspoons cornstarch

½ teaspoon baking soda

½ teaspoon salt

1 stick (8 tablespoons) unsalted butter, at room temperature

¾ cup speculoos cookie butter

¼ cup granulated sugar

½ cup plus 1 tablespoon brown sugar

¼ cup pasteurized egg whites, at room temperature

1½ teaspoons vanilla extract

// **Make the puppy chow:** Pour the Chex into a large bowl. Set aside.

// In a medium microwave-safe bowl, melt the chocolate chips, cookie butter, and butter in the microwave at 50% power in 30-second intervals, stirring in between, until completely smooth. Stir in the vanilla. Pour the chocolate mixture over the cereal and mix with a rubber spatula until all the pieces are evenly coated. Add the confectioners' sugar in two additions and mix until everything is well coated. Spread on waxed paper to cool. Set aside.

// **Make the dough:** In a medium bowl, whisk together the heat-treated flour, cornstarch, baking soda, and salt. Set aside.

// In the bowl of a stand mixer fitted with the paddle attachment, beat the butter and cookie butter on medium speed until smooth and creamy, about 2 minutes. Add the granulated and brown sugars and mix on medium until light and fluffy; about 4 minutes will do the trick. Use a rubber spatula to scrape the bowl. Add the egg whites and vanilla and mix until fully incorporated, about 2 minutes.

// Add half of the flour mixture and mix on low just until the powdery texture of the flour disappears, about 15 seconds. Immediately add the rest of the flour mixture and mix until combined. Scrape the bowl and mix a final 15 seconds.

// Remove the bowl from the mixer and use a rubber spatula to fold in 1½ cups of the puppy chow. The rest is yours to snack on!

// Chow down! This speculoos snack is ready!

Craving some cookies? Have extra cookie dough? See My Go-To Baking & Storage DŌrections on page 48.

Store puppy chow in an airtight container at room temperature for up to 1 week.

Play Dough

They say playing with your food as an adult is a big "no-no." I'm not sure who "they" are, but you can go ahead and disregard their nonsensical "rules." Release your inner artist—this recipe is *meant* to be played with. Find the cookie cutters, roll it into shapes, get your hands messy, and quit listening to the haters! Grab the nearest kid (your own, or someone you know…not just, like, any random kid) and make a masterpiece you can eat before the real adults come home.

2½ cups heat-treated all-purpose flour (instructions on page 31)

1 tablespoon cornstarch

1½ teaspoons cream of tartar

¾ teaspoon salt

1½ sticks (12 tablespoons) unsalted butter, at room temperature

1 cup plus 2 tablespoons sugar

⅓ cup applesauce

1½ teaspoons vanilla extract

Gel food coloring, your choice of color(s)

// In a medium bowl, whisk together the heat-treated flour, cornstarch, cream of tartar, and salt. Set aside.

// In the bowl of a stand mixer fitted with the paddle attachment, beat the butter on medium speed until smooth and creamy, about 2 minutes. Add the sugar and mix on medium until light and fluffy; about 4 minutes will do the trick. Use a rubber spatula to scrape the bowl. Add the applesauce and vanilla and mix until fully incorporated, about 2 minutes.

// Add half of the flour mixture and mix on low just until the powdery texture of the flour disappears, about 15 seconds. Immediately add the rest of the flour mixture and mix until combined. Scrape the bowl and mix a final 15 seconds.

// If you want multiple colors, divide the dough into equal portions in separate bowls. Add 1 drop of food coloring at a time to a dough portion and knead to mix the color throughout. Continue adding drops until you've achieved your desired color. Repeat with each remaining portion, using one color per portion.

// This one's ready—let's play!

If you want to bake your shapes, follow My Go-To Baking & Storage DŌrections on page 48. If your shapes are small or thin, you might need to adjust the baking time. They are ready when they look set and the edges barely darken.

/////////// *Kristen's Tip* ///////////

Look, Ma! No eggs! That's right—you probably have all these ingredients in your pantry, so what are you waiting for? You can play with this one all day. No eggs = no need to refrigerate immediately! PLAY AWAY!

//

Sugar Rush

I think it's safe to say I'm addicted to sugar. My desk drawer in the DŌ office is full of all sorts of candy. I've considered naming my next dog Watermelon Sour Patch, Cotton Candy can be the nickname for my firstborn child, and Pop Rocks would be my porn star name...if I had one.

I'm not convinced that throwing sour watermelon candy into cookie dough is the best idea. (I mean, I definitely tried it out, and let's just say it didn't make the book.) However, I do know that making cookie dough with cotton candy sugar and Pop Rocks is a *wonderful* idea. It's colorful, it's sweet, and it packs a popping surprise. Who doesn't love a good sugar rush?

2½ cups heat-treated all-purpose flour (instructions on page 31)

1 tablespoon cornstarch

1½ teaspoons cream of tartar

¾ teaspoon baking powder

¾ teaspoon baking soda

¾ teaspoon salt

1½ sticks (12 tablespoons) unsalted butter, at room temperature

1 cup plus 2 tablespoons cotton candy sugar (I order it on Amazon)

⅓ cup pasteurized egg whites, at room temperature

1½ teaspoons vanilla extract

3 drops gel food coloring (pick the color based on the flavor of cotton candy sugar you use!)

½ cup sugar sprinkles

2 packs Pop Rocks

// In a medium bowl, whisk together the heat-treated flour, cornstarch, cream of tartar, baking powder, baking soda, and salt. Set aside.

// In the bowl of a stand mixer fitted with the paddle attachment, beat the butter on medium speed until smooth and creamy, about 2 minutes. Add the sugar and mix on medium until light and fluffy; about 4 minutes will do the trick. Use a rubber spatula to scrape the bowl. Add the egg whites, vanilla, and food coloring and mix until fully incorporated, about 2 minutes.

// Add half of the flour mixture and mix on low just until the powdery texture of the flour disappears, about 15 seconds. Immediately add the rest of the flour mixture and mix until combined. Scrape the bowl and mix a final 15 seconds.

// Remove the bowl from the mixer and use a rubber spatula to fold in the sprinkles and Pop Rocks.

// Bring on the sugar rush! Your dough is ready!

If you're planning on finishing this later, see My Go-To Baking & Storage DŌrections on page 48.

/////////// **Kristen's Tip** ///////////

The Pop Rocks are the most exciting part of this recipe—but if they get too wet, they lose their pop. Make sure to keep the Pop Rocks separate from other ingredients and add them to the dough only once the flour is well incorporated. Then, watch your friends' faces light up when they take a bite!

//

When You're Salty but Need Something Sweet

When I set out to start DŌ, I thought my toughest challenge would be managing a small business. Boy, was I wrong.

During those early days, I was pricing out sugar and supplies on Monday and in the hospital fighting for my life on Wednesday. I had a severe reaction to an antibiotic prescribed by my doctor that was diagnosed as Stevens Johnson syndrome (SJS), a rare and often fatal disorder that affects only between one and five people per million. With those odds, I could have won the lottery, but instead, I found myself within inches of losing my life. My illness progressed to the worst possible level, known as severe toxic epidermal necrolysis syndrome (TENS). It's similar to sustaining extensive chemical burns all over your body—but I was burning from the inside out.

Weeks later, I woke up with a tube down my throat, unable to breathe or talk, a feeding tube up my nose, unable to eat or drink, and my eyes essentially sewn shut, blinded from an experimental eye surgery that attempted to save my eyesight. Sometimes I tried to communicate, writing chicken scratch on paper, only to fall unconscious mid-word. I was a prisoner in my hospital bed, trapped in a body battling with itself.

I wasn't the only one feeling isolated, lost, and alone. My family, friends, and soon-to-be husband felt just as helpless. They were forced to make decisions about my treatment without my input, while trying to stay positive and present for me. My mind blocked out a lot of the trauma, but my family experienced fear they'll never forget. I'll spare you the gory details of what happens when all of your skin falls off, and just say it was twenty-one days of excruciating physical and emotional trauma. But, because of my fighter's spirit, a wonderful medical team, and an even better support system, I won the real lottery. I survived.

This illness came with a silver lining, or, as I like to say, a crunchy sugar coating: a new perspective. I no longer cared about frivolous wedding planning details. I cared about things that mattered: loving the people around me, living a fulfilling life, and seizing each opportunity as though every day could be my last. I could see so clearly what was important and what was, well...bullsh*t.

Forget about how to bake a perfect cookie—if you take anything away from this book, let it be the realization of how truly lucky you are—you're alive and so loved. Give your loved ones a big hug—and a bigger batch of cookie dough—and let them know exactly what they mean to you. Out of the chaos of my illness, the most challenging and painful trial of my life, came the clarity I needed to make DŌ, my wildest dream, come true.

/// It's inevitable; life is sometimes going to be salty. But with the right perspective, you can also make it super sweet. And together, they're even better. These recipes are salty, making you appreciate the sweetness that much more.

Carnival Crunch

It wasn't until college that I realized you could pop popcorn without a machine. My mom, Karen, had a popcorn maker that we used daily—we had popcorn for dessert, popcorn after school, and if we were lucky, popcorn for dinner. On the rare occasion that my dad had a late meeting, my mom would skip cooking and make dinner-style popcorn. She'd pop it fresh, melt butter, sprinkle on LOTS of salt, and toss it all together with grated Parmesan. It was a treat—and is my second-favorite way to eat popcorn to this day.

My numba one way to eat it is caramel-coated, another Karen original. Karen's Killer Karamel Korn (see what I did there, Kris Jenner?). It's crunchy and salty and sweet and somehow still light and airy. I highly recommend making a double batch of popcorn when you're prepping for this cookie dough. If for some insane reason you have any left over (maybe you have that thing my friends are always telling me about—self-control), then just hand it right over to me, I'll help you out.

2 cups Karen's Killer Karamel Korn (divided; recipe follows)

2 cups heat-treated all-purpose flour (instructions on page 31)

1 tablespoon cornstarch

1½ teaspoons cream of tartar

¾ teaspoon baking powder

¾ teaspoon baking soda

¾ teaspoon salt

1½ sticks (12 tablespoons) unsalted butter, at room temperature

1 cup plus 2 tablespoons sugar

⅓ cup pasteurized egg whites, at room temperature

1½ teaspoons vanilla extract

// Make Karen's Killer Karamel Korn: Once cooled, place 1 cup of the caramel popcorn in a food processor and pulse until it has a flour-like texture. You may need to stir the popcorn a few times between pulses to make sure the popcorn "flour" has an even consistency.

// In a medium bowl, whisk together the ground popcorn "flour," heat-treated flour, cornstarch, cream of tartar, baking powder, baking soda, and salt. Set aside.

// In the bowl of a stand mixer fitted with the paddle attachment, beat the butter on medium speed until smooth and creamy, about 2 minutes. Add the sugar and mix on medium until light and fluffy; about 4 minutes will do the trick. Use a rubber spatula to scrape the bowl. Add the egg whites and vanilla and mix until fully incorporated, about 2 minutes.

// Add half of the ground popcorn mixture and mix on low just until the powdery texture of the flour disappears, about 15 seconds. Immediately add the rest of the ground popcorn mixture and mix until combined. Scrape the bowl and mix a final 15 seconds.

// Remove the bowl from the mixer and use a rubber spatula to fold in the remaining 1 cup caramel corn.

// Dough's done. Time to get poppin'!

If you happen to have some dough left over, see My Go-To Baking & Storage DŌrections on page 48.

KAREN'S KILLER KARAMEL KORN

*Makes **4 cups***

*Active time: **20 minutes***

*Time 'til caramel corn: **1 hour***

⅔ cup popcorn kernels

1 stick (8 tablespoons) unsalted butter

¼ cup light corn syrup

1 cup brown sugar

½ teaspoon baking soda

½ teaspoon vanilla extract

¼ teaspoon salt

// Pop the popcorn according to the package instructions. Set aside in a large metal bowl.

// Preheat the oven to 200°F. Line at least two baking sheets (more if your sheets are small) with parchment paper or silicone baking mats.

// In a large, heavy-bottomed pot, melt the butter over low heat. Stir in the corn syrup and brown sugar and continue to stir as you bring the mixture to a boil over medium-high heat. Reduce the heat and simmer for 3 minutes, stirring constantly. Add the baking soda, vanilla, and salt. Stir vigorously to incorporate. The mixture will foam up. Immediately pour the caramel mixture over the popcorn and stir to coat evenly.

// Spread the popcorn in a single layer on the baking sheet and bake for 15 minutes. Stir the popcorn on the baking sheet and bake for an additional 15 minutes. Remove from the oven and let the popcorn cool on the baking sheet.

// Store the popcorn in an airtight container for up to 5 days.

The Everything

NATURALLY
GF

I've been making The Everything for a very, very long time. This recipe has seen me through high school heartbreak, school fund-raisers, broken bones, marathon TV binges, countless birthdays and friendsgivings...you get the picture.

The Everything is one that *everyone* likes. It's an oatmeal cookie meets peanut butter cookie meets butterscotch blondie meets chocolate chip cookie. Not to mention, it's naturally gluten-free, which is a huge plus for me. It's the perfect recipe for all of those almost-empty bags of chocolate chips, extra nuts, and leftover jars of random ingredients in your pantry. Anything and everything (get it!?) goes with this one.

3 cups oats (if you're gluten-free, check that the oats also are gluten-free!)

1¼ teaspoons baking soda

½ stick (4 tablespoons) unsalted butter, at room temperature

1 cup peanut butter

¾ cup granulated sugar

¾ cup brown sugar

½ cup pasteurized egg whites, at room temperature

½ teaspoon vanilla extract

½ cup butterscotch chips

½ cup semisweet chocolate chips

// In a food processor or blender, pulse the oats 3 to 4 times, until they have a roughly chopped consistency. The oats shouldn't be as fine as flour but definitely should be finer than whole oats. Heat-treat the oats according to the instructions on page 31.

// Once the oats have cooled completely, whisk together the oats and baking soda. Set aside.

// In the bowl of a stand mixer fitted with the paddle attachment, beat the butter and peanut butter on medium speed until smooth and creamy, about 2 minutes. Add the granulated and brown sugars and mix on medium until light and fluffy; about 4 minutes will do the trick. Use a rubber spatula to scrape the bowl. Add the egg whites and vanilla and mix until fully incorporated, about 2 minutes.

// Add half of the oat mixture and mix on low just until the powdery texture of the oats disappears, about 30 seconds. Immediately add the rest of the oat mixture and mix until combined. Scrape the bowl and mix a final 15 seconds.

// Remove the bowl from the mixer and use a rubber spatula to fold in the butterscotch chips and semisweet chips.

// This dough is everything, and it's ready to eat!

If fresh-baked cookies are more your thing, see My Go-To Baking & Storage DŌrections on page 48.

Salt & Pepper Perfection

GREAT MADE GF

KRISTEN'S *Fav*

EASY TO MAKE *Vegan*

If you've shared a meal with anyone from my family, then you know all about our obsession with salt and pepper. We like A LOT of it, all over everything we eat. You'll know when the dish has enough pepper on it because my papa will sneeze, no less than five times, from his own pepper grinding ways. He does it to himself. No judgment, though, I'm the same way—it's clearly part of my DNA.

You probably think that putting pepper in cookie dough is super strange, but did you ever stop to think that it could be the secret spicy gem that's been missing from your classic cookie dough all along? Hear me out. No one thinks a jalapeño in your margarita is gross, or that fried chicken on your waffles is weird, so quit questioning and trust my expert, pepper-loving opinion.

1 cup Kick Ya in the Nuts Brittle (recipe follows)

1¼ cups heat-treated all-purpose flour (instructions on page 31)

2 teaspoons cornstarch

½ teaspoon baking soda

¾ teaspoon ground black pepper

½ teaspoon salt

1 stick (8 tablespoons) unsalted butter, at room temperature

¾ cup peanut butter

¼ cup granulated sugar

½ cup plus 1 tablespoon brown sugar

¼ cup pasteurized egg whites, at room temperature

1½ teaspoons vanilla extract

// Make a batch of Kick Ya in the Nuts Brittle: Once completely cooled, roughly chop the brittle and set aside.

// In a medium bowl, whisk together the heat-treated flour, cornstarch, baking soda, ground pepper, and salt. Set aside.

// In the bowl of a stand mixer fitted with the paddle attachment, beat the butter and peanut butter on medium speed until smooth and creamy, about 2 minutes. Add the granulated and brown sugars and mix on medium until light and fluffy; about 4 minutes will do the trick. Use a rubber spatula to scrape the bowl. Add the egg whites and vanilla and mix until fully incorporated, about 2 minutes.

// Add half of the flour mixture and mix on low just until the powdery texture of the flour disappears, about 15 seconds. Immediately add the rest of the flour mixture and mix until combined. Scrape the bowl and mix a final 15 seconds.

// Remove the bowl from the mixer and use a rubber spatula to fold in the chopped brittle.

// Boom! You have some pepper-perfect dough ready to devour!

Craving some cookies? Have extra cookie dough? See My Go-To Baking & Storage DŌrections on page 48.

CONTINUES ▶

/////////////////////////////////////

KICK YA IN THE NUTS BRITTLE

Makes *12 servings*
Active time: *10 minutes*
Time 'til brittle: *25 minutes*

2 cups granulated sugar

½ teaspoon sea salt

1¼ teaspoons ground black pepper

1¼ cups chopped peanuts (salted, unsalted, roasted, or not—whatever you like best)

// Line a baking sheet with parchment paper or a silicone baking mat.

// In a medium saucepan, warm the sugar over medium heat while stirring constantly with a rubber spatula.

// The sugar will begin to melt and gather in dry clumps. Keep stirring until the sugar is completely melted and the liquid turns light brown. Do. Not. Stop. Stirring. The mixture will bubble and thicken. Stir for 8 to 12 minutes, until it develops into a deep amber hue.

// Remove from the heat, add the salt and pepper, and stir until well incorporated (the pepper clumps easily, so stir well!). Once thoroughly combined, stir in the peanuts.

// Use a rubber spatula to scrape the caramel into the center of the lined baking sheet. It will be thick, but do your best to spread the hot brittle until the peanuts are in a single layer. It will not fill the whole baking sheet. Cool to room temperature. When the brittle is hard enough to shatter, it's ready!

// Break by hand or use a sharp knife to slice before serving. The brittle can be stored in an airtight container at room temperature for up to 1 week.

It's Always Samoa® Season

GREAT MADE GF

What's your favorite season? They all bring something to the table—winter is for holiday cheer and building snowmen; spring is all flowers blooming and birds singing; summer has long days and beach trips; and fall brings you delightfully basic pumpkin spice lattes. There's a secret fifth season that happens during the worst time of year—after you're so over winter but spring is still so far away. It's the absolute best season of all: Girl Scout Cookie season. It's probably for the best that Girl Scout Cookies are only around for a couple of weeks; it would be dangerous if I could get my hands on them year-round. I used to settle for the "stock up and store them in your freezer" approach, until I had one of my greatest ideas of all time: reimagine my favorite Girl Scout Cookie as cookie dough. This recipe is my take on the classic Samoas (also called Caramel deLites). Get ready to enjoy Girl Scout Cookie season all year long!

⅓ cup Homemade Salted Caramel Sauce (recipe on page 70)

2½ cups shredded unsweetened coconut

1 cup dark chocolate chips

2¼ cups heat-treated all-purpose flour (instructions on page 31)

2¼ teaspoons cornstarch

1 teaspoon baking soda

¾ teaspoon salt

1½ sticks (12 tablespoons) unsalted butter, at room temperature

¼ cup granulated sugar

1 cup brown sugar

⅓ cup pasteurized egg whites, at room temperature

1 tablespoon vanilla extract

// Make the Homemade Salted Caramel Sauce. Let the caramel cool completely.

// Toast the coconut: Preheat the oven to 300°F. Line a baking sheet with parchment paper or a silicone baking mat.

// Spread the coconut in a single layer and bake for 10 minutes, stirring every 3 minutes to make sure all the coconut pieces turn over at least once during baking. Remove from the oven and set aside on a plate to cool.

// Melt the chocolate: In a small microwave-safe bowl, heat the chocolate chips in the microwave on 50% power in 30-second increments. Stir well between each increment. Repeat just until the chocolate is melted. Lay a sheet of waxed paper on the countertop or another flat surface. Use a rubber spatula to scoop the melted chocolate into a piping bag or a ziplock bag. Cut the tip or corner so there's only a small hole. Pipe thick lines of chocolate onto the waxed paper. Set aside to cool.

// Measure 1½ cups of the cooled, toasted coconut and place it in a food processor. Pulse until the coconut has a crumb-like texture.

// In a medium bowl, whisk together the ground coconut, heat-treated flour, cornstarch, baking soda, and salt. Set aside.

// In the bowl of a stand mixer fitted with the paddle attachment, beat the butter on medium speed until smooth and creamy, about 2 minutes. Add the granulated and brown sugars and mix on medium until light and fluffy; about 4 minutes will do the trick. Use a rubber spatula to scrape the bowl. Add the egg whites and vanilla and mix until fully incorporated, about 2 minutes.

// Add half of the coconut mixture and mix on low just until the powdery texture of the flour disappears, about 15 seconds. Immediately add the rest of the coconut mixture and mix until combined. Scrape the bowl and mix a final 15 seconds.

// Use your hands or a knife to break the cooled dark chocolate strips.

// Remove the bowl from the mixer and use a rubber spatula to fold the dark chocolate pieces and the rest of the toasted coconut into the dough. Drop ⅓ cup caramel in tablespoon-size scoops in four different locations in the bowl. Use a rubber spatula to gently swirl until you see thick ribbons of caramel. Don't overmix—you're finished!

// At last, Girl Scout Cookie season is here!

If you didn't eat it all in one sitting, see My Go-To Baking & Storage DŌrections on page 48.

Dessert Focaccia

GREAT MADE GF   EASY TO MAKE *Vegan*

Bread is kind of like cookie dough—you can take something that's already amazing and jazz it up with mix-ins to elevate it to a whole new level. I love a good zucchini bread, and I crave tangy cheese bread, but most of all, I obsess over fresh rosemary focaccia.
The kind at restaurants that comes with olive oil for dipping that you ask them to refill again and again and then can they please bring you one more basket so you can throw some in your to-go box? That kind.

If focaccia bread and cookie dough made some badass offspring, it would be this recipe.

2½ cups heat-treated all-purpose flour (instructions on page 31)

1 tablespoon cornstarch

1½ teaspoons cream of tartar

¾ teaspoon baking powder

¾ teaspoon baking soda

¾ teaspoon salt

¾ stick (6 tablespoons) unsalted butter, at room temperature

¼ cup olive oil

1 cup plus 2 tablespoons sugar

⅓ cup pasteurized egg whites, at room temperature

1½ teaspoons vanilla extract

1 tablespoon finely minced fresh rosemary

½ cup roughly chopped dark chocolate bar

¼ teaspoon coarse sea salt

// In a medium bowl, whisk together the heat-treated flour, cornstarch, cream of tartar, baking powder, baking soda, and salt. Set aside.

// In the bowl of a stand mixer fitted with the paddle attachment, beat the butter and olive oil on medium speed until smooth and creamy, about 2 minutes. Add the sugar and mix on medium until light and fluffy; about 4 minutes will do the trick. Use a rubber spatula to scrape the bowl. Add the egg whites and vanilla and mix until fully incorporated, about 2 minutes.

// Add half of the flour mixture and mix on low just until the powdery texture of the flour disappears, about 15 seconds. Immediately add the rest of the flour mixture and mix until combined. Scrape the bowl and mix a final 15 seconds.

// Remove the bowl from the mixer and use a rubber spatula to fold in the rosemary and dark chocolate. Sprinkle with the sea salt.

// Call Oprah, it's savory dough time!

If you're planning on finishing this later, see My Go-To Baking & Storage DŌrections on page 48.

IT TAKES A
village

It takes a lot of work to run a business, and I certainly can't take all the credit. Over time, I've slowly and steadily built a team of people who have become like family to me.

A family mentality is a priority when it comes to building a team and choosing partners and new locations. It doesn't matter what the role, or how long you've been part of the group, each employee has made a difference to me, the business, and our customers.

My employees have worked (literally) around the clock during holiday season. They have given up their nights and weekends and sanity to travel across the country for pop-ups and festivals. They have scooped thousands of pounds of cookie dough for customers. They have filled more than one million containers for online shipping. They have washed more dishes than I even want to count. They are the ones connecting with thousands of fans a day, the ones who really shape every individual DŌ experience. All while being my best source of inspiration, my everyday heroes. I can't say it enough: I truly appreciate my crew—each and every one of them. I am so lucky to have my incredible DŌ family.

Kristen's TIP

If you don't have fresh rosemary but still want savory sweet dough, substitute 1 teaspoon dried rosemary for the fresh rosemary, or if rosemary is out of the question, use 1 teaspoon dried thyme.

When It's Bathing Suit Season but There's Still Cookie Dough to Eat

My ideal vacation is a trip to the beach. I need that sunscreen smell that sticks between the creases of your fingers, the hot-to-the-touch feeling of freshly sun-kissed skin, and an extra-large frozen margarita—with salt—in my hand (and at least one in my belly).

So, for my bachelorette party, the obvious choice was Hilton Head Island, my favorite beach. I and twenty-one of my gal pals planned on catching plenty of vitamin sea and extra-large margaritas in a beachfront house over Memorial Day weekend (thanks to my best friend Liz's parents!).

At this point I had finalized the cookie dough recipes for DŌ's menu. In fact, I had made and frozen heaping batches of the final product. I was planning to bring it to my bachelorette for one last round of taste-testing. Plus, what better way to soak up all that tequila? But I was admitted to the ICU ten days before the trip. My dream bachelorette party was canceled and the cookie dough stayed locked up in my tiny NYC freezer.

Once I left the hospital, I was on a mission to gain back some of the weight I had lost. I binged on my freezer full of cookie dough. "Doctor's orders," I mumbled between bites. After clearing out the original freezerful (hey, I had a lot of weight to gain!), I thought, if I couldn't party at the beach, at least I could eat summer-inspired cookie dough. Using things like rosé and fresh berries, I made a ton of new recipes.

Don't worry. The beach trip happened, about a year and a half late. We called it "Kristen said 'I DŌ,'" since both my marriage to Chris and my business were going strong!

/// Lucky for you, your own beach trip is just a mixing bowl away! With these flavors, it's easier than ever to whip up a batch of cookie dough that's perfect for a summer getaway (or a stay-cation at home).

Kristen's
TIP

If you make this recipe with frozen fruit, put the strawberries in first and heat them alone for 3 minutes. Then add the rest of the berries and heat for 3 minutes. Add the sugar and follow the rest of the recipe.

Best Berry Crisp

GREAT MADE GF

Fruit is my jam. I started stuffing my face with berries at an early age. I have vivid memories of fighting off mosquitoes while picking raspberries in my grandma's backyard. My siblings and I would raid her raspberry bushes, making sure not to leave even one tiny piece of fruit behind. While I don't get to pick many berries fresh off the vine these days, one of my favorite things about summer is having fresh berries in season! It's the perfect time to make a pie, a cobbler, and, most often in my kitchen, this cookie dough.

FOR THE BERRY COMPOTE

½ cup blueberries

½ cup raspberries

½ cup chopped strawberries

¼ cup granulated sugar

2 tablespoons cornstarch

FOR THE CRISP TOPPING

¼ cup all-purpose flour

¼ cup oats (if you're making this gluten-free, check that the oats also are gluten-free!)

½ cup brown sugar

½ teaspoon ground cinnamon

¼ cup chopped pecans

½ stick (4 tablespoons) unsalted butter, melted

FOR THE DOUGH

2¼ cups heat-treated all-purpose flour (instructions on page 31)

2¼ teaspoons cornstarch

1 teaspoon baking soda

¾ teaspoon salt

1½ sticks (12 tablespoons) unsalted butter, at room temperature

¼ cup granulated sugar

1 cup brown sugar

⅓ cup pasteurized egg whites, at room temperature

1 tablespoon vanilla extract

// Make the berry compote: Place the berries, sugar, and cornstarch in a medium saucepan over medium heat, and stir to coat. Stir occasionally and gently mash to release some of the juices. Once the mixture begins to boil, stir continuously for about 2 minutes, until the compote is thick and jam-like. Remove from heat and cool in the refrigerator.

// Make the crisp topping: Preheat the oven to 350°F and line a baking sheet with parchment paper or a silicone baking mat.

// In a medium bowl, whisk together the flour, oats, brown sugar, cinnamon, and pecans. Pour in the melted butter and stir to combine. Scrape the mixture onto the lined baking sheet and spread into an even layer, about ¼ inch thick. Bake for 7 minutes, or until the topping looks bubbly and lightly golden brown around the edges. Remove from the oven and let cool in the refrigerator.

// Make the dough: In a medium bowl, whisk together the heat-treated flour, cornstarch, baking soda, and salt. Set aside.

// In the bowl of a stand mixer fitted with the paddle attachment, beat the butter on medium speed until smooth and creamy, about 2 minutes. Add the granulated and brown sugars and mix until light and fluffy; about 4 minutes. Use a rubber spatula to scrape the bowl. Add the egg whites and vanilla and mix until fully incorporated, about 2 minutes.

// Add half of the flour mixture and mix on low just until the powdery texture of the flour disappears, about 15 seconds. Immediately add the rest of the flour mixture and mix until combined. Scrape the bowl and mix for a final 15 seconds.

// Remove the bowl from the mixer and use a rubber spatula to fold in the crisp topping. Drop the cooled compote in 2 tablespoon–size scoops in four different locations in the bowl. Use the rubber spatula to gently swirl until you see thick ribbons of compote. Don't overmix!

// Grab a spoon—this one is berry good!

Trust me, you'll want to bake this dough too! See My Go-To Baking & Storage DŌrections on page 48.

128 \ WHEN IT'S BATHING SUIT SEASON BUT
THERE'S STILL COOKIE DOUGH TO EAT
\ MAKES
25 scoops
\ TIME 'TIL DOUGH
22 minutes
\ TIME 'TIL COOKIES
2 hours 40 minutes

Cookies and Cream

Being gluten-free isn't all that difficult, but I do miss a few things: bread, pizza, and Oreos. Sadly, I have to say no to cookies and cream everything: ice cream, McFlurries, cupcakes, frosting—I could go on all day. As I'm writing this, there are no gluten-free Oreo cookies. I guess since Oreos are already vegan (still shocked about that btw), Oreo ticked the dietary accommodation box and left us gluten-free-ers out in the cold. Bummer. (If you're reading this, and Nabisco has started to make gluten-free Oreos, then I'm probably at least ten pounds heavier and 10 percent happier.)

While I've never quite been able to make the perfect gluten-free Oreo cookie replica, I have cracked the code for the copycat cream filling, thanks to Stella Parks (check out her first book, *BraveTart*!); and we all know the cream is the best part of the sandwich cookie anyway. For all my non-gluten-free friends (and my gluten-free-ers willing to use Oreo knock-offs), this recipe is a little bit crunchy, a little bit creamy, and a little bit chocolate-y. Add all those "little bits" together and you get something that's a whole lotta delicious!

FOR THE COPYCAT CREAM FILLING

1 stick (8 tablespoons) unsalted butter

½ teaspoon vanilla extract

2 cups confectioners' sugar

FOR THE DOUGH

2¼ cups heat-treated all-purpose flour (instructions on page 31)

2¼ teaspoons cornstarch

1 teaspoon baking soda

¾ teaspoon salt

1½ sticks (12 tablespoons) unsalted butter, at room temperature

¼ cup granulated sugar

1 cup brown sugar

⅓ cup pasteurized egg whites, at room temperature

1 tablespoon vanilla extract

½ cup Oreo baking crumbs (or any brand chocolate cookie crumb, found in the baking section)

// Make the copycat cream filling: In a small microwave-safe bowl, microwave the butter on 50% power for five 30-second intervals, stirring well between each interval. Continue with all five intervals even if the butter is fully melted. Let the butter cool slightly.

// Pour the melted butter into the bowl of a stand mixer fitted with the paddle attachment. Add the vanilla and beat on medium for 30 seconds. Add the confectioners' sugar 1 cup at a time, beating on low speed. Then increase the speed to medium and beat until the mixture has the consistency of a thick frosting. Set aside.

// Make the dough: In a medium bowl, whisk together the heat-treated flour, cornstarch, baking soda, and salt. Set aside.

// In the bowl of a stand mixer fitted with the paddle attachment, beat the butter on medium speed until smooth and creamy, about 2 minutes. Add the granulated and brown sugars and mix on medium until light and fluffy; about 4 minutes will do the trick. Use a rubber spatula to scrape the bowl. Add the egg whites and vanilla and mix until fully incorporated, about 2 minutes.

// Add half of the flour mixture and mix on low just until the powdery texture of the flour disappears, about 15 seconds. Immediately add the rest of the flour mixture and mix until combined. Scrape the bowl and mix a final 15 seconds.

// Remove the bowl from the mixer and use a rubber spatula to fold in the Oreo baking crumbs. Drop the copycat cookie cream filling in tablespoon-size scoops in four different locations in the bowl. Use the rubber spatula to gently swirl until you see thick ribbons. Don't overmix—you're finished!

// Dig right into double-stuffed dough.

If you happen to have some dough left over, see My Go-To Baking & Storage DŌrections on page 48.

Kristen's
TIP

Don't waste time shelling nuts. You can find pre-shelled pistachios in your grocery store. If you don't see them, ask! Sometimes they are hidden in bulk sections or with health food items.

Papa's Pistachio

Our annual family vacation for the first eighteen years of my life took my extended family to Hilton Head Island, South Carolina. We would head out early to the beach each morning with no plans to return until we were fully sunburned and our hands and feet were completely prune-y. We had to be sure to pack enough to sustain us for a long day of sandcastle building, beach walking, and swimming in the ocean. Each of the adults had a different responsibility: Grandma packed us sandwiches and water; my aunt was tasked with licorice and Diet Pepsi; my uncle was in charge of Bloody Marys and beer; my mom grabbed the sunscreen and towels (plus her not-so-secret stash of gin). My dad carried the beach chairs and toys, and Papa only had to remember one very important thing—the pistachio nuts.

We would eat handful after handful of those pistachio nuts, passing the bag around, arguing about who got it next or whose sandy hand ruined the whole damn bag. We'd toss the shells on the sand, marking our spot on the beach and leaving the only trace of our day of fun in the sun. Pistachios will always remind me of those unforgettable family vacations and of my nut-loving grandfather. Here's to you, Papa!

1 cup shelled pistachios

2½ cups heat-treated all-purpose flour (instructions on page 31)

1 tablespoon cornstarch

1½ teaspoons cream of tartar

¾ teaspoon baking powder

¾ teaspoon baking soda

¾ teaspoon salt

1½ sticks (12 tablespoons) unsalted butter, at room temperature

1 cup plus 2 tablespoons sugar

⅓ cup pasteurized egg whites, at room temperature

1½ teaspoons vanilla extract

1 (4-ounce) bar of dark chocolate, roughly chopped

// In a food processor, pulse the pistachios 3 to 6 times, until the nuts are crumbly but not yet flour. Transfer to a small bowl. Set aside.

// In a medium bowl, whisk together the heat-treated flour, cornstarch, cream of tartar, baking powder, baking soda, and salt. Set aside.

// In the bowl of a stand mixer fitted with the paddle attachment, beat the butter on medium speed until smooth and creamy, about 2 minutes. Add the sugar and mix on medium until light and fluffy; about 4 minutes will do the trick. Use a rubber spatula to scrape the bowl. Add the egg whites and vanilla and mix until fully incorporated, about 2 minutes.

// Add half of the flour mixture and mix on low just until the powdery texture of the flour disappears, about 15 seconds. Immediately add the rest of the flour mixture and mix until combined. Scrape the bowl and mix a final 15 seconds.

// Remove the bowl from the mixer and use the rubber spatula to fold in the nuts and chocolate.

// You'd be nutty not to eat the dough now!

If fresh-baked cookies are more your thing, see My Go-To Baking & Storage DŌrections on page 48.

132 WHEN IT'S BATHING SUIT SEASON BUT THERE'S STILL COOKIE DOUGH TO EAT

MAKES
30 scoops

TIME 'TIL DOUGH
35 minutes

TIME 'TIL COOKIES
2 hours 30 minutes

Mixing Bowl Cherry Cola Slurpee®

GREAT MADE GF

I didn't choose the Cherry Cola Slurpee life, the Cherry Cola Slurpee life chose me. My obsession started as a Friday carpool treat. Our moms would rotate pickup days, and whoever was lucky enough to get the Friday afternoon shift had to make the stop at 7-Eleven on the way home to prevent a riot.

There is a right way to make a Cherry Cola Slurpee: first goes the layer of Cola, then cherry, then Cola on top. Always use a regular straw (those spoon straws don't allow you to slurp up the last inch at the bottom). It's a science.

Now, years later, if I pull into a 7-Eleven to get gas or walk by one in the city, you better believe I stop in to get the same Slurpee I've been sipping on for years. I proudly walk my thirty-year-old butt out of that fine establishment with one big ol' smile and one Super Gulp Slurpee.

FOR THE CHOCOLATE-COVERED CHERRIES

1½ cups semisweet chocolate chips

1 cup dried cherries

FOR THE DOUGH

2¼ cups heat-treated all-purpose flour (instructions on page 31)

2¼ teaspoons cornstarch

1 teaspoon baking soda

¾ teaspoon salt

1½ sticks (12 tablespoons) unsalted butter, at room temperature

¼ cup granulated sugar

1 cup brown sugar

⅓ cup pasteurized egg whites, at room temperature

2 tablespoons cherry soda syrup (found online or in stores by the SodaStreams)

1 tablespoon vanilla extract

// **Make the chocolate-covered cherries:** In a medium microwave-safe bowl, heat the semisweet chips in the microwave on 50% power in 30-second increments. Stir well between each increment. Repeat just until the chocolate is melted.

// Use a toothpick or fork to dip the cherries into the melted chocolate. Place on waxed paper in a single layer to dry.

// **Make the dough:** In a medium bowl, whisk together the heat-treated flour, cornstarch, baking soda, and salt. Set aside.

// In the bowl of a stand mixer fitted with the paddle attachment, beat the butter on medium speed until smooth and creamy, about 2 minutes. Add the granulated and brown sugars and mix on medium until light and fluffy; about

4 minutes will do the trick. Use a rubber spatula to scrape the bowl. Add the egg whites, cherry soda syrup, and vanilla and mix until fully incorporated, about 2 minutes.

// Add half of the flour mixture and mix on low just until the powdery texture of the flour disappears, about 15 seconds. Immediately add the rest of the flour mixture and mix until combined. Scrape the bowl and mix a final 15 seconds.

// Check that the chocolate on the cherries has set. Remove the bowl from the mixer and use a rubber spatula to fold in the chocolate-covered cherries.

// Slurp this one up! It's ready!

If you're planning on finishing this later, see My Go-To Baking & Storage DŌrections on page 48.

/////////// *Kristen's Tip* ///////////

Not a Cherry Cola fan? You can use any concentrated soda syrup (look for SodaStream)—try root beer or orange-flavored syrup! Make a "float" flavor by swapping the chocolate-covered cherries for white chocolate chips! Call me when it's ready:)

///

Rosé All Day,
page 134

Mixing Bowl
Cherry Cola Slurpee®,
opposite page

Kristen's
Lemonade
Stand, page 135

Rosé All Day

GREAT MADE **GF**

One of my favorite annual traditions is a trip my husband, Chris, and I take each summer to the Hamptons. We stay at the same place, eat at the same restaurants, and visit the same wineries. Of all the wineries Long Island has to offer, our favorite is Wölffer Estate—partially for the beautiful views, partially for their banging cheese plate, but mostly for their Summer in a Bottle rosé. This rosé is crisp, refreshing, and bursting with flavors of the fruits like apple and pear that reach peak ripeness at the height of summer. Wölffer's celebrated rosé might be called Summer in a Bottle, but for me, rosé season doesn't end! I crave it all day, every day, winter, spring, summer, and fall. If you can relate, this is the cookie dough for you.

FOR THE STRAWBERRIES

2 cups sliced strawberries (about ¹/₈ inch thick)

FOR THE ROSÉ REDUCTION

1½ cups strawberries (Fresh or Frozen)

4 tablespoons sugar

1 cup rosé

FOR THE CRÈME

½ cup white chocolate chips

¼ cup heavy cream

FOR THE DOUGH

3 cups heat-treated all-purpose flour (instructions on page 31)

1 tablespoon cornstarch

1½ teaspoons cream of tartar

¾ teaspoon baking powder

¾ teaspoon baking soda

¾ teaspoon salt

1½ sticks (12 tablespoons) unsalted butter, at room temperature

1 cup plus 2 tablespoons sugar

⅓ cup pasteurized egg whites, at room temperature

1½ teaspoons vanilla extract

// Prepare the strawberries: Preheat the oven to 225°F. Line a baking sheet with parchment paper or a silicone baking mat.

// Spread the strawberries in an even layer over the lined baking sheet. Bake for 30 minutes. Flip the strawberries and bake for an additional 30 minutes, until strawberries appear dehydrated. Set aside.

// Make the crème: Place white chocolate chips in a small bowl. Heat the cream in the microwave in 30-second increments, stirring well between each increment until it boils. Pour the hot cream over the white chocolate and let sit briefly. Then stir vigorously, until the chocolate and cream are well combined. Chill in the refrigerator.

// Make the rosé reduction: In a medium saucepan, warm the strawberries and sugar over low heat. Give the mixture a few stirs, pour in the rosé, and increase the heat while stirring constantly until the mixture boils. Then turn the heat to medium high. Continue to cook, stirring occasionally, until the strawberries are soft and the mixture has the appearance of a compote, 15 minutes. For the final 10 minutes, stir constantly, breaking up the strawberries until the mixture is thick and jam-like. Chill in the refrigerator.

// Finish the crème: Transfer the white chocolate mixture from the refrigerator to the bowl of a stand mixer fitted with the paddle attachment. Whip on high, scraping the bowl as needed, until the mixture is fluffy and resembles a thick cream, like frosting. Set aside.

// Make the dough: In a medium bowl, whisk together the heat-treated flour, cornstarch, cream of tartar, baking powder, baking soda, and salt. Set aside.

// In the bowl of a stand mixer fitted with the paddle attachment, beat the butter on medium speed until smooth and creamy, about 2 minutes. Add the sugar and mix on medium until light and fluffy; about 4 minutes will do the trick. Use a rubber spatula to scrape the bowl. Add the egg whites, vanilla, and ¾ cups of the rosé reduction and mix until fully incorporated, about 2 minutes.

// Add half of the flour mixture and mix on low just until the powdery texture of the flour disappears, about 15 seconds. Immediately add the rest of the flour mixture and mix until combined. Scrape the bowl and mix a final 15 seconds.

// Remove the bowl from the mixer. Roughly chop the dehydrated strawberries and fold them into the dough. Then swirl in the crème.

If Rosé All Day is your motto, what are you waiting for?

If you have more willpower than I do and find yourself with extra, see My Go-To Baking & Storage DŌrections on page 48.

Kristen's Lemonade Stand

EASY TO MAKE *Vegan*

GREAT MADE GF

Adding fruit to something automatically makes it healthy in my book. Throw a raspberry in my champagne, some strawberries in my milkshake, or some fresh lemon in my cookie dough, and you can tick off a serving of fruits and vegetables for the day.

No need to wait until summer to stumble by a local lemonade stand. Get your lemonade fix—and a daily serving of fruit—right here.

3 whole lemons

2½ cups heat-treated all-purpose flour (instructions on page 31)

1 tablespoon cornstarch

1½ teaspoons cream of tartar

¾ teaspoon baking powder

¾ teaspoon baking soda

¾ teaspoon salt

1½ sticks (12 tablespoons) unsalted butter, at room temperature

1 cup plus 2 tablespoons sugar

1½ teaspoons vanilla extract

1 teaspoon lemon extract

2 tablespoons finely chopped fresh basil (optional)

// Zest the lemons into a small bowl until you have 1 tablespoon zest. Set aside.

// Juice the lemons until you have ⅓ cup juice. Use a juicer or my favorite cheap-o method: Stick a spoon into the lemon and squeeze. Move the spoon back and forth while squeezing until all the juice is out. (This works so well because the spoon creates leverage and breaks the membranes of the juice sacks. Max juice for the low price of a spoon!)

// In a medium bowl, whisk together the heat-treated flour, cornstarch, cream of tartar, baking powder, baking soda, and salt. Set aside.

// In the bowl of a stand mixer fitted with the paddle attachment, beat the butter on medium speed until smooth and creamy, about 2 minutes. Add the sugar and mix on medium until light and fluffy; about 4 minutes will do the trick. Use a rubber spatula to scrape the bowl. Add the lemon juice, vanilla, and lemon extract and mix until fully incorporated, about 2 minutes.

// Add half of the flour mixture and mix on low just until the powdery texture of the flour disappears, about 15 seconds. Immediately add the rest of the flour mixture and mix until combined. Scrape the bowl and mix a final 15 seconds.

// Remove the bowl from the mixer and use a rubber spatula to fold in the lemon zest and basil.

// Lemon-y fresh dough, let's go!

If fresh-baked cookies are more your thing, see My Go-To Baking & Storage DŌrections on page 48.

//////////// **Kristen's Tip** ////////////

The fresh basil is optional, but it's my favorite twist on this lemon-y dough. Fresh herbs always add a bright, herbal zing— and they remind me of my mom's garden every time!

Kristen's
TIP

You can use either a
Microplane or a cheese
grater to get fine
chocolate shavings.

Always Room for Mint Chip

Why is it that you can finish eating dinner and feel completely stuffed—like physically unable to fit one more bite in your stomach—but still have room for ice cream? It's like your stomach reserves this little pocket where only ice cream is allowed, so that there is always room for a delectable dessert post-dinner. Mint chip ice cream (and cookie dough!) is a meal-finishing must-have. It's light and refreshing and has juuuuustt the right amount of little chocolate shavings sprinkled throughout. I'm going to need an extra pocket!

2¼ cups heat-treated all-purpose flour (instructions on page 31)

2¼ teaspoons cornstarch

1 teaspoon baking soda

¾ teaspoon salt

1½ sticks (12 tablespoons) unsalted butter, at room temperature

¼ cup granulated sugar

1 cup brown sugar

⅓ cup pasteurized egg whites, at room temperature

1 tablespoon vanilla extract

1 teaspoon peppermint extract

3 drops mint green food coloring

1 (4-ounce) bar semisweet chocolate, finely grated (1 cup)

// In a medium bowl, whisk together the heat-treated flour, cornstarch, baking soda, and salt. Set aside.

// In the bowl of a stand mixer fitted with the paddle attachment, beat the butter on medium speed until smooth and creamy, about 2 minutes. Add the granulated and brown sugars and mix on medium until light and fluffy; about 4 minutes will do the trick. Use a rubber spatula to scrape the bowl. Add the egg whites, vanilla, peppermint extract, and food coloring and mix until fully incorporated, about 2 minutes.

// Add half of the flour mixture and mix on low just until the powdery texture of the flour disappears, about 15 seconds. Immediately add the rest of the flour mixture and mix until combined. Scrape the bowl and mix a final 15 seconds.

// Remove the bowl from the mixer and use a rubber spatula to fold in the shaved chocolate.

// You know you have room! Dig in!

If you didn't eat it all in one sitting, see My Go-To Baking & Storage DŌrections on page 48.

AROUND THE world

DŌ's customers aren't just NYU students and local New Yorkers, they hail from around the globe, traveling to Greenwich Village to visit our flagship shop. I've met countless excited people from nearly every continent that "just had to come" to see what DŌ was all about.

Once, a couple flew all the way from Australia just to come to DŌ. They came straight from the airport to the shop, loaded up on cookie dough, and were flying back to Australia three hours later. That's twenty hours in one-way flight time, just for my cookie dough. Unreal!

A couple from Germany even got engaged in the shop! This wonderful man came over to Chris when he was working the door one afternoon. He spoke broken English, but Chris was able to make out the general idea: He wanted us to hold up a series of signs and hide a diamond ring in his special lady's cookie dough. "I'm sorry, what? He just handed you this diamond ring and wants us to get it covered in cookie dough?" I asked Chris. "That's awesome! Let's dough this!" I proclaimed. (You know me, I'm here to make dreams come true.) And we did. We gave this woman a proposal she would never forget—and a cup of cookie dough to enjoy while she was at it. Too bad every cup of cookie dough doesn't come with a diamond in it!

When It's Finally Sweater Weather

Like any cautious entrepreneur, I took the scoop shop's initial success with a grain of salt. I was enjoying every second of the interviews, lines, celebrity sightings, and shout-outs. But surely it couldn't last forever. There wouldn't always be lines down the block, would there? I'd speculate about the day the line would disappear and what would be the cause. Two months later, I thought I'd found the answer.

A powerful blizzard, forecasted to dump three feet of snow, was set to roll over New York City. This was uncharted territory. Should we open? Would anyone show up? In a blizzard? I decided to take the risk. If some dedicated customers NEEDED cookie dough bad enough to trek out into the storm…we had BETTER be open for them. Besides, the weathermen were probably wrong anyway.

I called my staff and crushed their dream of a snow day with my plan to open. Promising a chill day (no pun intended), I scrounged up a skeleton crew of team members. *Who is going out in a blizzard for cookie dough, anyway?* they mumbled. Thank god they showed up.

You know who else showed up? Customers. Lots of them. Hoping they could finally get into DŌ because there "surely wouldn't be a line in these conditions." Kids who were off school, adults who didn't have work, and tourists who were stranded in a blizzard came flocking to Greenwich Village for the ~~hottest~~ coldest dessert in town.

Since my customers were outside, so was I. Shoveling the snow, handing out hot chocolate samples, and managing the door as people tried to push their way inside for relief from the intense wind. Fun fact: The Instagram picture we posted to let customers know we'd open during the storm is still our most-liked Instagram picture! (At the time of typing this sentence, at least.)

/// These cookie dough recipes are so good you'd trek out into a blizzard for them—but luckily you no longer have to!

Caramel Apple Harvest

The best part of autumn in New York is apple picking. Apple picking is a family tradition that dates back to before I can remember. Every September we'd spend a day in the orchard picking apples and spend the next few months attempting to eat them all. Every year when it starts to feel chilly out, I grab a bunch of girlfriends and head to New York's best upstate farms to continue the tradition.

Whether you've picked them yourself, or picked them up from the grocery store, with this dough you'll need only two apples from your haul to be ready for fall!

1½ cups oats (if you're making this gluten-free, check that the oats also are gluten-free!)

2 apples

1 cup Sprite

1 cup plus 1 tablespoon heat-treated all-purpose flour (instructions on page 31)

1 teaspoon cornstarch

½ teaspoon baking soda

½ teaspoon ground cinnamon

½ teaspoon salt

1 stick (8 tablespoons) unsalted butter, at room temperature

¼ cup granulated sugar

¾ cup plus 2 tablespoons brown sugar

¼ cup pasteurized egg whites, at room temperature

1 tablespoon vanilla extract

⅓ cup caramel bits

¼ cup cinnamon chips

// In a food processor or blender, pulse the oats 3 or 4 times, until they have a roughly chopped consistency. The oats shouldn't be as fine as flour but should be visibly chopped, about a quarter of the size of whole oats. Heat-treat the oats according to the instructions on page 31.

// While the oats cool, core and dice the apples, then fully submerge them in the cup of Sprite to soak.

// Once the oats have cooled completely, in a medium bowl, whisk together the oats, heat-treated flour, cornstarch, baking soda, cinnamon, and salt. Set aside.

// In the bowl of a stand mixer fitted with the paddle attachment, beat the butter on medium speed until smooth and creamy, about 2 minutes. Add the granulated and brown sugars and mix on medium until light and fluffy; about 4 minutes will do the trick. Use a rubber spatula to scrape the bowl. Add the egg whites and vanilla and mix until fully incorporated, about 2 minutes.

// Add half of the flour mixture and mix on low just until the powdery texture of the flour disappears, about 15 seconds. Immediately add the rest of the flour mixture and mix until combined. Scrape the bowl and mix a final 15 seconds.

// Remove the bowl from the mixer and use a rubber spatula to fold in the caramel bits and cinnamon chips.

// Drain the apples and arrange in a single layer on paper towels. Pat the apples dry, then fold into the dough.

// Let's grab a spoon and live apple-y ever after.

Trust me, you'll want to bake this dough too! See My Go-To Baking & Storage DŌrections on page 48.

/////////// **Kristen's Tip** ///////////

Using Sprite to keep apples from browning is one of my favorite tricks. Sprite has all the anti-gross-brown-spots power of lemon juice, without the acidic flavor.

///

142 \ WHEN IT'S FINALLY
SWEATER WEATHER

\ MAKES
33 scoops

\ TIME 'TIL DOUGH
25 minutes

\ TIME 'TIL COOKIES
2 hours 50 minutes

PSB(londie)

You're either a pumpkin spice kinda person, or you're just not. When leaves start to fall and there's a crispness in the air...you are counting down the days until Starbucks releases their notorious lattes, or you could care less. You start making more frequent trips to Trader Joe's, hoping that the grocery store fairies will magically stock the shelves with pumpkin spice everything, or you don't even notice.

I can guarantee that you will like this recipe even if PSL isn't in your vocabulary. It's got everything you love about a blondie—all the chewy, brown sugary, buttery flavors—mixed with everything you love about fall—the spices, the warmth of that new scarf, the smell of your favorite harvest candle—and it's cookie dough! Move over, PSL. PSB is here, and we're super excited.

FOR THE PUMPKIN PIE SPICE

1 tablespoon ground ginger

2 teaspoons ground cinnamon

1 teaspoon ground allspice

1 teaspoon ground cloves

1 teaspoon ground nutmeg

FOR THE DOUGH

1½ cups heat-treated all-purpose flour (instructions on page 31)

1½ teaspoons cornstarch

½ teaspoon baking soda

½ teaspoon salt

¾ stick (6 tablespoons) unsalted butter, at room temperature

1 cup brown sugar

½ cup unsweetened 100% pumpkin puree (I use Libby's, but any 100% pumpkin will work)

2 teaspoons vanilla extract

// Make the pumpkin pie spice: In a small bowl, whisk together the ginger, cinnamon, allspice, cloves, and nutmeg. Measure 1 tablespoon of pumpkin pie spice. Store the rest in an airtight container for later use.

// Make the dough: In a medium bowl, whisk together the pumpkin pie spice, heat-treated flour, cornstarch, baking soda, and salt. Set aside.

// In the bowl of a stand mixer fitted with the paddle attachment, beat the butter on medium speed until smooth and creamy, about 2 minutes. Add the brown sugar and mix on medium until light and fluffy; about 4 minutes will do the trick. Use a rubber spatula to scrape the bowl. Add the pumpkin puree and vanilla and mix until fully incorporated, about 2 minutes.

// Add half of the flour mixture and mix on low just until the powdery texture of the flour disappears, about 15 seconds. Immediately add the rest of the flour mixture and mix until combined. Scrape the bowl and mix a final 15 seconds.

// Pumpkin spice dough is anything but basic—let's eat!

Craving some cookies? Have extra cookie dough? See My Go-To Baking & Storage DŌrections on page 48.

Kristen's TIP

/////////////////////

/////////////////////

If you prefer your blondies—especially pumpkin spice blondies—in bar form, you're in luck! This recipe will yield one 8"x8" pan. Line with my Picture-Perfect Parchment Method on page 42, spread the cookie dough evenly throughout, and bake at 350°F for 25 minutes.

Mint to Be Stress-Free, page 146

A Hot Cocoa Holiday, opposite page

Kristen's
TIP

Like a bit of spice? For a twist on Mexican hot chocolate, whisk 1 teaspoon each of ground cayenne pepper, chili powder, and ground cinnamon into the flour mixture, then follow the recipe instructions as written.

A Hot Cocoa Holiday

SUPER *Quick*

GREAT MADE *GF*

Can we talk about all these national food holidays? What the hell is National Carbonated Beverage with Caffeine Day (November 19) all about!? Seriously, did you run out of all the good food and drinks that deserve to be celebrated? National Hot Cocoa Day, on the other hand, should be on everyone's calendar (December 13), as a day to celebrate drinking sugar in the form of liquid chocolate. *Now that's* a national day I can get behind.

In fact, I think this hot cocoa cookie dough deserves its own day. Let's sub out National Carbonated Beverage with Caffeine Day for this non-carbonated, caffeine-free, beverage-inspired cookie dough. You heard it here first—November 19 is now a day to celebrate, so get mixing!

2¼ cups heat-treated all-purpose flour (instructions on page 31)

½ cup cocoa powder

1 teaspoon baking powder

1 teaspoon baking soda

1 teaspoon cornstarch

1 teaspoon salt

1½ sticks (12 tablespoons) unsalted butter, at room temperature

⅓ cup granulated sugar

1 cup brown sugar

½ cup pasteurized egg whites, at room temperature

1 tablespoon vanilla extract

1 cup mini marshmallows

// In a medium bowl, whisk together the heat-treated flour, cocoa powder, baking powder, baking soda, cornstarch, and salt. Set aside.

// In the bowl of a stand mixer fitted with the paddle attachment, beat the butter on medium speed until smooth and creamy, about 2 minutes. Add the granulated and brown sugars and mix on medium until light and fluffy; about 4 minutes will do the trick. Use a rubber spatula to scrape the bowl. Add the egg whites and vanilla and mix until fully incorporated, about 2 minutes.

// Add half of the flour mixture and mix on low just until the powdery texture of the flour disappears, about 15 seconds. Immediately add the rest of the flour mixture and mix until combined. Scrape the bowl and mix a final 15 seconds.

// Remove the bowl from the mixer and use a rubber spatula to fold in the mini marshmallows.

// Cuddle up with a bowl of this hot cocoa dough—it's ready to eat!

If you have more willpower than I do and find yourself with extra, see My Go-To Baking & Storage DŌrections on page 48.

Mint to Be Stress-Free

No one has time to spare around the holidays. There are parties to go to, family to see, gifts to purchase, champagne to drink, and lots and lots of food to eat. Luckily for you (and me), this Pretend You're Put Together Peppermint Bark is the easiest recipe ever. It can be whipped up in no time, whether you need to bring a last-minute treat to the office potluck, make a cute hostess gift, or say a special thank you to someone.

   And while it's super delicious mixed into this cookie dough, it can also be packaged all alone, which means you can save all the cookie dough for yourself.

1 batch Pretend You're Put Together Peppermint Bark (recipe follows)

2¼ cups heat-treated all-purpose flour (instructions on page 31)

2¼ teaspoons cornstarch

1 teaspoon baking soda

¾ teaspoon salt

1½ sticks (12 tablespoons) unsalted butter, at room temperature

¼ cup granulated sugar

1 cup brown sugar

⅓ cup pasteurized egg whites, at room temperature

1 tablespoon vanilla extract

½ teaspoon peppermint extract

// Make the Pretend You're Put Together Peppermint Bark. Roughly chop so the pieces are no larger than ½ inch. Set aside.

// In a medium bowl, whisk together the heat-treated flour, cornstarch, baking soda, and salt. Set aside.

// In the bowl of a stand mixer fitted with the paddle attachment, beat the butter on medium speed until smooth and creamy, about 2 minutes. Add the granulated and brown sugars and mix on medium until light and fluffy; about 4 minutes will do the trick. Use a rubber spatula to scrape the bowl. Add the egg whites, vanilla, and peppermint extract and mix until fully incorporated, about 2 minutes.

// Add half of the flour mixture and mix on low just until the powdery texture of the flour disappears, about 15 seconds. Immediately add the rest of the flour mixture and mix until combined. Scrape the bowl and mix a final 15 seconds.

// Remove the bowl from the mixer and use a rubber spatula to fold in the peppermint bark pieces.

// This dough is mint to eat...now!

If you have more willpower than I do and find yourself with extra, see My Go-To Baking & Storage DŌrections on page 48.

PRETEND YOU'RE PUT TOGETHER PEPPERMINT BARK

Makes *16 servings*
Active time: *25 minutes*
Time 'til bark: *45 minutes*

1 cup semisweet chocolate chips

¼ teaspoon peppermint extract

1 cup white chocolate chips

2 tablespoons crushed peppermint candies

1 tablespoon holiday sprinkles

// Cover a baking sheet with aluminum foil with the shinier side facing up. Set aside.

// In a small microwave-safe bowl, heat the semisweet chips in the microwave on 50% power in 30-second increments. Stir well between each increment. Repeat just until the chocolate is melted. Once the chocolate is melted, stir in the peppermint extract.

// Pour the chocolate onto the lined baking sheet and use a spatula to spread it evenly into a ¼-inch-thick layer. Let stand at room temperature until it is set, about 10 minutes.

// Meanwhile, in a second small microwave-safe bowl, melt the white chips in the microwave using the microwave method above. Carefully spread the white chocolate over the set semisweet chocolate. Immediately sprinkle with the crushed peppermint candies and holiday sprinkles.

// Let stand at room temperature for at least 45 minutes, then slice and serve. Store in an airtight container in the refrigerator for up to 1 week.

148 \ WHEN IT'S FINALLY
SWEATER WEATHER

\ MAKES
30 scoops

\ TIME 'TIL DOUGH
1 hour 15 minutes

\ TIME 'TIL COOKIES
3 hours 45 minutes

Triple B (BOURBON, BACON, BROWN SUGAR)

GREAT MADE GF

If I'm not eating sugar, I'm eating bacon. If I'm not eating bacon, I'm drinking bourbon. Or at least I'm wishing that I had one of the three. My best-case scenario? Putting brown sugar *on* bacon with a bourbon in hand. The success of DŌ makes it clear that I'm a sugar connoisseur, but you may not know that I also consider myself a bona fide bacon connoisseur. If it were possible to become a sommelier of bacon, I would take the test immediately. And, if it weren't so "off brand" for me to sneak different bacon recipes into this cookbook, I would write a dozen of them and load this baby up with my favorite meat. But sadly, you'll have to wait until my next cookbook—its working title is *The Bacon Diaries*—for those.

Since you're getting some bourbon out for this recipe anyway, why don't you make yourself an Old Fashioned to go with this Triple B bacon bomb—you won't regret it.

1 (1-pound) package uncooked bacon (Don't worry! There will be extra to eat along the way.)

2½ cups heat-treated all-purpose flour (instructions on page 31)

1 tablespoon cornstarch

1 teaspoon baking soda

¾ teaspoon salt

¾ stick (6 tablespoons) unsalted butter, at room temperature

¼ cup granulated sugar

1 cup brown sugar

¼ cup pasteurized egg whites, at room temperature

1 tablespoon vanilla extract

¼ cup bourbon (save the good stuff for your cocktail)

2 ounces dark chocolate (half a 4-ounce bar), chopped

2 ounces milk chocolate (half a 4-ounce bar), chopped

// Remove the bacon from the refrigerator and allow it to come to room temperature.

// In a medium bowl, whisk together the heat-treated flour, cornstarch, baking soda, and salt. Set aside.

// Heat a large skillet over medium heat and add the bacon in a single layer, making sure not to crowd the pan. (You may need to do a few batches depending on your skillet.) Cook the bacon on both sides until extra-crispy.

// Transfer the bacon from the skillet to a plate lined with paper towels. Drain the bacon fat from the skillet into a small bowl before adding more bacon to the skillet and reserve the fat for later use.

// Once all the bacon is cooked, measure 6 tablespoons of the reserved bacon fat into a clean bowl or cup and place in the refrigerator to chill. Discard the rest of the bacon fat. (Go ahead and eat a slice or two of bacon while you're at it to stop your mouth from watering!)

// In the bowl of a stand mixer fitted with the paddle attachment, beat the chilled bacon fat and butter on medium speed until smooth and creamy, about 2 minutes. Add the granulated and brown sugars and mix on medium until light and fluffy; about 4 minutes will do the trick. Use a rubber spatula to scrape the bowl. Add the egg whites and vanilla and mix until fully incorporated, about 2 minutes. Add the bourbon and mix until completely combined. We're adding a lot of liquid to the dough, so it will need extra mixing. Once the dough no longer separates when the mixer is turned off, you're ready to move to the next step.

// Add half of the flour mixture and mix on low just until the powdery texture of the flour disappears, about 15 seconds. Immediately add the rest of the flour mixture and mix until combined. Scrape the bowl and mix a final 15 seconds.

// Finely chop or crush the bacon strips until you have ⅓ cup bacon with a small crumb-like consistency. Roughly chop more bacon strips into ¼-inch pieces until you have ⅔ cup. The rest of the bacon is your snack!

// Remove the bowl from the mixer and use a rubber spatula to fold in the crumbled and chopped bacon bits. Once well mixed, fold in the chopped dark and milk chocolate.

// Your bacon-y boozy dough is ready to enjoy!

For a savory twist on chocolate chip cookies, try baking this one! See My Go-To Baking & Storage DŌrections on page 48.

Kristen's
TIP

If you don't have enough bacon grease to make 6 full tablespoons, add in an extra tablespoon of butter for every tablespoon of bacon fat that is missing. Your cookies will be less bacon-y, but still to die for!

Gingerbread Man of My Dreams

EASY TO MAKE *Vegan*   **GREAT MADE** *GF*   **SHOP** *Special*

Holiday gingerbread is typically dry and hard as a rock. Like, hard enough to use as a weapon at your family's holiday gathering. (Wait...is that the real intention?!) For real, though, no one enjoys biting the arm off of a gingerbread man—he's only around for his good looks!

Clearly, I couldn't make any old gingerbread cookie dough for the shop. THIS gingerbread recipe is extra-soft and extra-special. It's got all the cinnamon-y, ginger-filled, molasses depth that warms you from the inside out; plus, there are two ways to bake it (this girl loves some options). You can either drop it on a cookie sheet and make soft, chewy, thick cookies, or (with an easy modification) roll it out to make the cutest—actually yummy—gingerbread shapes.

Skip the family drama and the potential gingerbread weapons this year. The only reason you'll have to launch these bad boys across the table is because you're too full to get up and pass them to your sister.

1½ cups heat-treated all-purpose flour (instructions on page 31)

1 teaspoon cornstarch

1 teaspoon baking soda

1 teaspoon ground ginger

1 teaspoon ground cinnamon

¼ teaspoon ground cloves

¼ teaspoon ground nutmeg

¼ teaspoon salt

1½ sticks (12 tablespoons) unsalted butter, at room temperature

¾ cup brown sugar

⅓ cup dark molasses

¼ cup pasteurized egg whites, at room temperature

2 teaspoon vanilla extract

// In a medium bowl, whisk together the heat-treated flour, cornstarch, baking soda, ginger, cinnamon, cloves, nutmeg, and salt. Set aside.

// In the bowl of a stand mixer fitted with the paddle attachment, beat the butter on medium speed until smooth and creamy, about 2 minutes. Add the brown sugar and molasses and mix on medium until light and fluffy; about 4 minutes will do the trick. Use a rubber spatula to scrape the bowl. Add the egg whites and vanilla and mix until fully incorporated, about 2 minutes.

// Add half of the flour mixture and mix on low just until the powdery texture of the flour disappears, about 15 seconds. Immediately add the rest of the flour mixture and mix until combined. Scrape the bowl and mix a final 15 seconds.

// Make some holiday memories with this fresh gingerbread dough!

If fresh-baked cookies are more your thing, see My Go-To Baking & Storage DŌrections on page 48. Or keep reading to learn how to make the cut-out version!

GINGERBREAD CUT-OUT COOKIES

// To make cut-out cookies, prepare a batch of gingerbread dough with 3 cups of flour (1½ cups more than what is called for in the recipe) and omit the baking soda.

// Divide the dough in half, cover with plastic wrap, and chill in the freezer.

// While the dough chills, lay out a large sheet of plastic wrap or waxed paper, preheat the oven to 350°F, and line a baking sheet with parchment paper or a silicone baking mat.

// Drop one half of the chilled dough into the center of the waxed paper and cover with another sheet of waxed paper. Roll the dough to ¼-inch thickness and cut with floured cookie cutters. Place on the lined baking sheet. Repeat with the other half of the dough.

// Bake for 9 minutes. Different sizes of cookies may bake differently. Keep your eyes on the edges—once they look dry and a shade darker, they are ready to come out of the oven.

When You Want to Have Your Cake and Eat Cookie Dough Too

//

So how dough we come up with our flavors?

When it comes to recipe development and testing, we turn to you, our customers and fans. You submit flavor ideas through the website, on social media pages, and at the store. Anything can serve as inspiration: childhood favorite treats, nostalgic candy, and desserts from other parts of the world. All of this information goes into a spreadsheet and gets sorted, categorized, and narrowed down. Unrealistic suggestions go to the digital trash bin (sorry, no Four Loko Cookie Dough anytime soon), and repeat suggestions get highlighted. Then, my team gets to add their ideas and we all vote. Next, we get down to the best part of the process, testing and tasting.

Most of the time, we have dough-y recipe successes, including a few of my favorites in this book: Carnival Crunch (page 114) and It's Always Samoa® Season (page 120). And sometimes we end up with complete failures, like Champagne (RIP). We spent weeks recipe testing to try to make champagne work. Champagne extract made the dough taste the way green apple soap from Bath & Body Works smells. Boiling it down smelled so much like the morning after a frat party, I couldn't even add it to the recipe without gagging. After about thirty "yuck" results, I finally decided I'd have to stick to drinking my champs instead!

As much as I enjoy tinkering around with inventive new ideas, my favorite source of inspiration is classic desserts. I love desserts so much that the only aspect of my wedding I was adamant about was a jam-packed, totally stocked dessert table. I couldn't pick cake, or pie, or brownies, or soufflé—I had to have them all! As it turns out, the Tomlans also are dessert-aholics, so Chris was 100 percent on board. I married into the right family.

/// If you're craving a particular dessert but also a bowl of cookie dough, these classic flavors are just the ones for you.

Classic Red Velvet

Normally I'm too busy eating cookies to waste my time on cake...unless we're talking red velvet. A red velvet cupcake and you'll see my ears perk up and my mouth start to water. There is something about the luxurious combo of the tangy frosting mixed with the light, barely chocolate-y cake that I can't resist.

This recipe has all of those traits plus a healthy dose of cookie dough. The base is light and filled with cocoa-powder-y DŌliciousness, and the ribbons of homemade cream cheese buttercream add a tangy complement. You could save this one to indulge in on a special occasion, or you could declare tonight a special occasion and treat yourself to a big bowl. Your call.

1⅔ cups heat-treated all-purpose flour (instructions on page 31)

3 tablespoons cocoa powder

2 teaspoons cornstarch

1 teaspoon baking soda

½ teaspoon salt

1 stick (8 tablespoons) unsalted butter, at room temperature

⅓ cup granulated sugar

¾ cup plus 1 tablespoon brown sugar

¼ cup pasteurized egg whites, at room temperature

1 tablespoon vanilla extract

1½ teaspoons red food coloring

1 cup milk chocolate chips

1 cup Classic Cream Cheese Buttercream (recipe follows)

// In a medium bowl, whisk together the heat-treated flour, cocoa powder, cornstarch, baking soda, and salt. Set aside.

// In the bowl of a stand mixer fitted with the paddle attachment, beat the butter on medium speed until smooth and creamy, about 2 minutes. Add the granulated and brown sugars and mix on medium until light and fluffy; about 4 minutes will do the trick. Use a rubber spatula to scrape the bowl. Add the egg whites, vanilla, and food coloring and mix until fully incorporated, about 3 minutes.

// Add half of the flour mixture and mix on low just until the powdery texture of the flour disappears, about 15 seconds. Immediately add the rest of the flour mixture and mix until combined. Scrape the bowl and mix a final 15 seconds.

// Remove the bowl from the mixer and use a rubber spatula to fold in the chocolate chips.

// Make the Classic Cream Cheese Buttercream. If baking cookies, set aside buttercream until after cookies are baked and cooled.

// If you're eating this as red velvet-y dough, drop the buttercream in tablespoon-size scoops in four different locations in the bowl. Use the rubber spatula to gently swirl until you see thick ribbons of buttercream, which are totally decadent and reminiscent of a big slice of cake. Don't overmix—you're finished!

// Decadent cookie dough, ready to go!

Craving some cookies? See My Go-To Baking & Storage DŌrections on page 48.

// Once the cookies are completely cooled, drop 1 tablespoon buttercream on each cookie. Use a butter knife or offset spatula to smooth the buttercream into an even layer on each cookie. Serve and enjoy!

Store the iced cookies in an airtight container in the refrigerator for up to 3 days.

156 \ WHEN YOU WANT TO HAVE YOUR CAKE AND EAT COOKIE DOUGH TOO

MAKES
5 cups

ACTIVE TIME
10 minutes

TIME 'TIL BUTTERCREAM
10 minutes

Classic Cream Cheese Buttercream

Buttercream is notoriously light and fluffy, like a sugar cloud softly landed on your ~~cupcake~~ cookie and added a simple whiff of sweetness. Take that American standard and add some tangy, smooth cream cheese, and suddenly you have a frosting that's luxurious and thick and adds some pizzazz to whatever you're eating. It's just as quick and easy to make as standard buttercream but with a tangy flavor punch to balance out the sweetness!

1 (8-ounce) package cream cheese, at room temperature

1 stick (8 tablespoons) unsalted butter, at room temperature

4 cups confectioners' sugar

1 teaspoon vanilla extract

// In the bowl of a stand mixer fitted with the paddle attachment, whip the cream cheese and butter on high speed until the mixture becomes fluffy, about 5 minutes. Every other minute, stop the mixer and scrape the bowl with a rubber spatula.

// Turn the mixer to low and slowly add the confectioners' sugar. You should be adding about ½ cup at a time to avoid a mess and a collapsed buttercream!

// Once all the sugar is incorporated, add the vanilla and turn the mixer to medium speed. Whip until the buttercream has doubled in size, scraping every 1 to 2 minutes to make sure you have an even creamy texture.

// Scoop into a piping bag for frosting cookies or cupcakes. Or freeze in an airtight container for up to 2 months. To use frozen buttercream, thaw in the refrigerator and re-whip before using.

//////////// *Kristen's Tip* ////////////

If you don't have a piping bag in your kitchen, you can use a sturdy gallon-size ziplock bag instead. Put the buttercream into one corner of the bag and snip off just the tiniest bit of that corner. Test it out and continue to cut tiny slivers off the bag until you have the just-right size for your piping needs.

//

Kristen's TIP

If you want a carrot cake cookie that really reminds you of the real thing, frost these cookies with my Classic Cream Cheese Buttercream (page 156).

Kick Ass Carrot Cake

Carrot cake is my mom's all-time favorite dessert. My grandma's signature carrot cake is out of this world good. So, this recipe had a lot to live up to!

When I wrote the recipe for the shop, it took me test after test to get it right. Should it be pecans or walnuts? Which base works best? Could I do a cream cheese swirl, or is that too much? After countless batches, many trips to the grocery store, and endless dishwasher cycles…I cracked it. Carrot cake was added to the menu as a seasonal flavor, and people loved it.

But when I went to pull that exact recipe for this book, I couldn't find it. Somehow, after multiple moves, a ton of changes to the shop, and a couple of new computers, my beloved carrot cake recipe was gone. The team turned the whole shop upside down but still could not find it. It should have been in a vault somewhere, or saved in the fancy digital cloud, but no such luck.

And so I began round two. I started the testing process all over again. To this day, I have no idea if this recipe is anywhere near the same as the original, but I do know that it tastes just as delicious. This one's for you, Mom and Grandma! With love, your favorite child/grandchild.

FOR THE CANDIED PECANS

⅓ cup brown sugar

1½ cups chopped pecans

FOR THE DOUGH

1 cup oats (if you're making this gluten-free, make sure they're gluten-free!)

1¼ cups heat-treated all-purpose flour (instructions on page 31)

1 teaspoon ground cinnamon

1 teaspoon cornstarch

½ teaspoon baking powder

½ teaspoon baking soda

¼ teaspoon ground ginger

¼ teaspoon ground nutmeg

¼ teaspoon salt

1 stick (8 tablespoons) unsalted butter, at room temperature

¼ cup granulated sugar

½ cup brown sugar

¼ cup pasteurized egg whites, at room temperature

1½ teaspoons vanilla extract

¾ cup finely diced carrots

// **Make the candied pecans:** In a small saucepan, heat the brown sugar and pecans over medium heat, stirring constantly. The sugar will turn to a syrup, but keep stirring. Slowly the nuts will start to appear dry as the sugar fuses to them; keep stirring until all of the nuts are dry. Transfer the nuts to waxed paper to cool completely.

// **Make the dough:** In a food processor, pulse the oats 3 or 4 times, until they have a roughly chopped consistency. Heat-treat the oats according to the instructions on page 31.

// Once oats have cooled completely, pour them into a medium bowl and whisk with the heat-treated flour, cinnamon, cornstarch, baking powder, baking soda, ginger, nutmeg, and salt. Set aside.

// In the bowl of a stand mixer fitted with the paddle attachment, beat the butter on medium speed until smooth and creamy, about 2 minutes. Add the granulated and brown sugars and mix on medium until light and fluffy; about 4 minutes will do the trick. Use a rubber spatula to scrape the bowl. Add the egg whites and vanilla and mix until fully incorporated, about 2 minutes. Add the carrot and mix for 1 minute.

// Add half of the oat mixture and mix on low just until the powdery texture of the oats disappears, about 15 seconds. Immediately add the rest of the oat mixture and mix until combined. Scrape the bowl and mix a final 15 seconds.

// Remove the bowl from the mixer and use a rubber spatula to fold in the candied pecans.

// Carrot cake cookie dough time!

Craving some cookies? Have extra cookie dough? See My Go-To Baking & Storage DŌrections on page 48.

Flourless Chocolate Soufflé Cookie Thing

I wish restaurants would give you the dessert menu right when you sit down. I need to know how much room to save for dessert. Will we order one dessert or do we *NEED* a second? On the other hand, if the dessert menu leaves something to be desired, then we're going to need an extra appetizer. This is real important life shit.

There are two chocolate desserts that I will order no matter what: chocolate soufflé and flourless chocolate cake. So, I figured a mash-up between my two go-to orders would be DIVINE.

My advice: Bake this recipe into cookies!!! They're less like a cookie and more like an ooey gooey chocolate bomb that literally melts in your mouth. The edges are crispy and firm thanks to the whipped eggs in the recipe, and the inside is a magic fudge-filled warm molten chocolate center.

Forget dessert at the restaurant. Come home and make these.

3 cups confectioners' sugar

1 cup cocoa powder

½ cup pasteurized egg whites, at room temperature

¼ teaspoon salt

½ cup semisweet chocolate chips

1 teaspoon vanilla extract

// In a medium bowl, whisk together the confectioners' sugar and cocoa powder. Set aside.

// In the bowl of a stand mixer with the whisk attachment, whip the egg whites and salt on high speed until soft peaks form. At first it will foam, but continue for about 5 minutes, until the mixture more than doubles in size, becomes opaque, and when you turn your whisk upside down, the peaks are just starting to hold. They should still be soft and melt back into themselves after a second.

// Scrape the egg white mixture from the whisk and change to the paddle attachment.

// In a small microwave-proof bowl, heat the chocolate chips in the microwave on 50% power in 30-second increments. Stir well between each increment. Repeat just until the chocolate is melted.

// Add half of the melted chocolate and mix on medium speed until combined. Then add half of the sugar mixture and mix until combined. Repeat with the melted chocolate and the rest of the sugar mixture until you've used it all. Add the vanilla and mix to incorporate.

// Scrape the bowl and mix on medium one more time for 15 seconds. The dough will have a fudge-like texture.

// Your flour-free indulgence is ready to eat, but trust me, you'll want to bake this dough!

// To Bake: Scoop heaping tablespoons of the dough onto parchment paper and freeze the cookie dough balls, uncovered, for 2 hours. Do not skip this step! You must create a "skin" for these cookies to properly bake—they are fragile just like soufflé!

// Preheat the oven to 350°F. Line a baking sheet with parchment paper or a silicone baking mat.

// Place the dough balls on the prepared baking sheet, leaving about 3 inches of space between scoops. Let stand at room temperature for 15 to 20 minutes, until a thin skin forms on the dough.

// Bake for 5 to 7 minutes, until the crust has set. The middle will still be gooey and the cookies will look very soft when you take them out of the oven. If you overbake them, they will wind up with a brownie texture, which also is yummy, but not what we're going for!

// Remove from the oven and let cool on the baking sheets for 8 minutes, or until they can be moved with a spatula. Dust the cookies with confectioners' sugar and enjoy warm.

The cookies can be stored in an airtight container at room temperature and are best enjoyed within 3 days.

162 \ WHEN YOU WANT TO HAVE YOUR
CAKE AND EAT COOKIE DOUGH TOO

\ MAKES
37 scoops

\ TIME 'TIL DOUGH
45 minutes

\ TIME 'TIL COOKIES
3 hours 5 minutes

Lazy Girl Cheesecake

Now that I'm a New Yorker, I obviously have an opinion or two on cheesecake. I've sat through many cheesecake-eating sessions when family and friends have come to visit me in the Big Apple. I'm here to tell you, Junior's Cheesecake (strawberry, specifically) is as good as it gets.

Cheesecake making is a true science, and a pain in the ass. But with this Lazy Girl Cheesecake recipe, you get creamy cheesecake filling faster than you can put on eyeliner. Add some strawberry jam and a graham cracker crust crumble, and you've got a cheesecake recipe that New York would be proud of!

FOR THE GRAHAM CRACKER CRUST

1½ cups graham cracker crumbs

¼ cup brown sugar

¾ teaspoon ground cinnamon

¼ teaspoon salt

1 stick (8 tablespoons) unsalted butter, melted

FOR THE CHEESECAKE SWIRL

2 (8-ounce) packages cream cheese, at room temperature

1 cup granulated sugar

2 tablespoons cornstarch

⅓ cup pasteurized egg whites, at room temperature

¼ cup plus 2 tablespoons heavy cream, at room temperature

1½ teaspoons vanilla extract

FOR THE DOUGH

2½ cups heat-treated all-purpose flour (instructions on page 31)

1 tablespoon cornstarch

1½ teaspoons cream of tartar

¾ teaspoon baking powder

¾ teaspoon baking soda

¾ teaspoon salt

1½ sticks (12 tablespoons) unsalted butter, at room temperature

1 cup plus 2 tablespoons granulated sugar

⅓ cup pasteurized egg whites, at room temperature

1½ teaspoons vanilla extract

¼ cup strawberry jam

// Preheat the oven to 350°F. Line a baking sheet with parchment paper or a silicone baking mat.

// Make the graham cracker crust: Whisk the graham crumbs, brown sugar, cinnamon, and salt in a medium bowl. Pour the melted butter over the graham mixture and stir until well combined.

// Press the graham mixture onto the baking sheet in an even layer about ¼ inch thick. It will not fill the baking sheet. Bake for 8 minutes, or until lightly browned. Remove from the oven and set aside to cool.

// Make the cheesecake swirl: In the bowl of a stand mixer fitted with the paddle attachment, combine cream cheese, sugar, and cornstarch on low speed. Add the egg whites, cream, and vanilla and continue to mix until smooth.

// Grease an 8"x8" pan. Pour the filling into the pan and bake for 35 minutes, or until the top has begun to lightly brown and the filling is set throughout.

// Remove from the oven and run a knife along the edges of the pan. Set aside to cool.

// Make the dough: In a medium bowl, whisk together the heat-treated flour, cornstarch, cream of tartar, baking powder, baking soda, and salt. Set aside.

// In the bowl of a stand mixer fitted with the paddle attachment, beat the butter on medium speed until smooth and creamy, about 2 minutes. Add the sugar and mix on medium until light and fluffy; about 4 minutes will do the trick. Use a rubber spatula to scrape the bowl. Add the egg whites and vanilla and mix until fully incorporated, about 2 minutes.

// Add half of the flour mixture and mix on low just until the powdery texture of the flour disappears, about 15 seconds. Immediately add the rest of the flour mixture and mix until combined. Scrape the bowl and mix a final 15 seconds.

// Once the graham crust is cooled, use your hands or a knife to roughly break it into small pieces until you have 1 cup.

// Remove the bowl from the mixer and use a rubber spatula to fold in the graham crust.

// Measure 1¼ cups of the cheesecake swirl. Put it into a food processor and run on low speed until the cheesecake has a thick, spreadable consistency.

// Drop the strawberry jam in tablespoon-size scoops in two different locations in the bowl. Drop the cheesecake cream in tablespoon-size scoops throughout the bowl. Use the rubber spatula to gently swirl until you see thick ribbons of strawberry jam and cheesecake cream. Don't overmix—you're finished!

// You did it! Cheesecake dough is yours!

If you're planning on finishing this later, see My Go-To Baking & Storage DŌrections on page 48.

Kristen's Tip

You can make the quickest cheesecake in the world: Press the crust from this recipe into the bottom of an 8"x8" pan and bake for 8 minutes. Then make the filling from the recipe, top the crust, and bake for 15 minutes more. Let cool completely and you are ready to dig into some cheesecake bars.

NAMING
the brand

"How *did* you come up with the name?" is a question I hear a lot.

I wanted the name to be sweet and simple, driving home the point that this brand is all about cookie dough. I knew I didn't want to spell it d-o-u-g-h. "Doughs" are already everywhere, and my first-of-its-kind product deserved a one-of-a-kind name. The name had to be memorable, eye-catching, and cute. I started looking up the phonetic spellings of "dough" in every dictionary I could get my hands on: dou, doe, doh, doō, dōō, and dō.

I took one look at "dō," and a logo immediately started forming in my mind. Two lowercase letters in a hot pink circle with the line (called a macron) over the "o," signaling the long "o." A graphic representation of the brand: bright and colorful, playful yet sophisticated...I ran with the idea.

A circle was the perfect shape—everything in baking is round! Bowls, cakes, cookies, even cookie dough scoops! That circle logo became the polka dot in a number of DŌ designs, including the wallpaper at our flagship shop! The line over the "o" in DŌ was transformed into a sprinkle pattern, which appears all over the website, wraps our ice cream carts, and jazzes up business cards.

And who would have guessed how punny those two letters would turn out to be. DŌnt believe me? Flip through this book—you'll plenty of DŌlightful examples to prove my case. Or, for the real punny gems, take a scroll through our Instagram—warning, mouth-watering may occur when scrolling through the @cookiedonyc feed.

OOO Key Lime Pie

Raise your hand if you agree that warm vacations are much better than spending your well-earned days off somewhere cold. If you're in the tropical destination camp with me, then YEA! Feel free to DM me @kristentomlan with all your recommended spots (and thanks in advance).

Who also agrees that a trip to the beach is never complete without a slice of key lime pie? That crunchy, buttery crust and the chilled, tart, green center are all I need to make a trip down south worth the travel. But sometimes you don't even need to travel to get your favorite vacation treat—you might find it in your own backyard! I sure did! I found a slice of pie heaven right in Brooklyn: Steve's Authentic Key Lime in Red Hook. It's right near the water, so it feels beach-y enough (in a dirty, New York river kind of way) that I can almost trick myself into *thinking* I've gone on vacation just by heading over to Steve's shop.

This recipe is my take on key lime pie. Even when I'm stuck in the kitchen in the dead of winter, I can still switch my brain to the out of office (OOO) mentality and go on a mental vacation by whipping this one up. Take a break and enjoy...

FOR THE GRAHAM CRACKER CRUST

1½ cups graham cracker crumbs

¼ cup brown sugar

¾ teaspoon ground cinnamon

¼ teaspoon salt

1 stick (8 tablespoons) unsalted butter, melted

FOR THE DOUGH

3 key limes

2½ cups heat-treated all-purpose flour (instructions on page 31)

1 tablespoon cornstarch

1½ teaspoons cream of tartar

¾ teaspoon baking powder

¾ teaspoon baking soda

¾ teaspoon salt

1½ sticks (12 tablespoons) unsalted butter, at room temperature

1 cup plus 2 tablespoons granulated sugar

1½ teaspoons vanilla extract

// Preheat the oven to 350°F. Line a baking sheet with parchment paper or a silicone baking mat.

// Make the graham cracker crust: Whisk the graham crumbs, brown sugar, cinnamon, and salt in a medium bowl. Pour the melted butter over the graham mixture and stir until combined.

// Press the mixture onto the lined baking sheet in an even layer. Bake for 8 minutes, or until crisp and lightly browned on the edges. Remove from the oven and let cool completely.

// Make the dough: Zest the key limes into a small bowl. In a separate bowl, juice the limes until you have ⅓ cup juice. Set both aside.

// In a medium bowl, whisk together the heat-treated flour, cornstarch, cream of tartar, baking powder, baking soda, and salt. Set aside.

// In the bowl of a stand mixer fitted with the paddle attachment, beat the butter on medium speed until smooth and creamy, about 2 minutes. Add the sugar and mix on medium until light and fluffy; about 4 minutes will do the trick. Use a rubber spatula to scrape the bowl. Add the lime juice and vanilla and mix until fully incorporated, about 2 minutes. Add lime zest to taste and mix for an additional 30 seconds.

// Add half of the flour mixture and mix on low just until the powdery texture of the flour disappears, about 15 seconds. Immediately add the rest of the flour mixture and mix until combined. Scrape the bowl and mix a final 15 seconds.

// Once cooled, use your hands or a knife to roughly break the graham cracker crust into small pieces until you have 1 cup.

// Remove the bowl from the mixer and use a rubber spatula to fold in the crust pieces.

// Go on vacation—lick the spatula!

If you happen to have some dough left over, see My Go-To Baking & Storage DŌrections on page 48.

166

WHEN YOU WANT TO HAVE YOUR
CAKE AND EAT COOKIE DOUGH TOO

MAKES
28 scoops

TIME 'TIL DOUGH
55 minutes

TIME 'TIL COOKIES
3 hours 20 minutes

Pecan Pie for the Win

Let me explain the Great Pie DŌbate in my house. My husband will tell you that apple pie is hands down the best pie on the block. Chris, brilliant as he is, occasionally gets things wrong, and his pie choice is one of those things. Pecan pie is easily the best pie out there. Ooey gooey brown sugar pecan filling with just a little bit of nutty crunch—I'm going to stop there. I'm clearly on the right side of this issue.

Upon the invention of this recipe, the Great Pie DŌbate is officially over. Chris and I can both agree with cookie dough like this—pie doesn't matter anyway.

FOR THE PIE CRUST

½ cup all-purpose flour

1½ teaspoons sugar

⅛ teaspoon salt

½ stick (4 tablespoons) unsalted butter, cold

1½ teaspoons water, ice cold

FOR THE PECAN FILLING

½ stick (4 tablespoons) unsalted butter

½ cup brown sugar

½ cup maple syrup

¼ cup dark corn syrup

2 tablespoons heavy cream

¼ cup pasteurized egg whites, at room temperature

1 cup pecans, chopped

FOR THE DOUGH

2¼ cups heat-treated all-purpose flour (instructions on page 31)

2¼ teaspoons cornstarch

1 teaspoon baking soda

¾ teaspoon salt

1½ sticks (12 tablespoons) unsalted butter, at room temperature

¼ cup granulated sugar

1 cup brown sugar

⅓ cup pasteurized egg whites, at room temperature

1 tablespoon vanilla extract

// Preheat the oven to 375°F.

// Make the pie crust: In a food processor, combine the flour, sugar, and salt and pulse to mix. Add the butter in 1-tablespoon chunks and continue to pulse until a coarse meal forms. With the processor running, gradually add the ice water in ½-teaspoon increments just until moist clumps form. You may not need all the water.

// Remove the dough from the processor and form it into a ball. Place the dough between two sheets of parchment paper and use a rolling pin to flatten it to about ¼ inch thick. Place on a baking sheet and remove the top piece of parchment. Bake for 15 to 20 minutes, until golden and crisp but not yet brown.

// Remove from the oven and cool completely. Turn the oven temperature down to 350°F and grease an 8"x8" pan.

// Make the pecan filling: Heat a saucepan over medium heat. Add the butter, brown sugar, maple syrup, corn syrup, and cream and bring to a boil while stirring constantly. Remove from the heat and set aside.

// In a medium bowl, lightly whisk the egg whites. Add 4 tablespoons of the butter-cream mixture to the beaten egg, 1 tablespoon at a time, whisking well after each addition. Add the butter-cream mixture very slowly to make sure the egg incorporates with the filling instead of cooking into scrambled egg.

CONTINUES →

// Once the egg and 4 tablespoons of the butter-cream mixture have been well combined, slowly add this mixture to the rest of the filling, stirring constantly.

// Pour ½ cup of the filling into a small bowl. Set aside.

// Stir the pecans into the remaining filling. Pour the filling into the prepared pan and bake for 8 to 10 minutes. When you shake the pan and it is no longer wobbly, the filling is done; it will still be bubbly on the edges. Remove from the oven and let cool completely.

// Make the dough: In a medium bowl, whisk together the heat-treated flour, cornstarch, baking soda, and salt. Set aside.

// In the bowl of a stand mixer fitted with the paddle attachment, beat the butter on medium speed until smooth and creamy, about 2 minutes. Add the granulated and brown sugars and mix on medium until light and fluffy; about 4 minutes will do the trick. Use a rubber spatula to scrape the bowl. Add the egg whites, vanilla, and the reserved ½ cup of filling. Mix until fully incorporated, about 2 minutes.

// Add half of the flour mixture and mix on low just until the powdery texture of the flour disappears, about 15 seconds. Immediately add the rest of the flour mixture and mix until combined. Scrape the bowl and mix a final 15 seconds.

// Once the crust has cooled, use your hands or a knife to roughly break it into small pieces until you have 1 cup.

// Remove the bowl from the mixer and use a rubber spatula to fold in the crust pieces.

// Drop the baked pecan filling in 1-tablespoon scoops in four different locations in the bowl. Use the rubber spatula to gently swirl until you see thick ribbons of pie filling. Don't overmix— you're finished!

// Pie, oh my! Eat up!

If you're planning on finishing this later, see My Go-To Baking & Storage DŌrections on page 48.

Magic Peanut Butter Brownie

You know how sometimes you wake up in the morning and you aren't sure if your dream actually happened? It was so vivid that it makes you question everything. Were you in bed last night or were you gallivanting around a magical school that was like Hogwarts, but it wasn't Hogwarts? You don't know.

Eating this flavor is the opposite experience: It will make you question whether real life is actually a wonderful, surreal dream. Like when you drive somewhere and don't remember a single moment of going from point A to point B. Except this time you'll find yourself scraping the bottom of the bowl and you won't know how you got there. Magic, I tell you.

1 cup semisweet chocolate chips

¼ cup peanut butter

¼ stick (2 tablespoons) unsalted butter, at room temperature

1 cup plus 2 tablespoons heat-treated all-purpose flour (instructions on page 31)

¼ cup cocoa powder

1½ teaspoons cornstarch

1 teaspoon baking powder

½ teaspoon salt

¼ cup granulated sugar

1 cup brown sugar

½ cup pasteurized egg whites, at room temperature

2 teaspoons vanilla extract

1 cup peanut butter chips

// In a medium microwave-safe bowl, heat the chocolate chips, peanut butter, and butter in the microwave on 50% power in 30-second increments. Stir well between each increment until melted. Set aside.

// In a medium bowl, whisk together the heat-treated flour, cocoa powder, cornstarch, baking powder, and salt until well combined. Set aside.

// Pour the melted chocolate mixture into the bowl of a stand mixer fitted with the paddle attachment and mix until the mixture is smooth, about 30 seconds.

// Add the granulated and brown sugars and mix on medium until well combined, about 2 minutes. Use a rubber spatula to scrape the bowl. Add the egg whites and vanilla and mix just until well incorporated, about 2 minutes. The mixture will be very runny.

// Add the flour mixture and mix on low just until the powdery texture of the flour disappears, about 30 seconds. Scrape the bowl and mix a final 15 seconds. The "dough" will have a consistency that is more like batter.

// Remove the bowl from the mixer and use a rubber spatula to fold in the peanut butter chips.

// Dig in now for this classic peanut butter brownie batter mash-up.

// For a dough-like consistency, press plastic wrap onto the batter and chill the whole bowl in the refrigerator for at least 15 minutes before you dig in with a spoon!

If you happen to have some dough left over, see My Go-To Baking & Storage DŌrections on page 48.

////////// **Kristen's Tip** //////////

This recipe can also be made into magic brownie bars. Pour the finished dough into an 8"x8" pan and bake at 350°F for 25 minutes, or until set in the middle. Once cooled, cut it into squares, and voilà…watch them magically disappear.

///

When You're Trying Really Hard to Stick to Your New Year's Resolution

///

I've read plenty of self-improvement articles over the years. I believe that we should all strive to be the best versions of ourselves. HOWEVER, sometimes the way society tells us (especially women) to go about improving ourselves is flawed. For example: For years, I fell into a trap of believing that in order to be a better version of myself, I had to give part of the "real" me up.

Anyone who knows me or, really, has been in my general vicinity, knows I swear like a sailor. It's just who I am (don't break the news to my in-laws). But some people don't like it, so one year, I made it my New Year's resolution to quit.

To hold myself accountable, I decided that every time I said a cuss word, I had to run a mile. Best-case scenario: I'd get in better shape AND drop the habit. Spoiler alert: It didn't work out. Night one I found myself with a ten-mile run looming in front of me. Determined to see it through, I set off. When I finally hit mile ten, I used what felt like my dying breath to say, "F**k this. There's no way."

That same year, when Lent came rolling around, I decided that I'd join some of my girlfriends in giving up sweets (or, as I said, depriving myself of the finer things in life). I figured I could make it forty days, but I couldn't even come close.

What I've finally come to realize is that self-improvement isn't about giving things up. What about adding things in instead? Things that make you smile, that allow you to be more present, that bring you joy in some way. Searching for those little moments of joy in life. Now that's a resolution! Trust me, I'm definitely a happier person with all the cookie dough and all the cuss words—where in in the hell would I be without them?

/// If you're not ready to jump ship on New Year's resolutions and join me in saying HELLO to a life full of cookie dough, these recipes will make it easier for you to indulge guilt-free in a little something sweet.

MAKES
32 scoops

TIME 'TIL DOUGH
3 minutes

TIME 'TIL COOKIES
2 hours 15 minutes

WHEN YOU'RE TRYING REALLY HARD TO
STICK TO YOUR NEW YEAR'S RESOLUTION

173

Pain-less, Flour-less Peanut Butter

These days, I eat most of my meals at the office, which means my home fridge and pantry are both understocked and underwhelming. Living in New York, it's a little easier to get away with; on the rare occasion you do end up eating at home, there's always a local pizza joint, the corner deli, Seamless delivery, or a reliable bodega to pop into. The only time it really comes back to bite you is if you're like me and have a huge late-night cookie dough sweet tooth.

The last time this happened to me, I was really jonesing. Problem was, I had no white sugar, no butter, no flour, and only one egg. I had to come up with a recipe that had MINIMAL ingredients; I pulled out the peanut butter jar and got to work. I dumped in a little of this, a little of that, tasting it all along the way. A few minutes into mixing up this concoction, I knew I had a hit.

2 cups brown sugar

2 cups peanut butter

½ cup pasteurized egg whites, at room temperature

2 teaspoons vanilla extract

Flaky sea salt, like Maldon, for topping

// In a medium bowl, combine the brown sugar and peanut butter with a wooden spoon or hand mixer.

// Mix in the egg whites and vanilla until well combined. If eating as dough, sprinkle with flaky salt.

// The easiest dough of your life is done!

Trust me, you'll want to bake this dough! See My Go-To Baking & Storage DŌrections on page 48.

174   WHEN YOU'RE TRYING REALLY HARD TO
STICK TO YOUR NEW YEAR'S RESOLUTION

MAKES
25 scoops

TIME 'TIL DOUGH
15 minutes

TIME 'TIL COOKIES
2 hours 30 minutes

Chocolate Chip with a Vegan Twist

GREAT MADE GF

For the most part, I find vegan baked goods to be downright disgusting. They're dry, crumbly, and rarely worth the calories. You're better off saving those calories for some wine, which is already vegan (and gluten-free). So, when I was developing my own vegan cookie dough recipes, I knew I wouldn't settle for anything less than undeniably addicting.

And what better dough to start with than my Signature Chocolate Chip—my rock, my go-to, my ride or die? It took an immense amount of taste-testing at my old office and at my husband's office to perfect the recipe. I didn't just want people who typically follow vegan diets to approve, I needed *that guy*, the one in IT, who eats nothing but BLTs all day, to agree that this was a damn good cookie, vegan or not.

2¼ cups heat-treated all-purpose flour (instructions on page 31)

2 tablespoons cornstarch

1 teaspoon baking soda

1 tablespoon espresso powder (optional)

¾ teaspoon salt

⅞ stick (7 tablespoons) vegan butter, at room temperature

5 tablespoons coconut oil

¼ cup granulated sugar

1 cup brown sugar

¼ cup soy milk

1 tablespoon vanilla extract

1 cup vegan chocolate chips (I use Trader Joe's)

// In a medium bowl, whisk together the heat-treated flour, cornstarch, baking soda, espresso powder, and salt. Set aside.

// In the bowl of a stand mixer fitted with the paddle attachment, beat the vegan butter on medium speed until creamy, about 1 minute. Add the coconut oil and mix until smooth, about 1 minute. Add the granulated and brown sugars and mix on medium until light and fluffy; about 4 minutes will do the trick. Use a rubber spatula to scrape the bowl. Add the soy milk and vanilla and mix until fully incorporated, about 3 minutes.

// Add half of the flour mixture and mix on low just until the powdery texture of the flour disappears, about 15 seconds. Immediately add the rest of the flour mixture and mix until combined. Scrape the bowl and mix a final 15 seconds.

// Remove the bowl from the mixer and use a rubber spatula to fold in the chocolate chips.

// Classic dough with a vegan twist is ready to eat!

Store uneaten dough in an airtight container in the refrigerator for up to 1 week.

// To Bake: Press a piece of plastic wrap onto the top of the cookie dough. Place the whole bowl in the refrigerator to chill for 24 hours or in the freezer for at least 2 hours.

// Preheat the oven to 350°F.

// Line baking sheets with parchment paper or a silicone baking mat. Use a cookie scoop to portion the dough onto the baking sheets, leaving about 3 inches of space between scoops. Press down to create ½-inch-thick disks and bake for 7 to 10 minutes, until the edges are lightly golden brown and the centers are just set.

// Remove from the oven and let cool on the baking sheets for 5 minutes. Enjoy warm or transfer to a wire rack to cool completely.

Kristen's
TIP

If you want to kick this recipe up, don't leave out that bit of espresso powder. No, your cookies won't taste like coffee. Espresso powder just enhances the chocolate flavor, which is always a bonus in my book!

MAKES	TIME 'TIL DOUGH	TIME 'TIL COOKIES
30 scoops	15 minutes	20 minutes

Protein-Packed Cookie Dough

SUPER *Quick*   **NATURALLY** *GF*

As much as I would love some hard-as-a-rock six-pack abs, it's just not going to happen with my current job title. I've resigned myself to the fact that the only time I'll be seeing flawless model bodies and chiseled muscles is when I'm scrolling through Instagram, probably while snacking. While having a six-pack sounds great and all, living the six-pack lifestyle really just isn't for me. No wine, no sugar, no carbs, no cookie dough—no way.

BUT, if you're still striving for that six-pack (good for you) or trying to keep the one you've already got (bravo!), but need something sweet without having to cheat, I've got just the recipe for you.

1 cup vanilla-flavored protein powder (Tone It Up brand gave me the best results)

½ teaspoon baking soda

¼ teaspoon salt

2 cups cashew butter

¼ cup honey

½ cup pasteurized egg whites, at room temperature

1 tablespoon vanilla extract

⅓ cup sprinkles

// In a medium bowl, whisk together the protein powder, baking soda, and salt. Set aside.

// In the bowl of a stand mixer fitted with the paddle attachment, beat the cashew butter and honey on medium speed until smooth and creamy, about 2 minutes. Use a rubber spatula to scrape the bowl. Add the egg whites and vanilla and mix until fully incorporated, about 2 minutes.

// Add half of the protein powder mixture and mix on low just until the powdery texture of the flour disappears, about 15 seconds. Immediately add the rest of the flour mixture and mix until combined. Scrape the bowl and mix a final 15 seconds.

// Remove the bowl from the mixer and use a rubber spatula to fold in the sprinkles.

// Muscle-building dough is ready to be devoured!

Store uneaten dough in an airtight container in the refrigerator for up to 1 week.

// To Bake: Preheat the oven to 350°F.

// Line baking sheets with parchment paper or a silicone baking mat. Use a cookie scoop to portion the dough onto the baking sheets, leaving about 3 inches of space between scoops. Bake for **3 minutes** (yes, 3: one, two, three minutes only), or until the edges are just barely golden.

// Remove from the oven and let cool on the baking sheets for 5 minutes. Enjoy warm or transfer to a wire rack to cool completely.

//////// *Kristen's Tip* ////////

The bake time on these cookies is super short for a reason. Protein powder essentially turns to sawdust when overbaked. Three minutes is just enough time to set the cookies and give the edges a little crispness—trust me on this one.

MAKES
20 scoops

TIME 'TIL DOUGH
15 minutes

TIME 'TIL COOKIES
2 hours 15 minutes

WHEN YOU'RE TRYING REALLY HARD TO
STICK TO YOUR NEW YEAR'S RESOLUTION

179

Chick*peanut* Butter Chip

NATURALLY
GF

So, you read the title of this recipe and now you're hesitant, worried, and confused. I can see it from here. Well, relax! If you've made it this far, then you should know by now that you can trust me! Cookie dough is what I do. I wouldn't put a chickpea cookie dough recipe in this book and tell you to make it unless I 100 percent stood behind it.

While recipe testing, I made plenty of weird chalky, sweet hummus variations—needless to say, a lot of those recipe quickly met the inside of my trash can. But all the trials and tribulations, terrible taste tests, and disappointed friends led me here, to the chickpea cookie dough I always knew was possible: Chick*peanut* Butter Chip. So, enough with the worrying already—grab a can of chickpeas and enjoy!

1 **(15½-ounce)** can chickpeas

2 **tablespoons** honey

2 **tablespoons** maple syrup

2 **teaspoons** vanilla extract

1 **teaspoon** baking powder

1 **teaspoon** salt

⅔ **cup** peanut butter (we use the natural no-stir kind, but Skippy will work as well!)

½ **cup** vegan chocolate chips (I use the chips from Trader Joe's)

// Drain the chickpeas and rinse with water. Pat the chickpeas dry with a paper towel. In a food processor, grind the chickpeas until they are in small pieces.

// With the food processor on low, add the honey, maple syrup, and vanilla. Run the processor until the mixture is very smooth, scraping the sides several times with a rubber spatula to free any hidden chunks. Add the baking powder and salt. Run for 1 to 2 more minutes, until the mixture is well combined.

// Transfer the chickpea mixture to a large bowl. Use a rubber spatula to fold in the peanut butter. Continue to stir and fold until the peanut butter is dispersed throughout. Fold in the chocolate chips.

You've got some guilt-free chickpea dough ready to go!

Store uneaten dough in an airtight container in the refrigerator for up to 1 week.

// Trust me. Try baking these!

// To Bake: Press a piece of plastic wrap onto the top of the cookie dough. Place the whole bowl in the refrigerator to chill for 24 hours or in the freezer for at least 2 hours.

// Preheat the oven to 350°F. Line baking sheets with parchment paper or a silicone baking mat.

// Use a cookie scoop to portion the dough onto the lined sheets, leaving about 3 inches of space between scoops. These cookies will not spread much in the oven, so help them out by pressing them down so they are about ½ inch thick. Bake for 8 minutes and check the cookies. Continue to bake for 1 to 3 minutes, watching the cookies for edges that are lightly golden. They will still be VERY soft and gooey when finished.

// Remove from the oven and let cool on the baking sheets for 5 minutes. Enjoy warm or transfer to a wire rack to cool completely.

180

\ WHEN YOU'RE TRYING REALLY HARD TO
STICK TO YOUR NEW YEAR'S RESOLUTION

\ MAKES
28 scoops

\ TIME 'TIL DOUGH
15 minutes

\ TIME 'TIL COOKIES
2 hours 30 minutes

STACY-APPROVED
Peanut Butter Snickerdoodle

When I first started the business, I made and sold all the cookie dough out of my tiny Brooklyn apartment. I had dozens and dozens of orders from strangers, and I didn't even have time to look at the customers' names. "Stacy London's" third order of the Chick*peanut* Butter Chip (page 179) caught my eye, though, when she professed her love for DŌ in a run-of-the-mill email coordinating her order pickup. I embarrassingly asked if she was "THE Stacy London" that I grew up watching on TLC. When she confirmed that she was, I immediately professed *my* love to *her* and officially had my first freak-out moment.

A few weeks later, she was headed to a party at Whoopi Goldberg's house(!!!) and wanted to take some cookie dough treats to share. She asked what other vegan and gluten-free flavors I had. The real answer was "none," but I whipped up a bunch of new recipes and sent them over to Stacy for a taste test. She immediately called to let me know that "this peanut butter cinnamon chip one is like crack. You'd never know it's gluten-free and vegan!"

We became fast friends— yes, she's even more amazing and thoughtful and genuine and cool IRL than she is on TV! This flavor has stayed on our menu ever since that wonderful day. Hey, if this one's good enough for Stacy London, then it's sure as hell good enough for me (and you).

FOR THE CINNAMON SUGAR
1 cup granulated sugar

¼ cup ground cinnamon

FOR THE DOUGH
1⅓ cups heat-treated gluten-free flour (instructions on page 31)

2 teaspoons cornstarch

½ teaspoon baking soda

½ teaspoon salt

½ stick (4 tablespoons) vegan butter, at room temperature

¼ cup coconut oil

1¼ cups peanut butter

¼ cup granulated sugar

½ cup plus 1 tablespoon brown sugar

3 tablespoons soy milk

1½ teaspoons vanilla extract

½ cup vegan chocolate chips

// Make the cinnamon sugar: In a small bowl, whisk together the sugar and cinnamon. Set aside.

// Make the dough: In a medium bowl, whisk together the heat-treated gluten-free flour, cornstarch, baking soda, and salt. Set aside.

// In the bowl of a stand mixer fitted with the paddle attachment, beat the vegan butter on medium speed until creamy, about 1 minute. Add the coconut oil and peanut butter and mix until smooth, about 1 minute. Add the granulated and brown sugars and mix on medium until light and fluffy; about 4 minutes will do the trick. Use a rubber spatula to scrape the bowl. Add the soy milk and vanilla and mix until fully incorporated, about 3 minutes.

// Add half of the flour mixture and mix on low just until the powdery texture of the flour disappears, about 15 seconds. Immediately add the rest of the flour mixture and mix until combined. Scrape the bowl and mix a final 15 seconds.

// Remove the bowl from the mixer and use a rubber spatula to mix in ¼ cup of the cinnamon sugar. Reserve the rest for rolling cookies or for using later. Once combined, fold in the chocolate chips.

// Stacy says—spoon this straight from the bowl!

Craving some cookies? Have extra cookie daugh? See my Go-To Baking & Storage DŌrections on page 48 but make sure to watch the bake time on these—they bake fast!

Kristen's
TIP

These cookies bake faster than most recipes in this book. Check them after 5 or 6 minutes and keep that oven light on!

Kristen's TIP

You can find matcha powder online or at most grocery stores in the beverage aisle near the coffee or the health and wellness aisle. You'll have lots of extra matcha powder for your pantry—it's great in lattes.

Must Love Matcha

GREAT MADE GF

Matcha will always have a special place in my heart. Before I drank coffee at Starbucks, I would order only their nonfat Matcha Green Tea Latte. In college, when my now-husband, Chris, was pursuing me, going to "grab coffee" never worked as an excuse to spend time together. I wasn't interested in coffee (or really him)—at the time. (Sorry!) But, he knew about my weakness for Green Tea Lattes, so he used to surprise me by "dropping one off" on my desk in the studio before class started. It was amazing—I got to skip the whole date thing and I didn't have to spend $6 I didn't have on the latte. Win, win! Lucky for me, it all worked out in the end, and those lattes—along with many other meals—were well worth the expense, right, honey?

2½ cups heat-treated all-purpose flour (instructions on page 31)

3 tablespoons cornstarch

1 tablespoon matcha powder

1½ teaspoons cream of tartar

¾ teaspoon baking powder

¾ teaspoon baking soda

¾ teaspoon salt

¾ stick (6 tablespoons) vegan butter, at room temperature

⅓ cup coconut oil

1 cup plus 2 tablespoons sugar

¼ cup soy milk

1½ teaspoons vanilla extract

½ cup vegan chocolate chips

// In a medium bowl, whisk together the heat-treated flour, cornstarch, matcha powder, cream of tartar, baking powder, baking soda, and salt. Set aside.

// In the bowl of a stand mixer fitted with the paddle attachment, beat the vegan butter on medium speed until creamy, about 1 minute. Add the coconut oil and mix until smooth, about 1 minute. Add the sugar and mix on medium until light and fluffy; about 4 minutes will do the trick. Use a rubber spatula to scrape the bowl. Add the soy milk and vanilla and mix until fully incorporated, about 3 minutes.

// Add half of the flour mixture and mix on low just until the powdery texture of the flour disappears, about 15 seconds. Immediately add the rest of the flour mixture and mix until combined. Scrape the bowl and mix a final 15 seconds.

// Remove the bowl from the mixer and use a rubber spatula to fold in the chocolate chips.

// Mmmmmm...matcha dough is good to go!

Store uneaten dough in an airtight container in the refrigerator for up to 1 week.

// To Bake: Press a piece of plastic wrap onto the top of the cookie dough. Place the whole bowl in the refrigerator to chill for 24 hours or in the freezer for at least 2 hours.

// Preheat the oven to 350°F.

// Line baking sheets with parchment paper or a silicone baking mat. Use a cookie scoop to portion the dough onto the baking sheets, leaving about 3 inches of space between scoops. Press down to create ½-inch-thick disks and bake for 7 to 10 minutes, until the edges are lightly golden brown and the centers are just set.

// Remove from the oven and let cool on the baking sheets for 5 minutes. Enjoy warm or transfer to a wire rack to cool completely.

184 WHEN YOU'RE TRYING REALLY HARD TO STICK TO YOUR NEW YEAR'S RESOLUTION

MAKES
31 scoops

TIME 'TIL DOUGH
15 minutes

TIME 'TIL COOKIES
2 hours 30 minutes

NATURALLY
GF

Paleo People Deserve Cookie Dough Too

New DŌ employees always think that they are going to have to go on a diet when they start working for me. They think they'll need to restrain themselves from eating a ton of cookie dough every shift to avoid inevitably gaining a bunch of unwanted weight. Funny thing is, most employees end up losing weight when they start working at the shop. Whether you're in the kitchen, scooping cookie dough, or on our support team, your job is a legitimate workout—schlepping fifty pounds of sugar up a flight of stairs is no easy task!

I'm certainly no health or fitness expert; however, I do recommend this cookie dough as a flavor you don't have to feel bad about eating. It's refined sugar–free, gluten-free, and satisfyingly almond-butter-full. It's the perfect treat whether you're healthy, pretending to be healthy, or even if you don't care about being healthy at all.

2 cups almond flour

½ cup coconut flour

1 teaspoon baking soda

½ cup pasteurized egg whites, at room temperature

½ cup coconut oil

1 cup almond butter

1 cup coconut sugar

2 teaspoons vanilla extract

½ cup vegan chocolate chips

Flaky salt, like Maldon, for topping

// In a medium bowl, whisk together the almond flour, coconut flour, and baking soda. Set aside.

// In the bowl of a stand mixer fitted with the paddle attachment, whip the egg whites on high until very frothy and they have enough structure to form a shape but not enough to hold it, about 1 minute.

// Using a rubber spatula, scrape the egg whites into a small bowl.

// In the bowl of a stand mixer, beat the coconut oil and almond butter on medium speed until smooth and creamy, about 2 minutes. Add the coconut sugar and mix on medium until light and fluffy; about 4 minutes will do the trick. Use a rubber spatula to scrape the bowl. Add the egg whites and vanilla and mix until fully incorporated, about 2 minutes.

// Add half of the flour mixture and mix on low just until the powdery texture of the flour disappears, about 15 seconds. Immediately add the rest of the flour mixture and mix until combined. Scrape the bowl and mix a final 15 seconds.

// Remove the bowl from the mixer and use a rubber spatula to fold in the chocolate chips. Sprinkle with flaky sea salt.

// Paleo people, this dough is for you!

Store uneaten dough in an airtight container in the refrigerator for up to 1 week.

// To Bake: Press a piece of plastic wrap onto the top of the cookie dough. Place the whole bowl in the refrigerator to chill for 24 hours or in the freezer for at least 2 hours.

// Preheat the oven to 350°F.

// Line baking sheets with parchment paper or a silicone baking mat. Use a cookie scoop to portion the dough onto the baking sheets, leaving about 3 inches of space between scoops. Bake for 4 to 6 minutes, until the edges are lightly golden brown.

// Remove from the oven and let cool on the baking sheets for 5 minutes. Enjoy warm or transfer to a wire rack to cool completely.

Start Here →

HOW MUCH TIME DO YOU HAVE?

A little bit

FOR DŌ?
All the time in the world!

Cereal Bowl
page 82

cereal

I'm Bananas for Nutella®
page 90

bananas

Nutella®

Have you had cookie dough before?

Are you making this for just yourself?

Their go-to breakfast includes

I've been known to dabble.

First-timer!

All me

I might share.

Plus the kids

HOW DID YOU KNOW?

How ya feeling?

Frisky

Something classic

I'm craving

A cocktail

Is it before noon?

As #basic as it gets

Signature Chocolate Chip
page 60

Brookie Dough
page 66

A green juice

Wine?

Bourbon?

I need

Nope, after naps

Like matcha?

Extra berries?

Plus lemon?

Rosé All Day
page 134

Triple B
page 148

An activity

What's their favorite color?

Must Love Matcha
page 183

Best Berry Crisp
page 127

Kristen's Lemonade Stand
page 135

Pink

Rainbow

Blue

You are a Goddamn Magical Unicorn
page 104

Glitter-everywhere messy

How messy can you handle?

Sugar Rush
page 111

Me Want Cookie
page 100

No mess!

A little is OK.

DunkaDŌo
page 99

Play Dough
page 108

Best in the Morning

My aDŌrable packaging didn't always come from a factory. Chris and I fulfilled dozens, then thousands, of orders with hand-assembled cups finished with a handwritten label. When we needed help, our "Ohio branch" (aka my retired father-in-law, John) chipped in working five hours a day labeling cups.

I needed a manufacturer to save my X-Acto-knife-cut hands and my sanity, but I couldn't afford the minimum order. Until one salesman cut me an unbelievable deal. We'll call him Larry.

I paid a deposit so gigantic that my hand shook when I signed on the dotted line. But it was worth it; my hand-labeling days were numbered. Just before the shipment date, I called Larry to get the specifics. He never answered me.

Nice try, Larry, this girl does not get ghosted. My team and I used the social media stalking skills honed from years of investigating Tinder dates to track him down. Turns out Larry was into some shady shit. I stared at the cuts on my hands, trying not to cry as I realized the end was nowhere in sight and I was out thousands of dollars.

Several months later, I got a random sales call: "Listen, my factory in Asia just sent me one of your cups. I can get you a better price," he said.

"What, my cups? I haven't even seen my cups!" I exclaimed. It was not salesman Mitch's average cold call.

Turns out Mitch (whom I will always call Angel Mitch) could get everything to the US; he just couldn't get the split shipment I had been "promised" by Larry. I couldn't store the entire order of cups, but I said, "Send them my way!"

We made a plan to handle the giant shipment—the trucking company would call the day before the delivery. Then, Chris's dad would drive a U-Haul up from the "Ohio branch" to take extra boxes. Given the plan, I thought nothing of it when I got a ring on the buzzer at our Midtown kitchen. "Yes, miss, the eighteen-wheeler is ready for unloading."

My jaw dropped. Ninety thousand lids and containers were no longer in Asia, because they were right here on 2nd Avenue. I called in Chris, Bri, and Rikki (my OG DŌ team), and got down to sweating in the summer sun while lugging boxes to our tiny second-floor kitchen. We didn't have space for 360 large boxes, so we trekked up an additional two stories to an empty fourth-floor space, a temporary fix while I figured out storage.

It took six hours. Everyone was lying on the ground when I got upstairs with the last box. "We can't, Kristen; please, we can't move these again," Bri begged. The last thing I did that day was use my blistered hands to sign the lease on the fourth-floor space, then I found my place on the floor with the rest of the team.

/// For those hectic days when there's no time for breakfast, you might as well add a little breakfast to your cookie dough...and on all the other days, go ahead and add a little cookie dough to your breakfast!

192 \ BEST IN THE MORNING

\ MAKES
15 to 20 pancakes

\ ACTIVE TIME
45 minutes

\ TIME 'TIL PANCAKES
45 minutes

STACK 'EM HIGH &
Watch 'Em Fly Cakes

kids LOVE

When it comes to pancakes, everyone's got their own secret family recipe... even if that recipe is some good ol' Bisquick! Jack Johnson takes his with bananas, my sister is a chocolate chip gal, and I stuff mine with cookie dough. No surprise there.

To eat them, stack 'em high and top 'em with your favorite go-tos: classic butter and maple syrup or, if you want to dough it like me, some frosting and sprinkles!

FOR THE COOKIE DOUGH

¾ cup cake mix (¼ box)

¾ cup plus 1 tablespoon heat-treated all-purpose flour (instructions on page 31)

1 tablespoon cornstarch

½ teaspoon salt

¾ stick (6 tablespoons) unsalted butter, at room temperature

¼ cup granulated sugar

¼ cup brown sugar

2 tablespoons pasteurized egg whites, at room temperature

1 teaspoon vanilla extract

¼ cup sprinkles

FOR THE PANCAKES

2½ cups all-purpose flour

1 tablespoon plus 1 teaspoon baking powder

½ teaspoon salt

2 cups milk

2 whole eggs

2 tablespoons canola oil

¼ cup semisweet chocolate chips

¼ cup white chocolate chips

¼ cup sprinkles

// Make the cookie dough: Heat-treat the cake mix according to the instructions on page 31.

// Once the cake mix has cooled completely, in a medium bowl, whisk together the cake mix, flour, cornstarch, and salt. Set aside.

// In the bowl of a stand mixer fitted with the paddle attachment, beat the butter on medium speed until smooth, about 2 minutes. Add the sugars and mix on medium until light and fluffy; about 4 minutes. Use a rubber spatula to scrape the bowl. Add the egg whites and vanilla and mix until fully incorporated, about 2 minutes.

// Add half of the cake mix mixture and mix on low just until the powdery texture of the flour disappears, about 15 seconds. Immediately add the rest of the flour mixture and mix until combined. Scrape the bowl and mix a final 15 seconds.

// Remove the bowl from the mixer and use a rubber spatula to fold in the sprinkles. Set in the refrigerator to chill while you prepare the pancake batter.

// Make the pancakes: In a large bowl, whisk together the flour, baking powder, and salt. In a separate bowl, whisk together the milk, eggs, and oil. Create a well in the center of the flour mixture and pour the milk mixture into it. Whisk until the mixture is smooth. Add both chocolate chips and the sprinkles and stir to evenly disperse them throughout the batter.

// Heat a nonstick skillet or griddle over medium heat and remove the cookie dough from the fridge. Use a ¼-cup measuring cup to slowly pour the batter onto the skillet. Use your fingers to break off teaspoon-size chunks of cold cookie dough and drop 4 to 5 pieces of dough onto the top of each pancake. Cook until small bubbles form and the bottom is fully set and lightly golden. Flip and cook on the opposite side until lightly golden. Repeat with the remaining batter and cookie dough.

// Serve warm with your favorite pancake toppings.

Store uneaten pancakes in an airtight container in the refrigerator for up to 1 week. Reheat in a buttered skillet over medium heat, about 1 minute on each side.

/ MAKES
18 cinnamon rolls / ACTIVE TIME
55 minutes / TIME 'TIL ROLLS
3 hours 30 minutes / BEST IN THE
MORNING / 195

A Cinnamon Roll Worth Fighting Over

KRISTEN'S
Fav

Every visit to Grandma's house results in a full-on sibling war over one thing—the cinnamon roll in the middle of the pan. Sure, there are plenty of delicious edge cinnamon rolls to go around, but we all want that one perfectly soft and sticky middle roll. When it comes to cinnamon rolls, the gooier the better!

In order to really take cinnamon rolls to the next level, to their ultimate peak ooziness, you need to stuff them, and I mean STUFF them, with cookie dough. The result is a full layer of molten cookie dough, somewhere between half-baked and baked, spiraling throughout your fresh-out-of-the-oven rolls. And what's even better? There are THREE middles in this recipe...one for each of my siblings. Lauren, Maddie, and Trey: Each of you gets a middle roll, just like you've always wanted...and I'll take the other fifteen.

FOR THE CINNAMON ROLL DOUGH

2 (¼-ounce) packets active dry yeast

½ cup warm water

6 cups all-purpose flour (divided), plus more for dusting

1 stick (8 tablespoons) unsalted butter, plus more for greasing

¾ cup whole milk

½ cup sugar

1½ teaspoons salt

3 whole eggs, at room temperature

2 teaspoons canola oil (or any neutral oil)

FOR THE COOKIE DOUGH FILLING

1 cup plus 2 tablespoons heat-treated all-purpose flour (instructions on page 31)

1 teaspoon cornstarch

½ teaspoon salt

¾ stick (6 tablespoons) unsalted butter, at room temperature

2 tablespoons granulated sugar

½ cup brown sugar

2½ tablespoons pasteurized egg whites, at room temperature

1½ teaspoons vanilla extract

½ cup mini semisweet chocolate chips

FOR THE CINNAMON FILLING

1 cup brown sugar

2 teaspoons ground cinnamon

1 teaspoon salt

⅜ stick (3 tablespoons) unsalted butter, melted

FOR THE GLAZE

3 cups confectioners' sugar

1 teaspoon vanilla extract

6 tablespoons milk

// Make the cinnamon roll dough: In a small bowl, dissolve the yeast in the warm water and set aside for 5 to 10 minutes. Measure the flour by placing 5 cups of flour in one bowl and setting 1 cup aside.

// In a microwave-safe container, heat the butter, milk, sugar, and salt on 50% power in 30-second increments until the butter is melted and the mixture is warmed, stirring well between each increment.

CONTINUES →

// Pour the mixture into a medium bowl. Whisk in the eggs one at a time. Add the yeast mixture (it should appear frothy) and whisk well. Pour the liquid into the bowl of a stand mixer fitted with the dough hook attachment. Add half of the 5 cups of flour and mix on medium speed until nearly combined. Add the remaining half of the flour and mix to combine. Add the reserved 1 cup flour 1 tablespoon at a time. Stop adding flour when the dough no longer sticks to the sides of the bowl and is easy to handle.

// Place the dough on a lightly floured surface and knead for 5 to 8 minutes. Oil a bowl with the canola oil. Place the kneaded dough in the oiled bowl, turning in the bowl once to make sure it is oiled on all sides. Cover and let the dough rise in a warm place for about 1 hour.

// Make the cookie dough filling: Use the ingredients listed in this recipe and follow the method on page 60.

// Generously grease a 9"x13" pan and an 8"x8" pan with butter.

// After the dough has risen for 1 hour or doubled in size, punch it down and remove it from the bowl. Use a floured rolling pin on a floured surface to roll the dough into a 12"x18" rectangle about ¼ inch thick.

// Make the cinnamon filling: Combine the brown sugar, cinnamon, and salt in a small bowl. Brush the melted butter over the entire rectangle (all the way to the edges). Sprinkle the brown sugar mixture over the dough, leaving a 1-inch margin on one of the long sides.

// Remove the cookie dough from the refrigerator and use your hands to break off dime-size to quarter-size pieces of dough. Sprinkle the pieces evenly over the rectangle, leaving the 1-inch margin.

// Beginning at the long side without the margin, tightly roll the dough. When you reach the margin at the other end of the dough, pull it tightly over the roll to create a seam. Pinch the seam to seal. Cut the log into even 1-inch slices.

// Place 12 slices in the 9"x13" pan in a 3"x4" arrangement. Place the other 6 slices in the 8"x8" pan, with one in the center surrounded by the rest of the slices. It's OK if they don't touch. Cover and set aside to rise in a warm place for 1 hour.

// Preheat the oven to 350°F. Bake the rolls for 25 to 30 minutes, until the edges are lightly browned and the tops are set.

// While the rolls bake, make the glaze: In a medium bowl, whisk together the confectioners' sugar, vanilla, and 2 tablespoons of the milk. Add 1 tablespoon additional milk at a time until the glaze coats the back of a spoon and slowly runs off.

// Let the rolls cool for 5 minutes before drizzling the glaze over the entire pan. Enjoy immediately!

Store uneaten rolls in an airtight container in the refrigerator for up to 5 days. Reheat in a preheated 275°F oven for 12 minutes, or until warm throughout.

MAKES
9 pie pockets

ACTIVE TIME
45 minutes

TIME 'TIL POCKETS
1 hour 20 minutes

BEST IN THE
MORNING

197

Pie Pocket Perfection

Can we get real about Pop-Tarts for a second? Pop-Tarts are the gateway drugs that teach us to eat dessert for breakfast. They make us think that eating pie pockets stuffed with sugar and topped with icing is a perfectly nutritious way to start the day.

Jokes aside, I'm a huge fan of Pop-Tarts (and all desserts disguised as breakfast dishes like donuts, muffins, and coffee CAKE). Forget breakfast for dinner, it's all about dessert for breakfast!

FOR THE CRUST

2 cups all-purpose flour

2 tablespoons granulated sugar

½ teaspoon salt

2 sticks (16 tablespoons) unsalted butter, very cold

2 tablespoons milk, very cold

1 whole egg

1 teaspoon vanilla extract

FOR THE FILLING

1 stick (8 tablespoons) unsalted butter, at room temperature

½ cup brown sugar

1 tablespoon heavy cream

1 teaspoon vanilla extract

¾ cup heat-treated all-purpose flour (instructions on page 31)

⅓ cup mini chocolate chips

FOR THE EGG WASH

1 whole egg

1 teaspoon milk

2 teaspoons heavy cream

FOR THE GLAZE

1 tablespoon milk

½ cup confectioners' sugar

FOR THE TOPPING

¼ cup mini chocolate chips or sprinkles

// **Make the crust:** In a food processor, pulse together the flour, sugar, and salt.

// Remove the butter from the refrigerator and quickly cut it into cubes. Add to the food processor and continue to pulse until the mixture forms crumbles about the size of a corn kernel. Transfer the mixture from the processor into a large bowl.

// In a separate bowl, whisk together the milk, egg, and vanilla and pour over the butter mixture. Use two forks to cut the mixture to disperse the moisture evenly throughout and continue to break up the butter crumbles. Once the dough comes together, use your hands to form two large balls.

// Press each ball slightly to flatten into a disk shape. Wrap the disks in plastic wrap and rest in the refrigerator for 30 minutes. Meanwhile, line two baking sheets with parchment paper or a silicone baking mat and preheat the oven to 350°F.

// Lay a large sheet or two of waxed paper on the countertop. Remove one disk from the fridge and place in the center of the waxed paper. Cover with another sheet of waxed paper and use a rolling pin to roll the dough out to be roughly the size of a 9"x13" baking dish.

CONTINUES →

// Use a bench scraper or pizza cutter to cut off uneven edges so you have a perfect rectangle. Then cut the dough into even thirds. Then cut into even thirds again going the other direction. (You'll have 9 even rectangles.) Place the crusts on the lined baking sheet. Repeat the rolling and cutting process with the other half of the dough. Place all 18 crusts on a baking sheet and chill in the refrigerator.

// Meanwhile, make the filling: In the bowl of a stand mixer fitted with the paddle attachment, beat the butter and brown sugar on medium speed until smooth and creamy, about 2 minutes. Add the cream and vanilla and mix until fully incorporated, about 2 minutes.

// Add the flour and mix on low just until the powdery texture of the flour disappears, about 15 seconds. Scrape the bowl and mix a final 15 seconds. Remove the bowl from the mixer and use a rubber spatula to fold in the mini chocolate chips. Set aside.

// Make the egg wash: In a small bowl, whisk together the egg, milk, and cream. Set aside.

// Time to assemble the pie pockets! Remove the dough from the refrigerator. Coat the edges of 9 rectangles with egg wash. Put 2 tablespoons of filling in the center of each of those rectangles. Use the remaining rectangles to top each pie picket. With a fork, gently press the two layers of crust together, leaving crimping marks around the border of each pie pocket. Use the fork to poke holes into the center of the pie pockets in several places to allow steam to escape.

// Bake for 20 to 25 minutes and check for pie pockets that are puffed and lightly golden brown. Add an additional 3 to 5 minutes if needed. Remove from the oven and let cool.

// While the pie pockets cool, make the glaze: In a small bowl, whisk the milk into the confectioners' sugar. Stop when the glaze coats the back of a spoon and slowly runs off. Spoon a large dollop of glaze into the center of each pie pocket; if needed, tilt the pie pocket in a circular motion to spread the glaze over the pastry. Top with chocolate chips or sprinkles, if using, and enjoy right away (or wait about 30 minutes for the glaze to set).

Store uneaten pie pockets in an airtight container at room temperature for up to 3 days. To reheat, place in a preheated 200°F oven for 10 minutes.

MAKES
12 crêpes

ACTIVE TIME
50 minutes

TIME 'TIL CRÊPES
50 minutes

Cookie Dough Packed Crêpes

Crêpes are traditional French pancakes, which makes them sound fancier and more intimidating than they really are! Seriously, don't let them scare you! I started making this recipe when I was ten years old, so I can testify to the fact that it is kid (and non-French-pastry-chef-trained adult) friendly!

The best thing about crêpes? You can fill them with whatever you have on hand! Sweet or savory, they make an out-of-the-ordinary breakfast, snack, or dinner. My perfect crêpe has (lots of) cookie dough packed in it. Welcome to my world.

Suggested filling combinations:

NUTELLA CHIP

½ batch Signature Chocolate Chip dough (page 60)

6 tablespoons Nutella

CHOCOLATE STRAWBERRY

½ batch Brownie Batter dough (page 64)

1 (8-ounce) package fresh strawberries, hulled and sliced

SNICKERDOODLE

½ batch Snickerdoodle dough (page 68)

2 teaspoons cinnamon sugar, for topping

FOR THE BATTER

4 whole eggs, at room temperature

2 cups milk, at room temperature

½ cup sugar

1 teaspoon salt

1½ cups all-purpose flour

FOR PREPARING THE CRÊPES

¼ stick (2 tablespoons) unsalted butter

Confectioners' sugar, for topping

// Make the cookie dough to use for the filling. Set aside the dough and additional filling ingredients while you prepare the crêpes.

// Make the batter: Use a stand mixer fitted with the whisk attachment or a hand mixer in a large bowl to beat the eggs and milk until smooth and combined. Add the sugar and salt and beat to incorporate. Slowly add the flour and mix until smooth.

// Prepare the crepes: Heat an 8-inch skillet over medium heat until hot. Add a little butter to the pan and swirl. Use a measuring cup to pour ½ cup batter into the skillet. Swirl the pan so the batter covers the entire bottom of the pan. Cook for about 2 minutes, until the edges begin to pull away from the sides of the pan. Flip the crêpe and cook the other side for about 1 minute. The crêpe should be lightly golden on both sides.

// Repeat until all the batter is used, buttering the pan between crêpes as needed. Stack the cooked crêpes on a plate.

// Once all the crêpes are cooked, they are ready to fill! Soften your cookie dough of choice in the microwave for a few seconds so it's easy to spread. Spread evenly over the crêpes and top with the suggestions above (or make up your own!).

// Fold the crêpes in half, and then in half again. Sprinkle with confectioners' sugar and serve warm.

Unfilled crêpes can be wrapped in foil and stored in the refrigerator for up to 3 days and in the freezer for up to 1 month.

Eat with your eyes? See the photo on page 87.

DŌnuts

The caboose on the dessert for breakfast train is the one recipe this section wouldn't be complete without. Our signature DŌnuts: freshly fried, stuffed with cookie dough buttercream, and tossed in sugar.

I don't eat a lot of donuts, but somehow I've ended up surrounded by the ultimate donut lovers—my husband, Chris; our pastry chef, Brianna; and my assistant, Ally. The three people I spend the most time with happen to have the same love in common. This one is for you, guys.

FOR THE DONUTS

1 cup milk

2 teaspoons vanilla extract

1 (¼-ounce) packet active dry yeast

2 whole eggs

1 stick (8 tablespoons) unsalted butter, melted and cooled

1¼ cups sugar (divided)

½ teaspoon salt

4½ cups all-purpose flour

2 quarts plus 1 tablespoon neutral oil, like canola

FOR THE FILLING

½ batch Cookie Dough Buttercream (page 213)

// Make the donuts: In a medium bowl, heat the milk and vanilla in the microwave on 50% power in 30-second increments until it reaches a temperature between 100°F and 110°F. Add the yeast, stir lightly, and let sit for 5 to 10 minutes, until foamy.

// In the bowl of a stand mixer fitted with the dough hook attachment, mix the eggs, butter, ½ cup of the sugar, and the salt on medium until well combined. Add half of the flour and mix until combined. Pour in the yeast mixture and stir. Add the rest of the flour and stir until the dough pulls away from the sides of the bowl. Use a rubber spatula to scrape the bowl if needed.

// Place the dough on a lightly floured surface and knead for 2 to 3 minutes. Place in a bowl oiled with 1 tablespoon of the canola oil. Turn the dough in the bowl once to make sure it is oiled on all sides. Cover and let rise in a warm place for about 1 hour.

// Once the dough has doubled in size, punch it down and turn it out onto a well-floured surface. Roll the dough out into a ½-inch-thick rectangle. Use a cup or round cookie cutter to cut the donuts. Place the cut rounds onto floured waxed paper, cover with a kitchen towel, and let rise for 45 minutes to 1 hour, until the donuts appear puffed and slightly risen.

// Make the Cookie Dough Buttercream while the dough rises. Place the buttercream into a piping bag fitted with a wide piping tip. Set aside.

// Heat the oil in a Dutch oven or other heavy-bottomed pan over medium heat until it reaches 375°F. In batches of 3 to 5, use a metal spatula to slide the donuts into the oil. Fry until the bottoms are golden brown, about 1 minute, then flip to brown other side. Remove from the oil with a slotted spoon and roll in the remaining ¾ cup sugar. Place on paper towels to drain.

// Once the donuts have cooled slightly, fill them by inserting the tip of the piping bag into the side of each donut and piping about 1½ tablespoons buttercream into the center. Avoid overfilling by feel— when the donut feels full in your hand, stop piping!

These DŌnuts are best enjoyed immediately! Store them at room temperature for up to 2 days.

/////////// *Kristen's Tip* ///////////

Add some color to your breakfast by rolling these donuts in rainbow sanding sugar!

///

Best When Baked

I attended an all-girls Catholic high school with plaid skirts, cardigan sweaters, and all.

Being at a single-sex school might sound weird, but it was a truly formative experience. Without the distraction of boys, we girls could concentrate on school, form friendships that would last a lifetime, and basically never shave our legs. This school fostered a spirit of companionship and community that women can really find only with other women. It's where I discovered that every successful woman has an army of other women who have her back.

It's no surprise I joined a sorority in college, where I leaned on my sisters to get me through boy drama and late nights in design studio. Those women have been part of my life long after school—they were at my wedding, by my bedside in the hospital, and, of course, there with me when I started my business.

Even when DŌ was very new, it seemed like a buttoned-up company. We had a great website, official-looking email addresses for different "departments" (orders@, help@, hiring@, catering@ cookiedonyc.com), an active social media presence, fancy colorful packaging, etc. etc. etc. But what I really had was a knack for fooling everyone. The site? My friend Liz wrote, edited, and proofed. The photos? Taken on my iPhone. The KitchenAid mixer I used? A wedding gift from my good friend Su. The word-of-mouth marketing? Spread by my girlfriends and Mom. All those email addresses? Straight to one in-box—mine. The "printed" spoons? Painstakingly stamped by hand by my girl squad ninjas using pencil erasers dripped in ink. Bless that squad.

Over the years, my girl gang has expanded to include other badass entrepreneurs in the industry. My gals have helped me work through ideas, made sure I didn't jump off a cliff, and have even inspired recipes in this book.

/// If these friendships have taught me anything, it's that there's no one like your girl group to take your half-baked ideas and turn them into full-baked ones! This chapter is all about those recipes that are baked all the way through.

DŌin' It
FOR THE
'Gram

I know I'm known for my dough, but with the right tricks, the doughs can look and taste their best when baked. Follow these tips for the perfect 'gram-worthy cookies.

1 TOP THEM

At the shop, and when I'm going all-out on home baking projects, I top each cookie individually with extra mix-ins. If I'm baking up Gimme S'more cookies (page 58), I'll have extra chopped Hershey's bar and mini marshmallows on hand to press into the top of each dough ball. It makes for some seriously pretty cookies.

2 FROST THEM

Frosting adds a new texture and a pop of color to an otherwise plain Jane cookie. For a typical drop cookie, stiffer frosting like buttercream works best because of the cookie's dome-like shape. Thinner icings and glazes will run off the sides of the cookie before they have a chance to set. Use gel food coloring to dye your frostings so they stay thick and creamy.

3 SPRINKLE THEM

You can apply sprinkles to any cookie before it goes in the oven, or after cooling and frosting. Sprinkles are becoming ever more popular, and they come in so many fun shapes and colors (see page 38). You can find them online or in your local craft store.

4 SANDWICH THEM

Anything can make the filling in a cookie sandwich. Think: thick buttercream (page 156), homemade ice cream (page 273), cookie dough dip (page 264), or any of the doughs in this book. If you can spread it, you can sandwich it!

5 MAKE 'EM MINI OR MASSIVE

I suggest using a cookie scoop for consistent cookies every time. But if you're ready to go crazy in the kitchen, try a supersize cookie. Make a dough ball the size of about five to six scoops, flatten the bottom slightly, stick it in the middle of a lined baking sheet, and watch as it bakes up and out into a gigantic delicacy! For mini cookies, use half the amount of one cookie scoop. Reduce the baking time and watch them carefully in the oven. They're way better than potato chips to fill a bowl at your next party.

6 STUFF THEM

Shut the stuff up!...and take a bite of a surprise cookie with a surprise inside. To stuff any dough, roll a scoop into a ball, poke a hole into the middle, fill it with ½ teaspoon of your favorite spread, pinch the seam closed, and roll it in between your hands until the seam disappears. Chill for 2 hours and bake according to My Go-To Baking & Storage DŌrections (page 48). My go-to filling is Nutella, but peanut butter, sprinkles, and Fluff do the job nicely too.

7 DIP THEM

When cookies take a lil' dip in chocolate, they instantly become fancier. To decorate a cookie that really wows, dye some melted white chocolate with food coloring and then scatter on some sprinkles. These dipped cookies can match any themed party—green for St. Paddy's, pink for a baby shower, and white for me because I'm too lazy to pull out the food coloring, but you dough you!

Brookie Bar

If you're going to make only one recipe in this book...it should be the Brookie Bar. It's the most popular confection at DŌ and the inspiration behind one of our all-time best-selling dough flavors (Brookie Dough; page 66)—you don't want to skip this one.

Start by making our Signature Chocolate Chip dough (our all-time best-seller) and our Brownie Batter dough (which tastes exactly how you're imagining it would). Then layer those doughs to make the most decadent half-brownie, half-cookie combo (hence the name Brookie). It's a little bit baked and a little bit dough-y, showing off the best parts of a cookie and a brownie at the same time. You don't have to choose between these two tempting treats—you get both in every single bite.

FOR THE SIGNATURE CHOCOLATE CHIP

½ batch Signature Chocolate Chip dough (page 60) using mini semisweet chocolate chips

FOR THE BROWNIE BATTER

1½ cups semisweet chocolate chips (divided)

½ stick (4 tablespoons) unsalted butter, at room temperature

¾ cup plus 1 tablespoon heat-treated all-purpose flour (instructions on page 31)

3 tablespoons cocoa powder

1 teaspoon cornstarch

¾ teaspoon baking powder

¼ teaspoon salt

3 tablespoons granulated sugar

¾ cup brown sugar

¼ cup plus 2 tablespoons pasteurized egg whites, at room temperature

1½ teaspoons vanilla extract

FOR THE GANACHE

1½ cups semisweet chocolate

1 tablespoon unsalted butter, at room temperature

¾ cup heavy cream

1 teaspoon vanilla extract

// Make the Signature Chocolate Chip dough, referring to the ½ batch ingredients on page 63. Chill in the freezer for 15 minutes. Meanwhile, line an 8"x8" pan using my Parchment Paper technique (see page 42).

// Remove the dough from the freezer. Use a spoon to drop scoops of dough into the pan and press the dough to form a flat, even layer. Place it back in the freezer.

// Preheat the oven to 350°F.

// Make the Brownie Batter dough: In a small microwave-safe bowl, heat ¾ cup of the chocolate chips with the butter in the microwave on 50% power in 30-second increments. Stir well between each increment. Repeat just until the chocolate is melted. Set aside.

// In a medium bowl, whisk together the heat-treated flour, cocoa powder, cornstarch, baking powder, and salt until well combined. Set aside.

// Pour the melted chocolate mixture into the bowl of a stand mixer fitted with the paddle attachment. Add the granulated and brown sugars and mix on medium until well combined, about 2 minutes. Use a rubber spatula to scrape the bowl. Add the egg whites and vanilla and mix just until well incorporated, about 2 minutes. The mixture will be very runny.

// Add the flour mixture and mix on low just until the powdery texture of the flour disappears, about 30 seconds. Scrape the bowl and mix a final 15 seconds.

CONTINUES ➡

// Remove the bowl from the mixer and use a rubber spatula to fold in the remaining ¾ cup chocolate chips. Chill the Brownie Batter in the freezer for 40 minutes. Remove the cookie dough layer from the pan by pulling up on the edges of the parchment paper. Place it back into the freezer to continue chilling. Line the 8"x8" pan with parchment again.

// Once chilled and easy to handle, press the Brownie Batter dough into an even layer in the bottom of the lined 8"x8" pan. Bake for 30 to 35 minutes, until the center is set. Place in the refrigerator for 10 minutes to cool.

// Meanwhile, make the ganache: Chop the semisweet chocolate and place it in a medium bowl. Break the butter into 4 pieces and add to the bowl. Set aside.

// In a small microwave-safe bowl, heat the cream on 50% power in 30-second intervals just until the cream boils. As soon as the cream boils, pour it over the chopped chocolate. Use a whisk to stir, starting in the center of the bowl and moving slowly outward to incorporate the chocolate. Once the mixture is fully combined and begins to look glossy, stir in the vanilla. Set aside to cool slightly.

// Remove the cookie dough layer from the freezer and remove the parchment. Carefully place it on top of the cooled brownie in the 8"x8" pan. Bake for 10 to 12 minutes. The cookie dough layer should still look very gooey and underbaked.

// Let cool for 10 minutes. Pour the ganache over the cookie dough and use a rubber spatula to spread evenly. Freeze for 30 minutes, or until you can touch the ganache without it sticking to your finger.

// Remove the finished Brookie from the pan by pulling up on the edges of the parchment paper. Cut with a sharp knife by pushing straight down. Don't drag the knife. Dragging might shift the layers of the Brookie—perfect layers are what's going to give you that Insta-worthy dessert.

Store the Brookie in its original pan, covered in the refrigerator, for up to 5 days.

Coopcakes

Let me break it down for you: half cookie + half cupcake = Coopcake. And, I'll let you in on a little secret: It's as much fun to eat and make as it is to say. Say it with me, "Coopcakes!" Now, let's get baking.

FOR THE COOKIE BOTTOMS

1½ cups cake mix (½ box)

1⅓ cups all-purpose flour

2½ tablespoons cornstarch

½ teaspoon baking soda

½ teaspoon salt

1½ sticks (12 tablespoons) unsalted butter, at room temperature

½ cup granulated sugar

½ cup brown sugar

¼ cup pasteurized egg whites, at room temperature

2 teaspoons vanilla extract

1 cup mini semisweet chocolate chips

FOR THE CUPCAKE TOPS

1¾ cups all-purpose flour

1 teaspoon baking powder

¼ teaspoon baking soda

½ teaspoon salt

½ cup whole milk

½ cup sour cream

1 stick (8 tablespoons) unsalted butter, at room temperature

1 cup granulated sugar

⅓ cup pasteurized egg whites, at room temperature

1 tablespoon vanilla extract

½ cup rainbow sprinkles

FOR THE TOPPING

1 batch Cookie Dough Buttercream (page 213), using reserved cookie dough from this recipe

¼ cup rainbow sprinkles

// **Make the cookie bottoms:** Make the Cake Batter dough, using the ingredients listed in this recipe and following the method on page 76.

// Line a 12-hole cupcake pan with paper liners. Use a cookie scoop to portion 1 scoop (1½ tablespoons) into each cupcake liner. Spray your fingers with cooking spray or use the back of a spoon and lightly press the dough into the bottom of the liner in a flat layer. Chill in the refrigerator for 30 minutes. Reserve the rest of the cookie dough and set aside.

// Preheat the oven to 350°F.

// **Meanwhile, make the cupcake tops:** In a medium bowl, whisk together the flour, baking powder, baking soda, and salt. In a small bowl, whisk together the milk and sour cream until there are no lumps of sour cream. Set aside.

// In the bowl of a stand mixer fitted with the paddle attachment, beat the butter and sugar together on medium speed until light and fluffy, 3 to 4 minutes. Scrape the bowl.

// Add the egg whites and vanilla and beat for 2 minutes, or until the mixture is totally incorporated. Scrape the bowl halfway through if necessary.

// With the mixer on low, alternate additions of the flour mixture and the sour cream mixture, starting and ending with the flour. Scrape the bowl and beat for an additional 30 seconds, or until the batter appears smooth and creamy. Remove the bowl from the mixer and use a rubber spatula to fold in the sprinkles. Set the batter aside.

// Remove the cookie bottoms from the refrigerator and bake for 15 to 18 minutes. Remove when the edges are golden brown and the centers are lightly browned. Immediately use a cookie scoop to portion 1 scoop of the cupcake batter on top of each cookie.

// Bake for 15 minutes, or until the edges of the Coopcakes are golden brown and the tops are lightly golden.

// Remove from the oven and let cool in the cupcake pan for 5 minutes. Transfer to a wire rack to cool completely.

// **Make the Cookie Dough Buttercream** while the Coopcakes cool, using the reserved cookie dough. Transfer to a piping bag.

// Once completely cooled, top the Coopcakes with the Cookie Dough Buttercream and sprinkles.

Store the Coopcakes in an airtight container in the refrigerator for up to 5 days.

210 \ BEST WHEN BAKED

\ MAKES
12 cupcakes

\ ACTIVE TIME
1 hour

\ TIME 'TIL CUPCAKES
2 hours

Molten Cookie Dough Cupcakes

With Pinterest, Etsy, and Instagram sending us into party-planning wormholes, a regular old cupcake will not cut it at your kid's birthday party. Desserts must taste great AND have a special twist: mini, fancy decoration, glow-in-the-dark, on a stick, who knows—it just has to be special! When I set out to create a cupcake that would be the envy of any blogger, I knew I needed a cupcake aficionado in my corner. (Cookies, totally my thing! Cakes, not so much.) My friend Sally McKenney, of *Sally's Baking Addiction*, helped me perfect an always-moist-but-still-light cupcake. These molten cookie-dough-stuffed cupcakes are impressive, totally foolproof, and better than store-bought!

FOR THE COOKIE DOUGH

2¼ cups heat-treated all-purpose flour (instructions on page 31)

2¼ teaspoons cornstarch

¾ teaspoon salt

1½ sticks (12 tablespoons) unsalted butter, at room temperature

¼ cup granulated sugar

1 cup brown sugar

⅓ cup pasteurized egg whites, at room temperature

1 tablespoon vanilla extract

1 cup mini semisweet chocolate chips

FOR THE CUPCAKES

1¾ cups all-purpose flour

1 teaspoon baking powder

¼ teaspoon baking soda

½ teaspoon salt

½ cup whole milk

½ cup sour cream

1 stick (8 tablespoons) unsalted butter, at room temperature

1 cup sugar

⅓ cup pasteurized egg whites

1 tablespoon vanilla extract

FOR THE TOPPING

1 batch Cookie Dough Buttercream (page 213), using reserved cookie dough from this recipe

¼ cup mini chocolate chips

// **Make the cookie dough:** Use the ingredients listed in this recipe and follow the method on page 60. Freeze for 15 minutes, or until the dough is easy to handle. Roll the dough into 12 one-tablespoon-size balls, place on a plate lined with waxed paper, and refrigerate until later. Set the remaining cookie dough aside.

// Preheat the oven to 350°F and fit a 12-hole cupcake pan with liners.

// **Make the cupcakes:** In a medium bowl, whisk together the flour, baking powder, baking soda, and salt. In a small bowl, whisk together the milk and sour cream until there are no lumps of sour cream. Set aside.

// In the bowl of a stand mixer fitted with the paddle attachment, beat the butter and sugar together on medium until light and fluffy, 3 to 4 minutes. Scrape the bowl. Add the egg whites and vanilla and beat for 2 minutes, or until the mixture is totally incorporated. With the mixer on low, alternate additions of the flour mixture and the sour cream mixture, starting and ending with flour. Scrape the bowl and beat for an additional 30 seconds, or until the batter appears smooth and creamy.

// Use a cookie scoop to portion 2 scoops of batter into each liner to fill about three quarters of the liner. Bake for 16 to 19 minutes, until the cupcake edges are golden brown and the tops are lightly golden and completely set. Remove from the oven and let cool in the pan for 5 minutes.

// With the cupcakes still in the pan, press 1 chilled cookie dough ball into the center of each cupcake. The top of the cookie dough ball should be even with the top of the cupcake. Let the cupcakes continue to cool in the pan.

// Make the Cookie Dough Buttercream while the cupcakes cool, using the reserved cookie dough. Transfer to a piping bag.

// Once the cupcakes are completely cool, top with the buttercream, sprinkle with the mini chocolate chips, and serve.

// Enjoy that ooey gooey cookie dough center.

Store the cupcakes in an airtight container in the refrigerator up to 3 days.

Coopcakes,
page 209

Molten Cookie Dough
Cupcakes, opposite page

Cookie Dough Buttercream

No surprises here, I'll add cookie dough to anything. A morning yogurt? Why not? Mix it into whatever you're drinking? Coffee? Check. Hot Cocoa? Delicious! How about a cookie dough taco? Honestly, don't knock it till you try it. With so many confections needing a swirl of frosting, I just had to figure out a way to throw a little bit of cookie dough in the mix. Turns out the solution is to whip half the dough into the frosting and add half at the very last minute so you still get surprise cookie dough bits in every luscious bite!

2 sticks (16 tablespoons) unsalted butter, at room temperature

1 tablespoon vanilla extract

1 tablespoon milk or heavy cream—the higher the fat the better

1 teaspoon salt

3 cups confectioners' sugar, sifted

2 cups from 1 batch Signature Chocolate Chip dough (page 60; preferably made with mini chips), fresh or softened

// In the bowl of a stand mixer fitted with the paddle attachment, cream the butter on medium speed for 3 minutes, or until light, fluffy, and completely smooth. Add the vanilla, milk, and salt and mix until combined. Scrape the sides of the bowl as needed.

// With the mixer on low, add the confectioners' sugar ½ cup at a time. Once incorporated, turn the mixer to high and let the frosting get super light and fluffy. This will take at least 5 minutes. The frosting will become lighter in color as air is whipped into it.

// Break the dough into quarter-size chunks. With the mixer running on medium, add about 1 cup of the chunks to the frosting a few at a time. Mix on medium until all the chunks are added, then turn the mixer to high and mix until the chunks disappear and are completely blended into the frosting.

// Turn the mixer to low and drop the remaining 1 cup chunks into the frosting. Mix just until incorporated. You want that last cup of chunks to keep some of their shape so there are surprise cookie dough bites throughout your frosting.

// Slather this on anything and everything you can!

Store the buttercream in an airtight container in the refrigerator for up to 5 days.

The Cookie Bomb

From the first time I baked it, I knew this "cupcake thing" would be a hit. We finally came up with the name because of the reaction we got while taste-testing: "These are the *bomb*!" And it makes sense...it's an explosion of flavors, a cookie version of a cupcake stuffed on the inside with a yummy surprise—a total taste bud bomb! The bombs have been and continue to be a wildly popular DŌ item. They've made appearances on *The Chew*, on People.com, in *Food & Wine*, and on the Hallmark Channel—and now in your home kitchen!

FOR THE COOKIE DOUGH

3 cups plus 2 tablespoons heat-treated all-purpose flour (instructions on page 31)

1½ teaspoons cornstarch

¾ teaspoon baking soda

¾ teaspoon salt

2¼ sticks (18 tablespoons) unsalted butter, at room temperature

¼ cup plus 2 tablespoons granulated sugar

1½ cups brown sugar

½ cup pasteurized egg whites, at room temperature

1 tablespoon vanilla extract

¾ cup mini semisweet chocolate chips

FOR FILLING, TOPPING, AND GARNISH

⅓ cup Nutella

1 batch Cookie Dough Buttercream (recipe follows), using reserved cookie dough from this recipe

// Make the cookie dough: In a medium bowl, whisk together the heat-treated flour, cornstarch, baking soda, and salt. Set aside.

// In the bowl of a stand mixer fitted with the paddle attachment, beat the butter on medium speed until smooth and creamy, about 2 minutes. Add the granulated and brown sugars and mix on medium until light and fluffy; about 4 minutes will do the trick. Use a rubber spatula to scrape the bowl. Add the egg whites and vanilla and mix until fully incorporated, about 2 minutes.

// Add half of the flour mixture and mix on low just until the powdery texture of the flour disappears, about 15 seconds. Immediately add the rest of the flour mixture and mix until combined. Scrape the bowl and mix a final 15 seconds.

// Remove the bowl from the mixer and use a rubber spatula to fold in the chocolate chips. Remove 2 cups and set aside.

// Refrigerate the remaining dough for 1 hour, or until it is easy to handle and no longer sticky. Once chilled, divide the dough into 13 even portions. Use your hands to shape the portions into balls and freeze for 30 minutes.

// Meanwhile, preheat the oven to 350°F and place 12 liners in a cupcake pan.

// Remove 12 cookie dough balls from the freezer and use your thumbs to press into the middle of each ball, forming each into a nest or bowl shape in the palm of your hand. Fill each hole with 1 heaping teaspoon of Nutella. Once filled, use your fingers to pinch the cookie dough over the Nutella to form a seam. Roll the balls in your hands until the seam disappears. The Nutella will be completely concealed in the middle of the ball. Place the stuffed cookie dough balls into the cupcake liners.

// Bake for 15 to 20 minutes. The bombs will look like a set cookie with golden brown edges when they are done. Remove from the oven and let cool in the pan for about 5 minutes. Transfer to a wire rack to cool completely.

// While the bombs cool, make the Cookie Dough Buttercream using the reserved cookie dough. Transfer to a piping bag.

// Once the bombs are completely cool, pipe the buttercream onto each cookie bomb, forming a large, three-tiered dollop. Garnish with the remaining cookie dough ball by pulling off small chunks and topping each bomb off with a small piece. Serve and enjoy!

Store the Cookie Bombs in an airtight container in the refrigerator for up to 3 days.

Kristen's
TIP

For a fun alternative to Nutella, stuff these Cookie Bombs with whatever you're craving—sprinkles, peanut butter, caramel sauce—you name it!

Cookie Dough Macs

When my younger sister studied abroad in Europe, my whole family made a trip to visit her. While in Paris, we took a magical boat tour on the Seine and brought along all things "French," including cheeses, grapes, plenty of wine, cured meats, salted butter, a fresh baguette, and the most impeccable French macarons. Cruising by the sights of the city and picking at our picnic spread felt *magnifique*. I was trying to capture my extremely Parisian moment, macarons in hand, when my brother, Trey, exclaimed, "This is the best cheese I have ever, ever had! What is it?!" while shoving huge chunks into his mouth. I turned to find my brother eating fistfuls of straight-up butter!

I could barely stop laughing long enough to tell him that it wasn't cheese. It has remained a family joke to this day; anytime there's butter on the table, keep it away from Trey! Eating butter like it's cheese, not so chic. These delicate macarons, très chic!

FOR THE SHELLS

½ cup egg whites, from whole eggs (about 4 large)

1¾ cups (165g) superfine blanched almond flour (I use Bob's Red Mill)

1½ cups (165g) confectioners' sugar

¾ cup (150g) granulated sugar

¼ teaspoon salt

½ teaspoon cream of tartar

2 drops gel food coloring

FOR THE COOKIE DOUGH FILLING

½ batch Sugar Cookie dough (page 68)

FOR THE BUTTERCREAM

½ stick (4 tablespoons) unsalted butter, at room temperature

2 cups confectioners' sugar

½ teaspoon vanilla extract

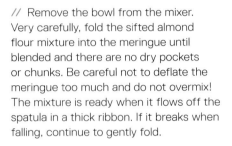

// Measure the egg whites and allow them to sit at room temperature for at least 2 hours or up to 2 days. Do not miss this step! Aging your egg whites is very important in macaron making.

// Make the shells: In a large bowl, whisk together the almond flour and confectioners' sugar. Pass the mixture through a fine-mesh sieve. There may be almond flour left behind in the sieve; throw it out.

// Sift the granulated sugar, salt, and cream of tartar into the bowl of a stand mixer. Add the aged egg whites to the bowl and whisk by hand to incorporate. Attach the bowl to a stand mixer fitted with the whisk attachment. Turn the mixer on high and beat until the mixture forms soft peaks. Add the food coloring and continue to beat until the mixture forms stiff, glossy peaks. You'll know it's ready when you lift the head of the mixer and the mixture no longer drips from the whisk and if you turn the bowl upside down, it does not slide or fall (thanks for the tip, Dana Pollack from @danasbakery!).

// Remove the bowl from the mixer. Very carefully, fold the sifted almond flour mixture into the meringue until blended and there are no dry pockets or chunks. Be careful not to deflate the meringue too much and do not overmix! The mixture is ready when it flows off the spatula in a thick ribbon. If it breaks when falling, continue to gently fold.

// Line two baking sheets with parchment paper or silicone baking mats. Transfer the batter into a piping bag fitted with a medium piping tip (Wilton #2a or Ateco 808 works great).

// Fill the piping bag with batter. Pipe directly down onto the baking sheet to form circles about 1 inch in diameter. Pipe 50 shells and tap the baking sheet on the counter 6 to 8 times to release air bubbles and help the batter settle. Let the macarons sit at room temperature for 45 minutes to 1 hour to create a "skin." The skin will be thin and glossy and dry to the touch.

// Meanwhile, preheat the oven to 325°F (if your oven has a convection setting, use it for this recipe!).

// Bake the shells for 10 to 15 minutes, until the macarons just lift from the baking sheet when moved. The centers will rise and the bottoms will have created little "feet" (the crinkly part), but there will not be any dark color indications apparent. Cool completely on the sheet away from the oven.

// Meanwhile, make the Sugar Cookie dough. Set in the refrigerator to chill.

// Make the buttercream: In the bowl of a stand mixer fitted with the paddle attachment, whip the butter until smooth. Add half of the confectioners' sugar and beat until smooth. Scrape the bowl and add the rest of the confectioners' sugar and the vanilla. Continue to beat until very fluffy, at least 4 minutes. Fill a piping bag with the buttercream.

// Assemble the macarons: Match similarly sized shells. You have a couple of extras in case any of the shells break. Place a dime-size ball of cookie dough in the center of the bottom shell. Pipe buttercream in a circle around the cookie dough. Top with the other shell. Et voilà! You have cute, cookie dough-y macarons ready to serve.

Store the macarons in an airtight container in the refrigerator up to 5 days.

//////////// *Kristen's Tip* ////////////

Macaroons can be finicky. I have the best results when I use exact measurements and a kitchen scale. I've provided you the ingredient weights so you can do the same!

//

THE HANDWRITING
test

So, I'm a little bit of a perfectionist. OK, a lot of a bit. Some might call me a tad neurotic; I like to think of myself as "detail-oriented," but whatever. Call it what you want.

When the business was just taking off, I needed help, and my friends were all ready to lend a hand. Now I know the saying "Beggars can't be choosers," but I was particular about divvying up the tasks that needed accomplishing based on my friends' skills. Not everyone was qualified to cut out circles, to put together orders, or to chop ingredients. It was better for me to know beforehand if you were terrible at something than for me to figure it out at the end when you had already ruined something. So, before I assigned a task, you had to pass its respective test. For example, the Handwriting Test.

We used to make every dough container by hand. The flavor name had to be meticulously handwritten on the side of each container. I didn't have a fancy printer, so I turned to a fine-point Sharpie for the labeling.

If you wanted this job, and its highly coveted wine payment, you absolutely had to write legibly and very small. I'd casually ask my (loyal, helpful) friends to write the words chocolate, cake, brownie, and nuts using the required Sharpie. If it looked nice, they were in, like Kate, my high school bestie. She got so, so much wine—and I got so many perfectly penned containers.

Win. Win.

Eat with your eyes? See a finished Lay-Her Cookie Cup on page 189.

Lay-Her Cookie Cups

Hello, hot stuff. The only thing you need to know about these layered cookie cups is that they are chock-full of all of our favorite things—luscious brownie, melty chocolate chip cookie, silky peanut butter filling, and warm cookie dough—in every sultry nibble.

The chef making these should beware. They might be an aphrodisiac, and anyone eating them will want to...

FOR THE SIGNATURE CHOCOLATE CHIP

2 batches Signature Chocolate Chip dough (page 60)

FOR THE BROWNIE BATTER

1 batch Brownie Batter dough (page 64)

FOR THE FILLING

1 cup creamy peanut butter

½ stick (4 tablespoons) unsalted butter, melted

1 cup confectioners' sugar

// Make the Signature Chocolate Chip dough, referring to the double batch ingredients on page 63.

// Meanwhile, preheat the oven to 350°F and fit two standard cupcake pans with liners.

// Make the Brownie Batter dough. Set in the refrigerator to chill.

// Make the filling: In a medium microwave-safe bowl, soften the peanut butter in the microwave for 10 seconds. Use a rubber spatula to stir in the butter and confectioners' sugar. Continue to stir until well incorporated.

// Assemble the cookie cups: Use a cookie scoop to portion one scoop (or 1½ tablespoons) of cookie dough into the bottom of each cup. Set aside the remaining cookie dough in the refrigerator for later. Lightly coat your fingers with cooking spray or use the back of a metal spoon to flatten the cookie dough into an even layer in the bottom of each cup. Spoon about 1½ tablespoons of filling onto each cookie dough bottom. Use the back of a metal spoon to spread the filling into an even layer. Use the cookie scoop to portion a heaping scoop of Brownie Batter into each cup. The cups will be almost full. Use a spoon or the back of the scoop to flatten the batter.

// Bake for 15 to 20 minutes, until the edges are baked and the centers are just set.

// Cool for 10 minutes in the pan. As the cookie cups cool, the centers will fall. Use a cookie scoop to portion a scoop of the remaining cookie dough into the center of each cookie cup. Let cool for 5 more minutes and serve warm!

Store the cookie cups in an airtight container in the refrigerator for up to 5 days.

220 \ BEST WHEN
BAKED

\ MAKES
16 bars

\ ACTIVE TIME
35 minutes

\ TIME 'TIL BARS
1 hour 35 minutes

Turnt Up Magic Bars

Depending on where you're from, you might call these Seven Layer Bars or you might call them Magic Bars. The name Seven Layer Bar is like when you were growing up and you named your stuffed bunny "Bunny" because that's exactly what it was. You know you're getting seven layers of something in a bar. Sounds great. "Magic Bar," on the other had, is the name I prefer because these taste like magic. Duh.

Whatever you call them, I've turned things up a bit by adding another magic layer—cookie dough. Let's get turnt.

FOR THE CRUST

1½ cups graham cracker crumbs

1 stick (8 tablespoons) unsalted butter, melted, slightly cooled

¼ cup brown sugar

¾ teaspoon ground cinnamon

¼ teaspoon salt

FOR THE LAYERS

1 cup semisweet chocolate chips

1 cup butterscotch chips

1½ cups shredded unsweetened coconut (divided)

1 cup raw pecans, chopped

1 (14-ounce) can sweetened condensed milk

FOR THE COOKIE DOUGH TOPPING

½ batch Signature Chocolate Chip dough (page 60)

// Preheat the oven to 350°F. Line a 9"x13" pan using my Picture-Perfect Parchment Paper technique (see page 42). If you plan to serve the bars straight from the pan, skip this step!

// Make the crust: In a medium bowl, mix together the graham cracker crumbs, melted butter, brown sugar, cinnamon, and salt. Press the mixture into the bottom of the lined pan.

// Assemble the 7 layers one at a time, sprinkling the items in an even layer on top of the graham cracker crust in this order: chocolate chips, butterscotch chips, ½ cup of the coconut, and the pecans. Drizzle the entire can of sweetened condensed milk over the layers. Sprinkle with the remaining 1 cup coconut. Bake for 25 to 30 minutes, until the sweetened condensed milk is golden brown and the top layer of coconut is nicely toasted.

// **Make the Signature Chocolate Chip cookie dough topping,** meanwhile, referring to the ½ batch ingredients on page 63. Once chilled, roll the cookie dough topping into dime-size balls. Set aside.

// Remove the bars from the oven and let cool for 15 minutes. Top with the cookie dough topping by sprinkling the balls over the entire surface of the bars. Allow to cool for 20 more minutes, or until the chocolate is set. Serve warm or let cool completely.

Store the bars in an airtight container in the refrigerator for up to 3 days.

Best Served Warm

Ask any New Yorker about their work-life balance, and they'll laugh and say, "What's that?" And that's just your typical full-time salaried employee. A small business owner? Yeah, you can kiss any "free time" good-bye.

As soon as I opened the shop, it took over my life. My dreams were all coming true, but other things quickly began slipping. I missed holidays, date nights, baptisms, birthday parties—I even skipped my honeymoon. That's right. That one trip you spend your whole life thinking about, your once-in-a-lifetime "If I could go anywhere in the world, I would go to…" vacation? We skipped it. Between getting sick and starting the business, we couldn't find the time. Besides, DŌ was my baby. I couldn't go jetting off to Europe and leave my newborn behind!

It took some time, but Chris and I finally did go on a honeymoon. Four years later. We escaped to Europe, successfully leaving both our DŌ baby and fur baby behind. After more than ten years together, it was our first-ever extended vacation for just the two of us. We spent two weeks driving up the coast of Italy, into the French Riviera, then on to Provence, with a final stop in Portugal on our way home. We got lost exploring new cities, still managed to eat our weight in dessert along the way, and at times we even forgot about our babies altogether.

People always ask me what I wish I'd known when I started DŌ. The short answer: Take breaks. Practicing a little self-care is essential, not just to being a successful business owner, but to being a healthy human. Plus, a break gives you a fresh perspective and more energy for when you get back to pursuing your professional dreams (aka, go on your honeymoon, people!).

/// The recipes in this section are the melt-in-your-mouth, good-for-the-soul kind that'll warm you up from the inside out. Perfect for a little R&R "me time." Kick back, take a load off, and enjoy.

SERVES
4 to 6

ACTIVE TIME
45 minutes

TIME 'TIL BREAD
1 hour 20 minutes

BEST SERVED
WARM

225

Ooh-Ooh Aah-Aah Bread

We're not monkey-ing around with this one. There's a surprise tucked inside those fluffy soft-baked biscuit pieces that are dripping with sweet caramelized cinnamon sugar. Don't tell your guests about the inside—it's best to see them ooh-ooh-ing and aah-aah-ing like a bunch of chimpanzees when they take their first bite!

FOR THE COOKIE DOUGH

1 cup plus 2 tablespoons heat-treated all-purpose flour (instructions on page 31)

1 teaspoon cornstarch

¾ teaspoon salt

¾ stick (6 tablespoons) unsalted butter, at room temperature

2 tablespoons granulated sugar

½ cup brown sugar

5 tablespoons pasteurized egg whites, at room temperature

1½ teaspoons vanilla extract

½ cup semisweet chocolate chips

FOR THE BISCUIT PIECES

⅓ cup ground cinnamon

2 cups granulated sugar (divided)

2 cans biscuits (I use Pillsbury)

1½ sticks (12 tablespoons) unsalted butter, at room temperature

FOR THE GLAZE

2 tablespoons milk, plus more as needed

¾ cup confectioners' sugar

// Make the cookie dough: Use the ingredients listed in this recipe and follow the method on page 60. Set in the freezer to chill briefly.

// Preheat the oven to 350°F and grease a 10" Bundt pan with cooking spray.

// Prepare the biscuit pieces: In a small bowl, use a fork to combine the cinnamon and 1 cup of the sugar. Set aside.

// Pull the biscuits apart and cut each biscuit in half horizontally. Once all the biscuits have been cut, wrap each slice around a 2 tablespoon–size piece of cookie dough. Pinch the biscuit dough to create a seam. Repeat with all the biscuit slices. (You may have some cookie dough left over—it's yours to snack on while you bake!) Roll each biscuit-covered cookie dough piece in the cinnamon sugar. Place on a baking sheet lined with parchment paper or a silicone baking mat and transfer to the refrigerator to chill.

// In a medium saucepan, heat the butter and the remaining 1 cup sugar. Once the butter has melted completely, stir the mixture constantly for 2 minutes. Remove the mixture from the heat.

// Remove the biscuit-covered cookie dough from the refrigerator. Place half of the dough balls into an even layer in the bottom of the Bundt pan. Pour half of the butter-sugar mixture over the dough balls. Cover with the remaining dough balls. Pour the rest of the butter-sugar mixture evenly over the entire pan.

// Cover with foil and bake for 15 minutes. Remove the foil and bake for 20 to 25 minutes more, until golden brown and the syrup appears thick and bubbly. Let cool in the pan for 15 minutes.

// Meanwhile, make the glaze: In a small bowl, mix together the milk and confectioners' sugar. Add more milk, as needed, until the glaze easily runs off the back of the spoon.

// Turn the pan with the bread upside down onto a plate and drizzle with the glaze. Serve immediately.

Store uneaten bread in an airtight container in the refrigerator for up to 2 days. Reheat in the microwave on 50% power.

I Love You Even S'more

Forgettabout the campfire. It's messy, requires the outdoors, and just really isn't practical in the concrete jungle, New York City. Even without it, this recipe will transport you back to summer camp—minus the bug spray, braces, or your awkward preteen years.

Just like the campfire classic, it's got Hershey's bars, graham crackers, and toasted marshmallows, but we've added a twist you could only dream of at camp—slowly melting cookie dough. Sandwiched between warm chocolate and a charred marshmallow, cookie dough has never felt so cozy.

FOR THE COOKIE DOUGH

½ batch Signature Chocolate Chip dough (page 60)

FOR THE S'MORES

10 graham crackers

5 chocolate bars (I use Hershey's)

10 to 20 large marshmallows

// Line an 8"x8" pan using my Picture-Perfect Parchment Paper technique (see page 42).

// Make the Signature Chocolate Chip dough, referring to the ½ batch ingredients on page 63.

// Scrape the dough out of the bowl into the lined pan. Use a rubber spatula or spray your fingers with cooking spray to form a flat, even layer of cookie dough. Place the dough in the freezer for 1 hour.

// Prepare the s'more ingredients by breaking the graham crackers and chocolate bars in half and counting out marshmallows.

// Once the cookie dough is frozen, pull up on the edges of the parchment to remove it from the pan. Use a sharp, hot knife to cut the dough. Use a graham cracker as a template and cut 3 even rows of 3, to make 9 squares. You'll have a little extra—cut that strip into 3 pieces and press together to make a square. Place the cookie dough squares on 10 graham crackers. Top with 2 toasted marshmallows (from a blowtorch, campfire, grill, or broiler). Press half of a chocolate bar and another graham cracker on top of the toasted marshmallows and enjoy!

The s'mores are best enjoyed immediately.

Kristen's
TIP

If you would love even s'more S'mores, check out my Gimme S'more cookie dough recipe on page 58.

MAKES
16 bars

ACTIVE TIME
30 minutes

TIME 'TIL BLONDIES
1 hour

Blondies Have More Fun

Hear me out. I get that people call them blondies because it's a cute way of saying they're chocolate-free brownies, but actually blondies and brownies aren't related at all. The defining characteristic of a blondie has nothing to do with chocolate. Blondies are a bar made with BROWN sugar only—no white sugar in the mix. So, if you're looking to the ingredients for the name, Brunette would be more fitting.

Call them what you like—blondies are my weakness. All that extra brown sugar makes blondies super soft and gooey and adds an unmistakable depth and richness to some of my other favorite flavors—vanilla and butterscotch. They say blondes have more fun, so maybe it makes sense after all.

3½ cups heat-treated all-purpose flour (instructions on page 31)

1 tablespoon cornstarch

1 teaspoon baking soda

1 teaspoon salt

1⅜ sticks (11 tablespoons) unsalted butter, at room temperature

2 cups brown sugar

½ cup pasteurized egg whites, at room temperature

2 tablespoons vanilla extract

2 cups butterscotch chips

Flaky sea salt, like Maldon, for topping

// Preheat the oven to 350ºF and line an 8"x8" pan using my Picture-Perfect Parchment Paper technique (see page 42).

// In a medium bowl, whisk together the heat-treated flour, cornstarch, baking soda, and salt. Set aside.

// In the bowl of a stand mixer fitted with the paddle attachment, beat the butter on medium speed until smooth and creamy, about 2 minutes. Add the brown sugar and mix on medium until light and fluffy; about 4 minutes will do the trick. Use a rubber spatula to scrape the bowl. Add the egg whites and vanilla and mix until fully incorporated, about 2 minutes.

// Add half of the flour mixture and mix on low just until the powdery texture of the flour disappears, about 15 seconds. Immediately add the rest of the flour mixture and mix until combined. Scrape the bowl and mix a final 15 seconds.

// Remove the bowl from the mixer and use a rubber spatula to fold in 1¾ cups of the butterscotch chips.

// Use a rubber spatula to spread the dough in the lined pan in an even layer. Top with the reserved ¼ cup butterscotch chips and sprinkle with flaky sea salt.

// Bake for 25 to 30 minutes, until the edges are golden brown and the center is lightly golden brown.

// Remove from the oven and let cool on a wire rack for 15 minutes. Slice into squares and serve warm!

Store the blondies in an airtight container at room temperature for up to 3 days.

//////////// **Kristen's Tip** ////////////

This recipe is also great in dough form, and it can be baked into chewy cookies. To make this recipe into cookies, see My Go-To Baking & Storage DŌrections on page 48.

///

The DŌpest Gooey Butter Cake

KRISTEN'S *Fav*

Gooey butter cake is a St. Louis staple. It started as a happy accident in the 1930s when a local baker put the wrong proportions of ingredients into his coffee cake batter. He ended up creating a gooey treat with a pudding-like texture that continues to delight everyone who tries it to this day!

If you're in STL, you can get it at a local bakery for breakfast or find it in a cookie version. STL is so crazy for this treat that there is a whole store dedicated entirely to serving gooey butter cake in a variety of flavors. My version has a sugar cookie dough secret that the St. Louis classic has been missing. Here's to you, my St. Louis crew!

FOR THE COOKIE DOUGH LAYER

1 batch Sugar Cookie dough (page 68)

FOR THE CAKE LAYER

1 box yellow cake mix

4 whole eggs, at room temperature (divided)

1 stick (8 tablespoons) unsalted butter, melted

1 teaspoon salt

1 (8-ounce) package cream cheese, softened

1 (1-pound) package confectioners' sugar, plus more for topping

½ cup rainbow sprinkles

// **Make the Sugar Cookie dough:** Remove the bowl from the stand mixer, place about 1½ cups of the dough in the refrigerator, and leave the rest at room temperature while you make the cake.

// Preheat the oven to 350°F.

// **Make the cake:** In a large bowl, mix the cake mix, 2 of the eggs, the melted butter, and salt. Stir with a rubber spatula until combined.

// In the bowl of a stand mixer fitted with the paddle attachment, beat the cream cheese until very smooth. Add the 2 remaining eggs and beat until combined. Add the confectioners' sugar and mix until smooth.

// **Assemble the cake.** Line a 9"x13" pan using my Picture-Perfect Parchment Paper technique (see page 42). If you plan to serve the bars straight from the pan, skip the parchment and lightly coat the pan with cooking spray. Use a rubber spatula to spread the cake mix on the bottom of the pan until you have one even layer.

// Take chunks of the room-temperature Sugar Cookie dough in your hands and flatten it out into disks. Place the disks on top of the cake layer, leaving a 1-inch border around the edges (the dough will spread as it bakes). Continue until you use all of the room-temperature cookie dough and you have almost completely covered the cake mix layer.

// Pour the cream cheese mixture over the pan and spread evenly. Tap the pan on the counter to release air bubbles and create an even layer.

// Bake for 35 to 45 minutes, until the edges are golden brown and a delicate crust has formed on the top. The middle should still be wobbly when shaken. Remove from the oven and allow to cool for 5 minutes. Sprinkle the rainbow sprinkles all over the top of the cake.

// Meanwhile, remove the reserved cookie dough from the refrigerator. Use your hands to break the dough into pea-size pieces and sprinkle the cookie dough pieces over the cake. Let cool for 15 more minutes. Liberally dust with confectioners' sugar just before serving. Cut into bars and serve warm.

Store the cake covered in the refrigerator for up to 5 days.

Cookie Dough
Cheesecake
Bars,
page 250

The DŌpest Gooey
Butter Cake,
page 229

Turnt Up Magic Bars, page 220

*Blondies Have
More Fun,
page 228*

Coffee Cup Cookie

SUPER *Quick*

GREAT MADE *GF*

It was a cruel, joyless human who came up with the rule of portioning. Clearly, I'm not a huge fan of portion control…I just don't have the willpower to stop eating once I get started. For those of you who can't help but finish the whole cake in one sitting (like me) or for those of you in desperate need of a pantry restock with only one spoonful of sugar left in the bag (definitely me), this Coffee Cup Cookie is for you. It's a single serving—like a personal pan pizza, only better!

Bonus: The cleanup's a breeze! You'll have to wash only three dishes: the measuring cup, mug, and spoon!

3 tablespoons milk (any except nonfat)

3 tablespoons neutral oil, like canola

2 tablespoons granulated sugar

1 tablespoon brown sugar

4 tablespoons all-purpose flour

2 tablespoons ground oats or oat flour

½ teaspoon baking soda

Pinch of salt

3 tablespoons chocolate chips (divided)

// In a large liquid measuring cup, stir together the milk, oil, and granulated and brown sugars until well combined. Add the flour, oats, baking soda, and salt and stir well until there are no clumps of flour. Stir in 1 tablespoon of the chocolate chips.

// Pour the mixture into a large coffee mug (reach for the biggest microwave-safe mug in your collection!). Top with 1 tablespoon of the remaining chocolate chips.

// Heat in the microwave for 60 seconds (the time will depend on your microwave and the shape of your mug). Let the cookie stand for a full minute before you open the microwave. Top with the final 1 tablespoon chocolate chips right before you dig in.

Enjoy your gooey, dough-y treat immediately!

/////////// *Kristen's Tip* ///////////

Any type of chips will work here. This recipe is for ridding your pantry of the random bits of chocolate left behind from the last recipe!

//

SERVES
8 to 10

ACTIVE TIME
55 minutes

TIME 'TIL BREAD PUDDING
3 hours

Bread Pudding of Champions

There's always a contestant on *Chopped* who sees the dessert round ingredients and decides to make bread pudding. If I could make it through the first two rounds, I know for a fact that I would be that person, because this recipe is a winner—guaranteed to keep me off the chopping block. Bring it on, Food Network.

FOR THE COOKIE DOUGH

½ batch Signature Chocolate Chip dough (page 60)

FOR THE BREAD

9 cups (about three quarters of a 1-pound loaf) brioche bread, crusts removed and cubed

FOR THE CUSTARD

4 whole eggs

2 egg yolks

1¾ cups whole milk

1½ cups heavy cream

¼ stick (2 tablespoons) unsalted butter, melted

¼ cup granulated sugar

2 tablespoons brown sugar

2 teaspoons vanilla extract

1½ teaspoons ground cinnamon

½ teaspoon salt

FOR THE TOPPING

1 cup semisweet chocolate chips

// Preheat the oven to 350°F.

// Make the Signature Chocolate Chip dough, referring to the ½ batch ingredients on page 63. Freeze for 10 minutes.

// Remove from the freezer and scoop the entire batch into 2 tablespoon–size balls onto a baking sheet lined with waxed paper. Transfer the baking sheet to the freezer and freeze completely.

// Toast the bread: Spread the bread on a baking sheet in a single layer and bake for 7 minutes. Flip the bread cubes and bake for an additional 8 minutes, or until the cubes are dry and just beginning to toast. Turn off the oven and transfer to a large bowl to cool.

// Make the custard: In a large bowl, lightly beat the eggs and egg yolks. In a separate bowl, whisk the milk, cream, and butter to combine. Add the milk mixture, granulated and brown sugars, vanilla, cinnamon, and salt to the eggs and whisk to combine. Set aside.

// Lightly grease a 9"x13" pan with cooking spray. Place about half of the bread cubes in a single layer in the bottom of the dish. Cover with ⅓ cup of the chocolate chips. Pour about one-third of the custard over the bread and chocolate chips. Top with the rest of the bread cubes. Pour another one-third of the custard over the bread. Chill the bread pudding and the remaining one-third of the custard in the refrigerator for 1 hour.

// Preheat the oven to 350°F.

// Remove the cookie dough from the freezer, and remove the bread pudding and the remaining custard from the refrigerator. Tuck two-thirds of the frozen chunks of dough throughout the dish of bread pudding. Scatter the last one-third of the dough over the top of the bread pudding. Lightly whisk the remaining custard and pour it over the bread pudding. Top with the remaining ⅔ cup chocolate chips.

// Cover with foil and bake for 25 minutes. Remove the foil and bake for an additional 15 to 25 minutes, until the bread tops look toasted and a knife inserted into a piece of bread about 1 inch from the edge of the pan comes out clean. (If you stick the knife into, the dough, it will come out covered in chocolate!)

// Cool for 20 minutes on a wire rack. Slice and serve warm.

Store the bread pudding in an airtight container in the refrigerator for up to 3 days. Reheat in the microwave on 50% power or in a preheated 250°F oven.

FIRST LOCATIONS:
Brooklyn, Herald Square, Midtown East

When DŌ first launched online, the options for getting your cookie dough were to have it shipped out of state ($$$), get it delivered anywhere in NYC ($$), or pick it up (free!). Originally, we had "three convenient pickup locations": 1. Brooklyn—aka my apartment; 2. Midtown East—aka my old office; and 3. Herald Square—aka Chris's office.

The pickup process was a bit of a joke. Chris and I commuted to work every day with suitcases crammed full of cookie dough to distribute to customers right out of our office lobbies. The two of us would offer "pickup windows" based on our work schedules, and customers were told to come during their window and send a text when they arrived.

The office doormen knew me as "the cookie dough lady," and everyone in our offices thought we were insane...or super-obvious drug dealers. I'm not sure what the customers thought of us, but if they had any reservations about the shady pickups, they certainly didn't let those concerns stand between them and their cookie dough. Even today, years later, when we no longer have those "locations" listed as pickup options, we'll still occasionally get emails from long-time customers asking if they "can pick up at that Brooklyn location where they got it last time," to which we have to politely decline.

Best Served Cold

//

I keep mentioning Chris, but let me truly introduce him. Oh, Chris. My lovely husband. I'm so glad we ended up together, because I almost sabotaged our relationship.

My sophomore year in college, Chris was my assigned teaching assistant (TA) for a small group project. I had a boyfriend at the time, so I didn't pay attention to him, although there were plenty of jealous people in my class who wished they were in the group with "the hot TA."

Shortly after the semester ended, Chris "happened" to get my number from the class list (sketch, much?) and began texting me to hang out. I left those texts "unread" and headed right out of town for an internship.

We were on opposite schedules with my internships and his travels. Until one winter we overlapped in Chicago. I didn't know many people in the city, so I finally agreed to have dinner with him. One dinner turned into many and there was some talk about "seeing where things could go," but I wasn't looking for anything serious or long distance.

I basically kept Chris on the backburner during this period, when "I liked to eat, and he liked to buy me dinner." His words, not mine! We continued having delightful yet infrequent dinners, every time picking up right where we left off. This worked for a while, but when Chris graduated he told me it was decision time: I finally had to be his girlfriend, or he had to start getting over me.

I was moving to NYC, and the timing wasn't right. So, I told him to get over me.

Months later he texted to say he was moving to Manhattan for a new job. I was surprised by how excited I felt about reconnecting.

We set a date and ended up closing down Rosa Mexicano with hours of tequila-fueled conversation. I went home that night full of margaritas and the feeling that I'd made a huge mistake. Maybe he was the one. He treated me better than anyone I had dated (and that was a lot of guys), and he was everything I was looking for in a partner—I just didn't see it before. This time, I confessed my love to him and asked him to give me another chance.

So officially, officially, we started dating-dating, and four years later said "I do." He's my rock, my absolute best friend, my most dedicated cheerleader, and it doesn't hurt that he's cute. Chris puts in more hours at DŌ than any of my actual employees, he's the best maintenance man Greenwich Village has ever seen, and somehow he's always "just a train stop away" when I need him.

The only thing I regret? Marrying someone with my same name. My nickname was Kris, but once I met my Chris, I dropped it and started going by Kristen. He can't say I've never done anything nice for him!

/// *My marriage is living proof that love doesn't have to start out all warm and fuzzy. Sometimes love is tucked away in something a little bit cold. True love just might be hiding in one of these chilly recipes.*

Ice Cream SanDŌ

The ice cream sandwich that will make you forget all other ice cream sandwiches. It's so addictive that some people ask if we make it with crack. Of course, we don't! But, I can guarantee you'll be thinking about this sugar high for days to come. And when you least expect it, you may just get that itch for an Ice Cream SanDŌ fix. It's the quintessential DŌ treat: something everyone loves, with a cookie dough twist.

I tell my customers exactly what I'll tell you if you're thumbing through this book and don't know where to start. Pick the SanDŌ!

1 batch Signature Chocolate Chip dough (page 60)

1 pint ice cream (I use vanilla; you can use whatever you want!)

// Line an 8"x8" pan using my Picture-Perfect Parchment Paper technique (see page 42). Set aside.

// Make the Signature Chocolate Chip dough. Chill in the refrigerator or freezer until cold and easy to handle.

// Once chilled, split the batch of dough in half. Press one half of the dough into an even layer in the 8"x8" pan. The layer will be rather thin, less than ½ inch. Freeze for 15 minutes. Remove from the freezer. Pull up on the parchment to remove the dough. Return the dough to the freezer.

// Line the 8"x8" pan again. Press the other half of the dough into the bottom of the pan, trying to make your layer as even as possible. Place the other, previously frozen, dough square (still in its parchment liner) into the pan. You now have two layers of cookie dough divided by a parchment liner. Freeze for at least 2 hours or overnight.

// Set the ice cream out to soften at room temperature to a spreadable consistency. For most ice creams, 15 to 20 minutes will do the trick. Once the ice cream is spreadable, take out the 8"x8" pan with the cookie dough layers from the freezer. Remove the top cookie dough layer, still in its parchment liner. Open the bottom parchment and spread the ice cream evenly over the bottom cookie dough layer. Flip over the other cookie dough layer, so the parchment is on top. Place on top of the ice cream to make a sandwich. Press down to smooth and remove the top parchment. Freeze for at least 5 hours or overnight.

// To serve, warm a knife by running hot water over it. Remove the SanDŌ from the freezer. Use the warmed knife to cut straight down and make 9 even sandwiches. Do not drag the knife, as this can cause the ice cream center to squish out.

Store the sliced SanDŌs covered in the freezer for up to 1 month.

/////////// *Kristen's Tip* ///////////

Once cut, wrap SanDŌs in individual pieces of parchment. Tape them shut or tie them with twine. You'll have ice cream sandwiches ready to go at all times!

\ MAKES
24 slices

\ ACTIVE TIME
40 minutes

\ TIME 'TIL FUDGE
5 hours

Oh, Fudge!

As a gluten-free-er, I can count on fudge as the one thing on the dessert table that is safe to eat. When it comes to fudge, I've eaten it all. Good fudge, bad fudge, stale fudge, white fudge, chocolate fudge, and especially Grandma Eleanor's famous peanut butter fudge. One year at Christmas, I ate the entire pan of her fudge by myself. Yes, I got called out for it by my in-laws.

Now, *this* fudge is next-level. You can use ANY of the cookie dough recipes in this book for your cookie dough fudge. Not to mention you also have two delicious fudge options to choose from—white chocolate or dark chocolate. My favorite combo? Swirling them together for a beautifully marbled creation. Double the fudge and therefore double my happiness. I'm not fudging around.

1 batch Signature Chocolate Chip dough (page 60) or any other dough you choose

3¼ cups chocolate chips (your choice; white chocolate or dark chocolate are my favorites)

3 cups Marshmallow Fluff

1½ cups sugar

1½ sticks (12 tablespoons) unsalted butter

¾ cup heavy cream

¾ teaspoon salt

// **Make the Signature Chocolate Chip dough.** Use your fingers to make dime-size pieces of dough; the pieces should not be perfectly uniform. Lay the pieces on a baking sheet in a single layer and chill in the freezer while you make the fudge.

// Make the fudge: Place the chocolate chips and Marshmallow Fluff in a large bowl and set aside. In a large microwave-safe bowl, combine the sugar, butter, cream, and salt. Heat the mixture in the microwave on 50% power for 2 minutes. Stir well and heat for an additional 30 seconds, or until the mixture comes to a boil. Pour the mixture over the chocolate chips and Fluff. Let sit for 5 minutes.

// Use a hand mixer or a stand mixer fitted with the whisk attachment to blend the ingredients on medium speed until smooth and soft. Continue to whisk until the chocolate is smooth. Set the warm fudge mixture aside for and let cool for 30 minutes.

// Meanwhile, line a 9"x13" pan using my Picture-Perfect Parchment Paper technique (see page 42).

// Once the fudge is cooled, remove the cookie dough from the freezer. Measure 1 cup of chunks and set aside. Fold the remaining cookie dough chunks into the cooled fudge. Do not overmix—the cookie dough should remain in large chunks.

// Pour the mixture into the prepared pan and use a rubber spatula to spread into a single layer. Top with the reserved 1 cup cookie dough chunks. Refrigerate on a level surface for 3 to 5 hours, until completely set. Cut into squares to serve.

Store the fudge in an airtight container in the refrigerator for up to 5 days or in the freezer for up to 2 months. To eat frozen fudge, let thaw in the refrigerator for at least 2 hours before serving.

MAKES
6 cups ice cream

ACTIVE TIME
1 hour

TIME 'TIL ICE CREAM
12 hours

Cookie Dough with a Side of Ice Cream

When it comes to cookie dough ice cream, I'm interested 94 percent in the cookie dough, 5 percent in the ice cream, and 1 percent in whatever other ingredients have been thrown in to jazz it up. I do my best archaeologist impersonation and excavate every cookie dough piece until all that's left is a carved-up mess of plain vanilla ice cream that goes right back into the freezer for my husband, Chris, to find and throw out once he realizes all of the good stuff is gone.

There should be way more cookie dough in cookie dough ice cream. At least three times more. And if no brand on the shelf is going to give me the proper ratio of cookie dough to ice cream, then I'm going to have to make my own!

FOR THE COOKIE DOUGH

1 batch Signature Chocolate Chip dough (page 60)

FOR THE ICE CREAM BASE

4 cups ice

2 cups water

3 whole eggs

1 vanilla bean

1 cup half-and-half

2 cups heavy cream

1 cup sugar

2 teaspoons vanilla extract

// Make the Signature Chocolate Chip dough. Chill in the freezer.

// Make the ice cream base: Fill a large bowl with ice and water. Set a medium bowl into the larger bowl. Set aside.

// In a small bowl, whisk the eggs until smooth and light yellow in color.

// Use a sharp knife to split the vanilla bean and scrape out the seeds. In a medium saucepan, combine the half-and-half, cream, sugar, vanilla bean husk, vanilla bean seeds, and vanilla extract and heat to 110°F.

// Slowly add 1 cup of this mixture to the beaten eggs, about 1 tablespoon at a time, whisking well between each addition. Be sure to go slow! If you add the warm mixture too quickly, the eggs can scramble.

// Add the egg mixture to the cream mixture in the saucepan, whisking vigorously to combine. Heat the mixture starting on low heat and very slowly increasing to medium heat, stirring constantly until it reaches 165°F. (This step pasteurizes the eggs.)

// Pour the mixture through a strainer into the medium bowl that is on ice. Rest in the ice bath for 20 minutes, stirring about once every minute so the mixture cools evenly. Transfer to an airtight container and let the base set in the fridge for at least 8 hours or overnight.

// Remove the dough from the freezer and break it into dime-size chunks. It's OK if they are uneven—it will make your ice cream more fun! Return to the freezer and freeze for at least 8 hours or overnight.

// Freeze the ice cream in an ice cream maker according to the manufacturer's instructions. Right as the freezing is coming to an end, add the frozen cookie dough chunks a handful at a time. Once the freezing is complete, place the ice cream into an airtight container and store in the freezer for at least 1 hour before serving.

// Enjoy from a chilled bowl or in a Cookie Dough Milkshake (recipe follows), sundae bar (page 292), or ice cream pie (page 267).

Store the ice cream in an airtight container in the freezer for up to 2 months.

244 \ BEST SERVED
COLD

\ *YIELD*
3 (8-ounce) milkshakes

\ *ACTIVE TIME*
10 minutes

\ *TIME 'TIL MILKSHAKE*
10 minutes

Cookie Dough Milkshake

If you thought a regular milkshake brings the boys to the yard, you better watch out. They will come out by the busload for this one...our line doesn't lie!

OPTION 1

3 tablespoons milk, any kind

2 cups ice cream (page 242)

½ cup any cookie dough (pages 54 to 184), chilled

OPTION 2

3 tablespoons milk, any kind

2 cups ice cream, any kind

1 cup any cookie dough (pages 54 to 184), chilled

OPTIONAL TOPPINGS

Whipped topping, like Cool Whip

Rainbow sprinkles

Maraschino cherries

Chocolate sauce

// Add the milk, ice cream, and cookie dough to a blender, in that order. Run the blender on low speed until you have a uniform creamy texture. Add more milk if the mixture is too thick (it shouldn't be!).

// Pour into a tall glass and top with whipped cream, sprinkles, cherries, or toppings of your choice. Enjoy immediately!

Cookie Dough with a Side of Ice Cream, page 242

Pop with a Chocolate Top

When I was young, summer wasn't complete until I'd had my fair share of sweet, sticky, make-a-mess-everywhere ice pops. Whether from the ice cream truck that jangled down the block or the concession stand at the pool, ice pops were a staple that I just don't get enough of in my adult life.

So, let's throw it back and cool off as we stroll down memory lane. As a bonus, these guys are so cute, you'll get a record number of likes on Instagram—if you didn't 'gram it, did you even eat it?!

FOR THE COOKIE DOUGH

1 batch Signature Chocolate Chip dough (page 60) using mini semisweet chocolate chips

FOR THE ICE POPS

1½ cups heavy cream

1½ cups whole milk

½ cup brown sugar

¼ teaspoon salt

2 teaspoons vanilla extract

FOR THE CHOCOLATE SHELL

1 cup semisweet chocolate chips

1 tablespoon coconut oil

// Make the Signature Chocolate Chip dough using mini semisweet chocolate chips. Freeze for 15 minutes, then use your hands to break it into dime-size chunks. It's OK if they are a little uneven—it will make your ice pops more fun.

// Make the ice pops: Whisk together the cream, milk, brown sugar, salt, and vanilla. Pour half of the mixture into ice pop molds or Dixie cups, then drop half of the cookie dough pieces into the molds. Use a butter knife to submerge the chunks of dough into the milk mixture. Freeze for 45 minutes. Store the remaining dough and milk mixture in the refrigerator while your pops freeze.

// Repeat with the rest of the milk mixture and cookie dough chunks. Insert ice pop sticks into each pop. Allow the pops to freeze completely, at least 2 hours.

// Make the chocolate shell: In a microwave-safe container, heat the chocolate chips and coconut oil on 50% power in 30-second increments, stirring well between each increment, until completely melted. Let the mixture cool in the refrigerator for about 5 minutes, until room temperature.

// Line a baking sheet with waxed paper. Dip each pop into the chocolate mixture and lay on the waxed paper. Freeze for at least 30 minutes. Serve very cold!

Store the pops on waxed paper in an airtight container in the freezer for up to 2 months.

////////// *Kristen's Tip* //////////

This ice pop is great with all kinds of cookie dough! Try using half a batch of your favorite dough in this recipe. You can bake the other half, or just eat it with a spoon while you wait for your ice pops to freeze.

//

248 \ BEST SERVED
COLD

\ MAKES
6 crème brûlées

\ ACTIVE TIME
35 minutes

\ TIME 'TIL CRÈME BRÛLÉE
2 hours

Three-Way Crème Brûlée

It's always nice to introduce two of your most beloved friends to each other. Cookie dough, meet one of my favorite desserts: crème brûlée. Crème brûlée, meet the love of my life: cookie dough. Great. Now that we've made the intro and I know you've become fast friends, I no longer have to pick between the two. Best three-way ever!

FOR THE COOKIE DOUGH

1 cup plus 2 tablespoons heat-treated all-purpose flour (instructions on page 31)

¾ teaspoon salt

¾ stick (6 tablespoons) unsalted butter, at room temperature

2 tablespoons granulated sugar

½ cup brown sugar

¼ cup pasteurized egg whites, at room temperature

1½ teaspoons vanilla extract

½ cup mini semisweet chocolate chips

FOR THE CRÈME BRÛLÉE

1 vanilla bean

4 cups heavy cream

½ teaspoon salt

7 egg yolks

½ cup granulated sugar

2 teaspoons vanilla extract

½ cup turbinado or other coarse sugar, for topping

// Make the cookie dough, using the ingredients listed in this recipe and following the method on page 60. Freeze for 15 minutes.

// Meanwhile, prepare 6 tall, 8-ounce ramekins by spraying them lightly with cooking spray. It is important to use ramekins that are very deep—this is not a job for a wide, shallow ramekin!

// Divide the cookie dough into 8 even portions. Reserve 2 portions in the fridge to be used for topping. Use your fingers to press the other 6 portions into an even layer in the bottom of each prepared ramekin. Chill in the freezer while you prepare the other ingredients.

// Preheat the oven to 325°F.

// Make the crème brûlée: Split the vanilla bean with a sharp knife. Scrape out the seeds of the bean.

// In a medium saucepan, combine the cream, vanilla bean husk (the outside), vanilla bean seeds, and salt and heat over medium heat until it comes to a boil. Once the mixture boils, immediately remove from the heat and allow to cool for 15 to 20 minutes.

// Meanwhile, in the bowl of a stand mixer fitted with the whisk attachment, whip the egg yolks, granulated sugar, and vanilla extract on medium speed for 5 minutes. When the mixture thickens, expands in size, and looks lighter in color, you'll know it's ready.

// Remove the vanilla bean husk from the cream mixture and discard. Turn the mixer to medium and very slowly add the warm cream mixture to the egg mixture, a little bit at a time, keeping the mixer going continuously. Don't go too quickly or your egg yolks may scramble. Transfer the mixture into a large liquid measuring cup with a spout.

// Pour the mixture into the ramekins over the cookie dough layer, distributing the cream mixture evenly among all six. Place the ramekins in a deep 9"x13" baking dish. Fill the baking dish with very hot water until it comes three quarters of the way up the sides of the ramekin.

// Bake for 40 to 45 minutes, until the crème brûlées look set on the top but still wobble when the pan is shaken.

// Remove the ramekins from the pan and refrigerate for at least 1 hour. Top each ramekin with a single layer of coarse sugar.

// Use a blowtorch to caramelize the sugar, waving the blowtorch over the ramekins about 5 to 6 inches from the surface. Be sure to keep the blowtorch moving so the sugar doesn't burn! If you don't have a blowtorch, broil in the oven for 5 minutes, or until the sugar caramelizes.

// Allow the caramelized sugar to set for 3 minutes. Roll the remaining cookie dough into teaspoon-size balls and add to each crème brûlée as a garnish. Serve immediately!

Store the crème brûlée without the caramelized tops covered in the refrigerator for up to 2 weeks. Topped crème brûlées should be served (and enjoyed!) immediately.

BEST SERVED
COLD

MAKES
12 bars

ACTIVE TIME
35 minutes

TIME 'TIL BARS
2 hours

No-Bake Cookie Dough Cheesecake Bars

Y'all know I think making traditional cheesecake can be a pain. I've already shared my lazy girl cheesecake trick (page 162). This one should be called The LAZIEST Cheesecake of All Time because you don't even have to turn on the oven to make it. It's got the classic graham cracker crust, it's light and whipped, and it's full of Cake Batter cookie dough with a generous dash of sprinkles. Trust me, not baking desserts is my thing.

FOR THE CRUST

13 graham crackers

1 stick (8 tablespoons) unsalted butter, melted

½ cup brown sugar

FOR THE COOKIE DOUGH

¾ cup cake mix (¼ box)

½ cup plus 2 tablespoons heat-treated all-purpose flour (instructions on page 31)

1 tablespoon cornstarch

½ teaspoon salt

¾ stick (6 tablespoons) unsalted butter, at room temperature

¼ cup granulated sugar

¼ cup brown sugar

2 tablespoons pasteurized egg whites, at room temperature

1 teaspoon vanilla extract

¼ cup sprinkles

FOR THE CHEESECAKE

2 (8-ounce) packages cream cheese, at room temperature

¼ cup granulated sugar

2 teaspoons vanilla extract

½ cup confectioners' sugar

½ container (4 ounces) whipped topping, like Cool Whip, slightly thawed

⅓ cup sprinkles

// Line an 8"x8" pan using my Picture-Perfect Parchment Paper technique (see page 42).

// Make the crust: Use a food processor to grind the graham crackers into fine crumbs. Add the melted butter and brown sugar and process until evenly moist throughout.

// Press the crumb mixture into the lined pan to form an even, flat layer. Freeze to harden.

// Meanwhile, make the cookie dough using the ingredients listed in this recipe and following the method on page 58.

// Place about three quarters of the dough in a bowl and chill in the refrigerator. Leave the remaining one quarter of the dough at room temperature.

// Make the cheesecake: In the bowl of a stand mixer fitted with the paddle attachment, whip the cream cheese on medium speed until very smooth and creamy, about 2 minutes. Add the granulated sugar and vanilla and continue whipping for 1 minute. Add the reserved ¼ batch of dough and whip for 30 seconds, or until the dough is evenly dispersed in the mixture. Scrape the bowl. With the mixer on low, add the confectioners' sugar ¼ cup at a time.

// Remove the bowl from the stand mixer and use a rubber spatula to fold in the whipped topping just until combined. Break the chilled cookie dough into dime-size pieces. Fold three quarters of the pieces and half of the sprinkles into the cheesecake. Pour the batter over the chilled crust. Top with the remaining cookie dough and sprinkles.

Freeze for at least 1 hour, until hard. Thaw in the refrigerator for at least 30 minutes before serving. Slice with a hot knife and serve cold!

Store the bars covered in the freezer for up to 1 month. Thaw in the refrigerator 30 minutes to 1 hour before serving frozen bars.

/////////// *Kristen's Tip* ///////////

If you don't want to pull out the food processor, you can crush the graham crackers in a plastic bag with a rolling pin. If you don't even want to do that, use 2¼ cups store-bought graham cracker crumbs.

Made to Share
Cakes, Pies & More

//

The cookie dough craze and four-hour lines at my shop began because of...sharing. Yes, nostalgia and a worldwide love of cookie dough helped, but without sharing, we never would have gotten to where we are today.

During our opening weekend, hundreds of customers Instagrammed their scoops of cookie dough, and faster than you can say "hashtag," *Thrillist, BuzzFeed,* and *Insider* came looking for interviews. Having video crews and lighting equipment packed in the shop was strange, but what came next was even stranger: all three videos went viral on Facebook. I got texts from friends in different states, family in other countries, and my grandma—who doesn't even have Facebook. It felt like everyone in the city, no...everyone I had ever known had seen the videos, and shared them.

Last time I checked, those videos have been viewed 158,593,238 times (That's 158 MILLION+ !!!), and the numbers are still growing. People showed up at that shop "their coworker tweeted about." Customers from all over the country placed orders so they "could try that cookie dough that's all over Facebook."

But when those online orders went from a handful a day to multiple a minute, I had to make the tough decision to temporarily shut down the online store. I was afraid I was making a huge mistake. I felt defeated. The online store had always been the backbone of my company, but I *had* to focus on the people who showed up and waited hours at the shop, at least for a few days. It took me three whole months to feel prepared to reopen the online shop. Even after the wait, customers who wanted a taste after those viral videos immediately flooded us with orders.

We still get comments about seeing our dough on *Insider*, and I'm so thankful to learn that people are still sharing them! All this sharing allowed me to accomplish DŌ's mission, "to sweeten the moment" for as many people as possible.

/// Sharing is powerful! Make the slice-able, spoon-able, and scoop-able recipes in this section and share them with your friends. Who knows what will happen next?!

The Ult-DŌ-Mate Cookie Lover's Cake

CUSTOMIZE
Me

GREAT
MADE
GF

We all have a signature dish we keep in our back pocket for special occasions or those moments when we want to "wow" everyone. It's the dish that, when brought to the office, you get multiple emails asking for the recipe details, to which the best response you can offer is an "oh that—I just whipped that up." Well, this cake is my signature.

I really did just whip it up one day. I needed a last-minute cake to take to a friend's dinner party, so I just kind of threw it together with things at the shop that I had on hand. Even after getting asked for the recipe more than a dozen times, I've only now officially written it down for this cookbook. Just for you. You're welcome.

FOR THE COOKIE DOUGH LAYERS

1 batch Cake Batter dough (page 76)

FOR THE COOKIE LAYERS

6¾ cups heat-treated all-purpose flour (instructions on page 31)

2 tablespoons cornstarch

2¼ teaspoons salt

4½ sticks (36 tablespoons) unsalted butter, at room temperature (divided)

¾ cup granulated sugar

3 cups brown sugar

1 cup pasteurized egg whites, at room temperature

3 tablespoons vanilla extract

1½ cups rainbow sprinkles, plus more for rolling

1½ cups semisweet chocolate chips

1½ cups white chocolate chips

FOR THE BUTTERCREAM

4½ sticks (36 tablespoons) unsalted butter, at room temperature

7 cups confectioners' sugar

3 tablespoons heavy cream

1½ teaspoons vanilla extract

// Make the cookie dough layers: Make the Cake Batter dough. Chill the dough in the freezer for 15 minutes, or until it is easy to handle.

// Meanwhile, line a 9" cake pan with plastic wrap. Divide the dough in half. Press half of the dough into the cake pan in a flat, even layer. Cover with plastic wrap. Freeze for 10 minutes, then pop the layer out of the pan. Cover and stick it back in the fridge. Repeat with the second half of the cookie dough. Set both layers aside in the fridge.

// Preheat the oven to 350°F.

// Make the cookie layers: In a medium bowl, whisk together the heat-treated flour, cornstarch, and salt. Set aside.

// In the bowl of a stand mixer fitted with the paddle attachment, beat the butter on medium speed until smooth and creamy, about 2 minutes. Add the granulated and brown sugars and mix on medium until light and fluffy; about 4 minutes will do the trick. Use a rubber spatula to scrape the bowl. Add the egg whites and vanilla, and mix until fully incorporated, about 2 minutes.

CONTINUES ➤

// Add half of the flour mixture and mix on low just until the powdery texture of the flour disappears, about 15 seconds. Immediately add the rest of the flour mixture and mix until combined. Scrape the bowl and mix a final 15 seconds.

// Remove the bowl from the mixer and use a rubber spatula to fold in the sprinkles, semisweet chips, and white chips.

// Line the bottom of three 9" cake pans with parchment paper, then spray the parchment and pan sides with cooking spray. Divide the dough into 3 equal portions and spread each portion evenly into the greased pan. If you don't have 3 cake pans, do these one at a time.

// Bake for 30 to 40 minutes, until the cookie layers look set with a golden brown edge. Remove from the oven and allow the cakes to cool completely in the pan—this will take several hours. You can speed it up by letting them cool in the fridge.

// Make the buttercream: In the bowl of a stand mixer fitted with the paddle attachment, whip the butter until very smooth and creamy. Add half of the confectioners' sugar and mix on low just until combined. Add the rest of the confectioners' sugar, the cream, and vanilla. Slowly turn the mixer up to medium and whip until very fluffy, about 5 minutes. Make sure the buttercream is a spreadable consistency; if it's too thick, add a teaspoon of cream. Transfer to piping bags.

// Remove the cookie dough layers from the refrigerator. Use an 8" cake cutter to cut out each layer. Take the excess cookie dough and roll it into tablespoon-size balls. Roll in sprinkles and set aside.

// Use an 8" cake cutter to cut completely cooled baked cookie "cake" layers. Place the outside "crust" in a medium bowl and use a wooden spoon or your hands to break the excess cookie into crumbs. Set aside.

// Assemble the cake: Place a baked layer on a turntable or cake plate. Pipe a single layer of buttercream onto the cookie layer, smooth with an offset spatula (rubber works too!), and top with a cookie dough layer. Repeat with the remaining layers, alternating baked and unbaked. Once you've piped and smoothed buttercream onto the top of the final baked layer, sprinkle it with cookie crumbs. In a pattern along the outside rim of the cake, arrange the cookie dough balls and use dollops of buttercream to keep them in place.

// Chill in the fridge until ready to serve. Use a warm knife and cut directly down to slice and serve.

Store the cake covered in the refrigerator for up to 2 days.

Kristen's TIP

You need an 8-inch round cake cutter for this recipe. It's the only way to make the naked cookie layers look baked and beautiful! They are relatively inexpensive on Amazon, or you can find them at your favorite specialty kitchen store.

Chris's Cookie Dough Dirt Cake

kids LOVE

Chris is the hardest person to buy gifts for. He doesn't need anything, he doesn't want anything, and it sincerely makes zero difference to him whether or not I get him anything at all. I swear, a homemade Funfetti cake is the only thing he asks for every year on his birthday. For our first wedding anniversary, I was stumped, so I made him dirt cake as a gift. That's right. In true Tomlan style, I made my husband homemade dirt cake—the classic childhood pudding dish with whipped topping, Oreos, and gummy worms—for one of the most important anniversary celebrations of all time.

Someday we'll grow up (or maybe not).

FOR THE CRUST AND TOPPING

3 cups semisweet chocolate chips (divided)

1⅛ sticks (9 tablespoons) unsalted butter, at room temperature

1⅔ cups Oreo crumbs

¼ cup plus 2 tablespoons cocoa powder

2 teaspoons cornstarch

1½ teaspoons baking powder

1 teaspoon salt

⅓ cup granulated sugar

1½ cups brown sugar

¾ cup pasteurized egg whites, at room temperature

1 tablespoon vanilla extract

FOR THE PUDDING

2 cups whole milk

4 tablespoons cornstarch

2 cups heavy cream

1 cup granulated sugar

¼ cup cocoa powder

1 teaspoon salt

1 cup dark chocolate chips

FOR THE WHIPPED TOPPING

1 (8-ounce) package cream cheese, at room temperature

1 (8-ounce) container whipped topping, like Cool Whip

1 cup confectioners' sugar

FOR THE LAYERS

2 cups mini gummy worms

1½ cups Oreo baking crumbs

// Preheat the oven to 350°F.

// Make the crust and topping: In a medium microwave-safe bowl, heat 1½ cups of the semisweet chips and the butter in the microwave on 50% power in 30-second increments. Stir well between each increment until melted. Set aside.

// In a medium bowl, whisk together the Oreo crumbs, cocoa powder, cornstarch, baking powder, and salt until well combined. Set aside.

// Pour the melted chocolate mixture into the bowl of a stand mixer fitted with the paddle attachment and mix until the mixture is smooth, about 30 seconds. Add the granulated and brown sugars and mix on medium until well combined, about 2 minutes. Use a rubber spatula to scrape the bowl. Add the egg whites and vanilla and mix just until well incorporated, about 2 minutes. The mixture will be runny.

// Add the Oreo mixture and mix on low just until the powdery texture of the crumbs disappears, about 30 seconds. Scrape the bowl and mix a final 15 seconds. Remove the bowl from the mixer and use a rubber spatula to fold in the remaining semisweet chips. Reserve 2 cups of the crust batter and set aside to chill in the freezer.

CONTINUES ▶

// Bake the crust: Pour the rest of the batter into a greased 9"x13" pan. Bake for 15 to 20 minutes, until the top is set and the edges are just getting crispy. Cool in the refrigerator.

// Make the pudding: In a small bowl, whisk together the milk and cornstarch until smooth. Set aside.

// In a medium saucepan, combine the cream, sugar, cocoa powder, and salt. Place over medium heat and bring to a simmer. Once the mixture simmers, stir in the dark chips. Continue stirring until the chips are melted and well incorporated. Slowly whisk in the cornstarch mixture. Continue simmering, stirring occasionally, until the mixture thickens, 1 to 2 minutes. Remove from the heat and cool in the refrigerator.

// Make the whipped topping: In the bowl of a stand mixer fitted with the paddle attachment, whip the cream cheese on high for 3 to 4 minutes, until smooth and creamy. Scrape the bowl and whip for an additional 1 minute. Add the whipped topping and beat on medium until fully combined. Scrape the bowl as needed to make sure the ingredients are thoroughly mixed.

// Set the mixer to stir. Add the confectioners' sugar in two ½-cup additions and stir until well combined.

// Assemble the dirt cake: Spread the cooled pudding in an even layer over the crust. Scatter dime-size pieces of the reserved cookie dough crust batter evenly on top of the pudding layer. Then sprinkle half of the gummy worms over the cookie dough. Spread the whipped topping over the worms in an even layer. Sprinkle the entire pan with Oreo baking crumbs. Top with the rest of the gummy worms and dig in!

Store the dirt cake covered in the refrigerator for up to 3 days.

SPEAKING OF
sharing

I love seeing Instagram stories, Facebook posts, and Snapchat videos featuring my cookie dough pop up daily. Every now and then I get totally surprised when someone like, oh, Kim Kardashian, Chrissy Teigen, Ryan Seacrest, or Bobby Flay shares some kind words about the joy edible cookie dough brings to the world. When Reese Witherspoon shared a story about the Frosted Fork (page 103), I was SHOCKED. I didn't even send her dough. Just goes to show everyone wants to say "Hello" to cookie dough!

Deep Dish Skillet Cookie

GREAT MADE GF

New York vs. Chicago might be the all-time great pizza debate, but honestly I'm not really part of it because I'm on team STL thin crust pizza all day long (#Imospizzaforlife). Unlike pizza, cookies are always better when they are thicker. No debate here. And when I want thick, I think skillet.

The best way to eat a skillet cookie is straight out of the oven and straight from the pan, which is why this dish is ideal for sharing. Plop a couple of scoops of ice cream on top, grab some spoons and your best pals, and dig in!

½ batch Signature Chocolate Chip dough (page 60)

½ cup Nutella

// Make the Signature Chocolate Chip dough, referring to the ½ batch ingredients on page 63. Freeze for 15 minutes.

// Remove the cookie dough from the freezer and divide it in half. Press one half of the dough into a 6" cast-iron skillet.

// On a sheet of waxed paper, shape the other half of the dough into a 6" disk—don't worry, it doesn't need to be a perfect circle! Freeze for 20 minutes, or until the disk easily lifts from the paper.

// Add the Nutella to the center of the dough in the cast-iron pan. Use a rubber spatula to spread the Nutella, leaving a 1-inch border around the edges. Top with the other half of the dough and lightly press around the edges of the disk to fuse the two halves together. Freeze the entire skillet for 30 minutes.

// Meanwhile, preheat the oven to 350°F.

// Bake for 25 minutes, or until the edges of the cookie are golden brown and the center is set. Let cool for 5 minutes and serve by topping with ice cream. Then hand out the spoons!

Store the cookie in the skillet, covered, in the refrigerator up to 2 days.

When I Dip, You Dip, We Dip

Why wait for dessert? Cookie dough makes a great appetizer for your next party. You can use any number of goodies as a vehicle to get the stuff into your mouth. I suggest trying graham crackers, pretzels, vanilla wafers, apples, celery—or frozen Reese's Cups if you're my dad. Hell, use your finger. Dip away, my friends!

FOR THE COOKIE DOUGH

1 cup plus 2 tablespoons heat-treated all-purpose flour (instructions on page 31)

½ teaspoon cornstarch

¼ teaspoon salt

¾ stick (6 tablespoons) unsalted butter, at room temperature

2 tablespoons granulated sugar

½ cup brown sugar

1½ teaspoons vanilla extract

FOR THE DIP

1 (8-ounce) package cream cheese, at room temperature

1 cup confectioners' sugar

1 teaspoon vanilla extract

1 cup mini chocolate chips

FOR DIPPING

Whatever you want! See photo for suggestions!

// Make the cookie dough: In a medium bowl, whisk together the heat-treated flour, cornstarch, and salt. Set aside.

// In the bowl of a stand mixer fitted with the paddle attachment, whip the butter on medium speed until it appears smooth and creamy, about 2 minutes. Add the granulated and brown sugars and beat on medium until light and fluffy; 3 to 4 minutes will do the trick. Use a rubber spatula to scrape the bowl. Add the vanilla. Beat on medium speed until well combined, about 1 minute.

// Add half of the flour mixture. Mix on low until the powdery flour texture disappears, about 15 seconds. Immediately add the rest of the flour mixture. Mix just until combined. Scrape the bowl and mix a final 15 seconds.

// Scrape the dough out of the bowl and set aside. Your dough will have a crumbly texture—don't worry if it doesn't seem like typical cookie dough! Transfer the "dough" to a separate bowl.

// Make the dip: In the same stand mixer bowl, whip the cream cheese on medium speed until smooth and creamy, 3 to 4 minutes. Scrape the bowl and add the confectioners' sugar. Beat on medium for an additional 2 minutes. Scrape the bowl, add the vanilla, and beat for 30 seconds, or until combined.

// With the mixer on stir, add the dough in four ½-cup additions. Scrape the bowl and mix for a final 30 seconds.

// Remove the bowl from the stand mixer. Use a rubber spatula to fold in the mini chocolate chips. Get to dippin'!

Store the dip in an airtight container in the refrigerator for up to 3 days.

SERVES
6 to 8

ACTIVE TIME
50 minutes

TIME 'TIL PIE
6 hours

MADE TO SHARE:
CAKES, PIES & MORE

267

Cookie DŌ
Ice Cream Pie

The year DŌ's storefront opened, I had a two-page spread in *People* and I featured this recipe!

We had lights, cameras, wardrobe, makeup artists, food stylists, catering, content producers, staff, publicists (and more), PLUS Chris and me in our tiny 450-square-foot apartment. Cue chaos.

The shoot started off smoothly. Hair, makeup, and wardrobe laid out on my bed. The lights came in and the couch went out...into the hallway. More lights were set up outside my window, and that's when my landlord lost it. I was half naked changing outfits and I hear, "Umm, Kristen, I think your landlord is calling the cops." Eventually, we talked him off the ledge and somehow all twelve of us survived ten hours crammed together. It was a surreal experience I'll never forget... for many reasons. I have the spread framed. So does my mom. So does my assistant's mom. If you didn't catch it in *People* magazine's July 2017 issue, here is the recipe you missed.

1 cup all-purpose flour

1½ teaspoons cornstarch

¼ teaspoon baking soda

¼ teaspoon salt

¾ stick (6 tablespoons) unsalted butter, at room temperature

2 tablespoons granulated sugar

½ cup brown sugar

1 large egg yolk, at room temperature

1½ teaspoons vanilla extract

½ cup semisweet chocolate chips

2 pints Cookie Dough with a Side of Ice Cream (page 242) or store-bought chocolate chip cookie dough ice cream

Sprinkles, for topping

// In a medium bowl, whisk together the flour, cornstarch, baking soda, and salt. Set aside.

// In the bowl of a stand mixer fitted with the paddle attachment, beat the butter on medium speed until smooth and creamy, about 2 minutes. Add the granulated and brown sugars and mix on medium until light and fluffy; about 4 minutes. Use a rubber spatula to scrape the bowl. Add the egg yolk and vanilla and mix until fully incorporated, about 2 minutes.

// Add half of the flour mixture and mix on low just until the powdery texture of the flour disappears, about 15 seconds. Immediately add the rest of the flour mixture and mix until combined. Scrape the bowl and mix a final 15 seconds.

// Remove the bowl from the mixer and use a rubber spatula to fold in the chocolate chips. Cover with plastic wrap and refrigerate for at least 4 hours.

// Preheat the oven to 350°F. Line a 9" round deep-dish pie pan with foil. Foil should extend over the lip of the pan to make handles. Lightly coat the foil with cooking spray.

// Remove dough from the refrigerator. Divide into 4 pieces and press into the bottom and sides of the pan to make an even crust. Coat a sheet of parchment paper with cooking spray on both sides and use to cover the crust and weigh down with pie weights.

// Bake for 15 minutes, then remove parchment paper and weights. Bake for an additional 5 to 10 minutes, until the crust is golden brown. Transfer to a wire rack to cool for 15 minutes. Use the foil to carefully remove the crust from the pan. Remove the foil from the crust and return the crust to the pan. Cool completely.

// Meanwhile, remove the ice cream from the freezer and soften on the counter for 15 minutes. Use a rubber spatula to transfer the ice cream to a large bowl. Stir with a rubber spatula until it is spreadable but not melted.

// Spoon the ice cream into the completely cooled crust and smooth the top. Top with sprinkles. Freeze the entire pie for at least 4 hours to harden. Remove the pie from the freezer just before serving. Use a warm knife to slice and serve immediately.

Store the pie covered in the freezer for up to 1 month.

268 \ MADE TO SHARE:
CAKES, PIES & MORE

\ *MAKES*
12 slices

\ *ACTIVE TIME*
30 minutes

\ *TIME 'TIL PIZZA*
1 hour

DŌssert Pizza Pie

One night in college, my friends and I came home late after a night out bar-hopping, ready to dig into some pizza—both the warm pizza we had just picked up and the cookie pizza I'd made earlier and left sitting on the counter. We walked into the house to see our friend (not to be named), who had clearly left the bar just before us, sitting silently in the dark dining room devouring the cookie pizza with a shard of plastic from a fork (the other part had broken off in her feverous attempt to dig into the cookie).

Luckily, we were able to lure her away from the cookie pizza with a fresh pepperoni slice and a bottle of ranch dressing, and we enjoyed every bite of what was left. Looking back, I think that might have been the last time I made a cookie pizza pie...until now.

1⅓ cups all-purpose flour

½ teaspoon baking powder

½ teaspoon baking soda

½ teaspoon salt

¾ stick (6 tablespoons) unsalted butter, melted

1 cup brown sugar

1 whole egg

2 cups mini marshmallows

½ cup M&M's

½ cup semisweet chocolate chips

// Preheat the oven to 350°F. Coat a pizza pan with cooking spray.

// In a medium bowl, whisk together the flour, baking powder, baking soda, and salt. Set aside.

// In a large bowl, stir the melted butter, brown sugar, and egg with a wooden spoon until well combined. Scrape the bowl with a rubber spatula. Add the flour mixture all at once and stir just until combined.

// Use a rubber spatula (or your hands!) to spread the mixture over the pizza pan in an even layer.

// Pile the mini marshmallows onto the "pizza crust," leaving a 1-inch border around the edges of the cookie, like a pizza crust. Bake for 15 to 20 minutes, until the edges are lightly golden and the marshmallows are lightly toasted on top. Remove from the oven and immediately sprinkle the M&M's and chocolate chips over the marshmallows. Let cool on a wire rack for at least 15 minutes. Slice like a pizza and enjoy warm or allow to cool completely.

Store the cookie pizza covered for up to 3 days.

Kristen's
TIP

You can choose your own toppings, just like you would with pizza. Add your favorite candies, chips, or sprinkles. Have fun with it!

270 \ MADE TO SHARE:
CAKES, PIES & MORE

\ MAKES
18 fur baby servings

\ ACTIVE TIME
12 minutes

\ TIME 'TIL DOGGY DOUGH
12 minutes

Doggy Dough

As much as I've always wanted a dog, having a puppy while working nonstop was not exactly an option for us. If I wasn't in the kitchen at the shop, I was downstairs in the basement, which functioned as our office / storage room / shipping center / dungeon. There was no time—and no space—for a furry little friend. It wasn't until we moved our offices to a pet-friendly space (big upgrade!) that I felt like I could finally add a dog daughter to our family. Once I finally let myself search rescue agencies, I found her quickly (on Instagram, no less)—a skinny tan "hound" puppy with floppy ears and a black snout, rescued with her siblings from the streets of Georgia.

From the first hug, I knew she was the one. Perfect little Penelope, nicknamed Nelly as a throwback to my St. Louis roots. She's the sweetest pup and rambunctious addition to the new office. Lucky Nelly, she's got no less than ten moms and more attention, and doggy-friendly dough, than she could ever need.

This dough is made to celebrate your pup's special days, whether you're celebrating her birthday, adopt-a-versary, or just being a very very good girl at the vet. Put a candle in the top, snap a pic, and let her scarf down this treat.

¾ cup plus 1 tablespoon canned pumpkin (unsweetened)

⅓ cup plus 1 tablespoon applesauce (unsweetened)

2 teaspoons honey

1½ cups peanut butter

½ cup ripe banana, mashed

2¾ cups oats, heat-treated according to the instructions on page 31

20 mini Milk-Bones or other small dog treat to top

// In the bowl of a stand mixer fitted with the paddle attachment, mix together the pumpkin, applesauce, honey, peanut butter, and banana on medium speed. Once well combined, add the oats. The mixture will become very thick. Continue to mix until the oats are evenly dispersed throughout.

// Use a spoon to portion the dough into 18 (3-ounce) Dixie cups. Top each cup with a small dog treat.

// The 2 extra treats are for your pup! She's being a very good girl while you make this recipe. Doggy dough can be served fresh, chilled, or frozen.

// Store Doggy Dough in its Dixie cup container in the refrigerator for up to 3 days or in the freezer up to 1 month.

You can bake these into adorable dog treats! See My Go-To Baking & Storage DŌrections on page 48.

SERVES
10 to 15

ACTIVE TIME
1 hour 15 minutes

TIME 'TIL CAKE
15 hours

MADE TO SHARE:
CAKES, PIES & MORE

273

My Homemade Ice Cream Cake

PLAN
Ahead

This Midwest gal is no stranger to chain restaurants and nationwide dessert brands. In fact, I might be a pro. Please pass the endless Olive Garden breadsticks, find me the nearest P.F. Chang's, order me a Domino's pizza, and hand over that Dairy Queen ice cream cake. Like, now. No shame here.

But New York City makes it a little bit harder. Chain restaurants are hard to stumble upon. Thank god for Postmates. With the closest ice cream cake option being in New Jersey, I was forced to come up with my very own version. The good news: It's even better than DQ.

FOR THE FUDGE TOPPING
1 cup heavy cream

½ cup sugar

2 tablespoons unsalted butter, at room temperature

1 cup semisweet chocolate chips

1 teaspoon vanilla extract

⅛ teaspoon salt

FOR THE LAYERS
1 batch Signature Chocolate Chip dough (page 60)

1½ quarts vanilla ice cream

1½ quarts chocolate ice cream

FOR THE COOKIE CRUMBLE
10 Oreo cookies, finely crushed

FOR THE TOPPING
3 tablespoons sprinkles

// Make the fudge topping: In a medium saucepan, whisk together the cream, sugar, and butter and heat over medium heat until melted. Bring the mixture to a boil, then reduce the heat to low. Stir in the chocolate chips, whisking constantly until smooth. Continue to whisk over low heat for about 2 minutes, until the mixture appears thick and glossy. Remove from the heat and stir in the vanilla and salt. Set aside to cool.

// Make the Signature Chocolate Chip dough. Chill in the freezer for 20 minutes. As your dough chills, remove the ice cream from the freezer and soften on the countertop for 15 to 20 minutes.

// Break the chilled cookie dough into dime-size chunks. Split the cookie dough chunks into 3 even portions.

// Use a rubber spatula to transfer each ice cream into its own medium bowl. Stir with a rubber spatula until the ice cream is spreadable but not melted. Add one portion of cookie dough chunks to each ice cream and stir with a rubber spatula to evenly disperse. Reserve the last portion of cookie dough.

// Make the cookie crumble: In a medium bowl, mix the crushed Oreos with 1 cup of the fudge topping. Set aside.

// Assemble the cake: Spread the chocolate ice cream mixed with chocolate chip cookie dough over the bottom of a 9"x13" pan. Top with all of the cookie crumble in a single layer. Sprinkle the reserved portion of cookie dough balls over the cake. Drop the vanilla ice cream mixed with chocolate chip cookie dough over the cake in 5 large scoops. Use a rubber spatula to spread the ice cream evenly over the cake.

// Garnish with a drizzle of chocolate fudge and the sprinkles. Place the entire cake in the freezer for at least 4 hours to harden.

// Remove the cake from the freezer just before serving. Use a warm knife to slice and serve immediately.

Store the cake covered in the freezer for up to 1 month.

/////////// *Kristen's Tip* ///////////

The best thing about a homemade ice cream cake is that you can personalize it, exactly to your liking. Sub out different ice cream flavors, use caramel or Nutella instead of fudge, and add whatever you want on top!

Made to Party

Customizable Treats & Serving Secrets

On June 21 each year, I have only one goal: to turn all of New York City (and beyond) into a giant cookie dough party. It's #NationalCookieDoughDay, and I won't let anyone forget it.

Any way you can serve cookie dough, we're doing it on June 21. We bring customized jar-fuls of cookie dough topped with extra-special sprinkles to surprise people in Madison Square Park, the High Line, Astor Place, and Times Square. Colorful party packs filled with our favorite flavors are sent to liven up lunch breaks across the country. And we plan all-out cookie dough extravaganzas that we can bring around the city: Our totally mobile cookie dough cart comes complete with a mix-ins bar and toppings scooped to order. It's the ultimate dessert spread. At the shop we get creative with festive cookie dough—maybe it's topping tiny ice cream cones or made into a special flavor that's mixed up for one day only. And, of course, the experience wouldn't be complete without an over-the-top photo wall to snap the most perfect pic!

But it's not just citywide celebrations that get a cookie dough treatment. Baby showers, engagement parties, and graduations can be sweetened with an unbaked creation. Like the wedding cake I made for my friends Stacy and Jeff—a giant fifteen-tiered cookie cake no less.

I was thrilled when Stacy asked me to make something for her special day. Being a cookie monster herself, she's always been one of my biggest DŌ supporters and fans. It was humbling. I couldn't believe that my cookie cake creation would be the star of her dessert table, surrounded by endless delicate containers filled with individual portions of cookie dough. That cake would live on in her memories of this special day and be immortalized in her wedding photos forever. What an honor!

I don't think I'll ever get tired of bringing cookie dough to the party, no matter what form it takes.

/// *These recipes are for any celebration, whether it's national, personal, or for no reason at all. You'll also find the serving secrets we use at DŌ to take our simple sweet cookie dough to party-ready dessert.*

276 \ MADE TO PARTY: CUSTOMIZABLE
TREATS & SERVING SECRETS

\ *MAKES*
24 treats

\ *ACTIVE TIME*
45 minutes

\ *TIME 'TIL TREATS*
1 hour 30 minutes

Cookie DŌ Crispies

In grade school, you didn't have to look far before you found the Rice Krispies Treats. They were at every bake sale, birthday party, and sports game. Although I ran into Rice Krispies Treats all the time, I never got tired of them. Their special place in my heart came down to a simple truth: They are so common because they are so easy— and so good when done right!

So, here's my spin on that childhood staple. They look seriously fancy dipped in chocolate and covered in cookie crumbles and sprinkles, but they come together faster than you can say "Snap, Crackle, Cookie Dough, Pop!"

FOR THE COOKIE DOUGH AND COOKIE CRUMBLES

1 batch Signature Chocolate Chip dough (page 60)

FOR THE TREATS

½ stick (4 tablespoons) unsalted butter

1 (10-ounce) bag mini marshmallows

6 cups crisp rice cereal (I use Rice Krispies)

FOR DIPPING

½ cup rainbow sprinkles (optional)

2 cups semisweet chocolate chips

2 tablespoons coconut oil

// **Make the Signature Chocolate Chip dough.** Preheat the oven to 350°F. Line a baking sheet with parchment paper or a silicone baking mat.

// Use a cookie scoop to portion 6 scoops of cookie dough onto the lined baking sheet and freeze for 30 minutes. Chill the remaining cookie dough in the refrigerator.

// Bake the cookies for 12 to 15 minutes, until golden brown all over. They need to be crispier than normal. Set aside.

// **Make the treats:** In a large saucepan or Dutch oven, melt the butter over medium heat. Add the marshmallows and stir constantly until the marshmallows are melted and the mixture is smooth. Remove from the heat and add the cereal. Stir until the cereal is well coated. Transfer to a large bowl and allow to cool for 5 minutes.

// Measure ¾ cup cookie dough. Drop tablespoon-size chunks of this cookie dough into the cereal mixture and gently stir to incorporate, making sure the cookie dough chunks stay intact. Too much stirring will cause the melted chocolate to spread too much!

// Use cooking spray to grease a 9"x13" pan, a ⅓-cup measuring cup, and your fingers (this will make the mixture easier to handle). Use the ⅓-cup measuring cup to make 15 portions of cereal mixture. Scatter these portions in the pan in a checkerboard formation, ensuring that the corners are filled with cereal mixture

and there are gaps between the cereal mixture portions.

// Remove the rest of the cookie dough from the refrigerator and use it to fill the gaps between the portions of cereal mixture. Once the cookie dough is used up, use a piece of waxed paper to smooth the treats into an even layer. Allow to chill in the freezer until very firm, about 30 minutes.

// **Prepare the chocolate dip and cookie crumbles:** Place the completely cooled cookies in a plastic bag and crush them with the back of a measuring cup or a rolling pin. Once the cookies have the consistency of crumbs, add sprinkles (if using) to the bag and shake to mix. Lay the crumb mixture on a plate.

// In a medium microwave-safe bowl, heat the chocolate chips with the coconut oil in the microwave on 50% power in 30-second increments. Stir well between each increment. Repeat just until melted. Let the chocolate cool slightly while you cut the treats into 24 even squares.

// Dip half of each treat into the chocolate. Remove from the chocolate and dip all sides into the cookie crumbs. Lay on waxed paper until the chocolate sets. Serve at room temperature.

These treats are best served the same day but can be stored in an airtight container at room temperature for up to 5 days.

SHOP
Special

Classic Red Velvet Cookie Bomb

Let me tell you about the greatest flying mishap of all time.

It started with me trying to transport some of our best-selling cookie bombs across state lines. Our cookie bombs are as adorable as they are delicious, but they're also very fragile. So, out of concern for my delicate desserts, I reminded Chris, while in the security line, to be very careful with that bag because (and I quote) "It's full of bombs." (Good job, Kristen.) NOT something you should say at the airport. Next to a TSA officer. Of all places. Needless to say, everyone around me was alarmed, and they weren't exactly reassured when I tried explaining that they weren't *bomb* bombs, they were cookie cupcakes that we *call* bombs because they *explode* in your mouth. Rookie mistake. Chris, the Bombs, and I all managed to make it out of the experience unscathed, but since then, no more traveling with Bombs of any kind!

1 batch Classic Red Velvet dough (page 155)

½ batch Classic Cream Cheese Buttercream (page 156)

Colorful sprinkles, for topping

// **Make the Classic Red Velvet dough.** Cover the bowl and chill in the refrigerator for 30 minutes, or until the dough is easy to handle. Once chilled, divide the dough into 12 even portions. Roll the portions into balls using your hands. Freeze for 30 minutes.

// Preheat the oven to 350°F and fit a standard cupcake pan with liners.

// Make ½ batch Classic Cream Cheese Buttercream, referring to the recipe directions on page 154. While the dough chills, transfer the buttercream to a piping bag.

// Stuff the bombs: Remove the cookie dough from the freezer and use your thumbs to press into the middle of each ball, forming each into a nest or bowl shape. Fill each hole with 1 heaping teaspoon of buttercream. Set the piping bag aside. Once filled, use your fingers to pinch the cookie dough over the buttercream to form a seam. Roll the balls in your hand until the seam disappears. The buttercream will be completely concealed in the middle of the ball. Place the stuffed cookie dough balls into the cupcake liners.

// Bake for 15 minutes, or until the bombs look risen and set but are not yet browning on the edges. Let the bombs cool in the pan for 5 minutes, then carefully transfer to a wire rack to cool completely.

// Once the bombs are completely cooled, pipe the buttercream onto each cookie bomb, forming a large 3-tiered dollop. Garnish with colorful sprinkles and serve.

// Enjoy your treats, they're the bomb!

// Store the bombs in an airtight container the refrigerator for up to 3 days. Let stand at room temperature for 15 minutes before serving.

278 \ MADE TO PARTY: CUSTOMIZABLE
TREATS & SERVING SECRETS

MAKES
12 bombs

ACTIVE TIME
1 hour

TIME 'TIL BOMBS
3 hours 10 minutes

Peppermint Hot Cocoa Bomb

SHOP
Special

When the holiday music starts playing and the temperatures start dropping, it's like my body—mainly my taste buds—knows what's coming. Christmas! Cookies and candy canes and chocolate, oh my! Even liquid sugar: hot cocoa, spiked cider, and eggnog—bring it on!

In the spirit of giving (to myself), this recipe combines a few holiday must-haves: a chocolate-y hot cocoa indulgence, a peppermint candy crunch, and a touch of Christmas cookie goodness, and a bonus—toasty, charred marshmallows to make me feel as if I'm cozied up next to a warm fireplace. Just when you thought the Bomb couldn't get better, it does! And my hibernation body DŌvelops even faster...'tis the season.

FOR THE BOMBS

2¼ cups heat-treated all-purpose flour (instructions on page 31)

½ cup cocoa powder

½ teaspoon baking powder

½ teaspoon baking soda

½ teaspoon cornstarch

1 teaspoon salt

1½ sticks (12 tablespoons) unsalted butter, at room temperature

⅓ cup granulated sugar

1 cup brown sugar

½ cup pasteurized egg whites, at room temperature

1 teaspoon vanilla extract

2 teaspoons peppermint extract

FOR THE STUFFING, TOPPING, AND GARNISH

2 cups Marshmallow Fluff

1 (8-ounce) package mini marshmallows

2 tablespoons crushed peppermint candies

FOR THE GANACHE

½ cup semisweet chocolate chips

1½ teaspoons unsalted butter, at room temperature

3 tablespoons heavy cream

¼ teaspoon vanilla extract

Classic Red Velvet Cookie Bomb, page 277

// Make the bombs: In a medium bowl, whisk together the flour, cocoa powder, baking powder, baking soda, cornstarch, and salt. Set aside.

// In the bowl of a stand mixer fitted with the paddle attachment, beat the butter on medium speed until smooth and creamy, about 2 minutes. Add the granulated and brown sugars and mix on medium until light and fluffy; about 4 minutes. Use a rubber spatula to scrape the bowl. Add the egg whites, vanilla, and peppermint extract and mix until fully incorporated, about 2 minutes.

// Add half of the flour mixture and mix on low just until the powdery texture of the flour disappears, about 15 seconds. Immediately add the rest of the flour mixture and mix until combined. Scrape the bowl and mix a final 15 seconds.

// Cover the bowl and chill in the refrigerator for 20 minutes. Once chilled, divide the dough into 12 even portions. Roll the portions into balls using your hands. Freeze for 30 minutes.

// Preheat the oven to 350°F and fit a 12-hole cupcake pan with liners. Fill a piping bag with Marshmallow Fluff. Cut the tip 1 inch from the bottom.

// Stuff the bombs: Remove the cookie dough from the freezer and use your thumbs to press into the middle of each ball, forming each into a nest or bowl shape. Fill each hole with 1 heaping teaspoon of Marshmallow Fluff. Once filled, use your fingers to pinch the cookie dough over the Marshmallow Fluff to form a seam. Roll the balls in your hand until the seam disappears. The marshmallow will be completely concealed in the middle of the ball. Place the stuffed cookie dough balls into the cupcake liners.

// Bake for 15 minutes. The bombs will look like a set cookie when they are done. Remove from the oven and let cool completely.

// Meanwhile, make the ganache: Place the chocolate chips and butter in a medium bowl. Set aside. Heat the cream in the microwave on 50% power in

30-second intervals just until the cream boils. Stir well between each increment. As soon as the cream boils, pour it over the chocolate chips and butter. Stir with a whisk, starting in the center of the bowl and moving slowly outward to combine. Once the mixture is fully incorporated and begins to look glossy, stir in the vanilla. Set aside to cool.

// To garnish: Pipe a small dollop of Marshmallow Fluff onto the center of each baked bomb. Place a small handfull of marshmallows onto the fluff, making a hefty mound. Use a handheld torch to toast the marshmallows, until they stick together and are browned on top. Drizzle with the ganache and sprinkle the peppermint candies on top.

Store the bombs in an airtight container in the refrigerator for up to 2 days. Unbaked bombs can be stored in the freezer for up to 2 months and baked a few at a time.

Peppermint Hot Cocoa Bomb, page 278

The Cookie Bomb, page 214

Super Soft Sugar Cookie Cut-Outs

My mother-in-law, Shawn, is a wonderful baker. She's famous in her Ohio town for her stuffed cupcakes, her extravagant holiday dessert tables, and her really yummy cut-out cookies. One year, a local bakery asked her to make holiday cookie trays for their customers, as her cookies were always such a huge hit. She agreed, but then immediately regretted it. Orders flooded in and she and my father-in-law, John, spent the next month, sunup to sundown, churning out cookies.

These days, she's retired from the cookie business, until I call her in an emergency to come lend me a hand in New York.

FOR THE COOKIES

2½ cups heat-treated all-purpose flour (instructions on page 31)

1 tablespoon cornstarch

¾ teaspoon salt

1½ sticks (12 tablespoons) unsalted butter, at room temperature

1 cup plus 2 tablespoons granulated sugar

⅓ cup pasteurized egg whites, at room temperature

1½ teaspoons vanilla extract

FOR THE ROYAL ICING

6 cups sifted confectioners' sugar

5 tablespoons meringue powder

¾ cup room-temperature water, plus more for thinning

Gel food coloring (optional)

// Make the cookies: In a medium bowl, whisk together the heat-treated flour, cornstarch, and salt. Set aside.

// In the bowl of a stand mixer fitted with the paddle attachment, beat the butter on medium speed until smooth and creamy, about 2 minutes. Add the sugar and mix on medium until light and fluffy; about 4 minutes will do the trick. Use a rubber spatula to scrape the bowl. Add the egg whites and vanilla and mix until fully incorporated, about 2 minutes.

// Add half of the flour mixture and mix on low just until the powdery texture of the flour disappears, about 15 seconds. Immediately add the rest of the flour mixture and mix until combined. Scrape the bowl and mix a final 15 seconds.

// Divide the dough in half, cover with plastic wrap, and chill in the freezer until easy to handle.

// Preheat the oven to 350°F and line a baking sheet with parchment paper.

// Lay out a large sheet of plastic wrap or waxed paper. Drop one half of the chilled dough into the center of the waxed paper and cover with another sheet of waxed paper. Roll the dough to ¼-inch thickness and cut with floured cookie cutters. Repeat with the other half of the dough.

// Place on the prepared sheet and bake for 10 to 12 minutes. Different sizes of cookies will bake differently. Keep your eyes on the edges; once they look set and barely golden, they are ready to come out of the oven.

// Let cool on the baking sheet for 5 minutes, then transfer to a wire rack to cool completely.

// Meanwhile, make the royal icing: In the bowl of a stand mixer fitted with the whisk attachment, whip the confectioners' sugar, meringue powder, and room-temperature water on low speed until well combined. Increase the speed to medium and mix for 7 to 10 minutes, until the icing forms stiff, glossy peaks. Use additional water, a drop or two at a time, to thin the icing to desired consistency. I know mine is ready when it drizzles off the whisk in a thick ribbon and disappears back into the bowl.

// For a single color, add gel food coloring (less is more!) to the mixing bowl and whip, or divide the icing into several bowls and add color to each bowl for multiple colors.

// Transfer the icing to a piping bag with a decorating tip. Pipe a border around the edges of the completely cooled cookies. Add lines of icing to the center of each cookie and use a toothpick to spread the icing to fill the cookie center. Allow the icing to set at room temperature for 2 hours. Snap a pic for Instagram and enjoy!

Store the cookies in an airtight container at room temperature for up to 5 days.

282 \ MADE TO PARTY: CUSTOMIZABLE
TREATS & SERVING SECRETS

\ *MAKES*
35 scoops \ *TIME 'TIL DOUGH*
15 minutes \ *TIME 'TIL COOKIES*
2 hours 30 minutes

You Dough You

EASY TO MAKE *Vegan* GREAT MADE GF *kids* LOVE

This recipe is for you...to dough you. You pick the base, then the candy, the mix-in, or the sauce and go to town creating the ultimate customized cookie dough of your dreams.

We start with whatever base tickles your taste buds—and then you fill in the rest. Giving it as a gift? Find out the lucky recipient's favorite candy. Taking it to a party? Go along with the theme. Treating yourself? Get whatever you've craving.

It's totally up to you!

1 **Pick** your favorite cookie dough base to start:

Signature (page 58)

Brownie Batter (page 64)

Sugar Cookie (page 68)

Peanut Butter (page 72)

Oatmeal (page 74)

Cake Batter (page 76)

2 **Add 1 cup** of your favorite mix-ins (I like to do 3 mix-ins, ⅓ cup of each!)

// Follow the recipe for the base you selected.

// Remove the bowl from the mixer and use a rubber spatula to fold in your chosen mix-ins!

// You're ready for a party in your mouth with this cookie dough combo!

If you're dying to bake some and try this as cookies, see My Go-To Baking & Storage DŌrections on page 48.

Kristen's
TIP

If you're making something for me (hint, hint), start by adding Nutella and then layer the flavors from there. Think crunchy! Chewy! Salty! Sweet! More is more. 😊

Cookie Milk Shots

GREAT MADE GF

Fun for all ages and a showstopper on a dessert table, I give you: cookie milk shots—complete with a chocolate-coated cookie dust rim and chock-full of tantalizingly sweet cookie milk. These are the ultimate cookies and milk combo.

What's cookie milk? It's inspired by Milk Bar's famous Cereal Milk, except less breakfast-y, more dessert-like, but equally nostalgic. It's got the same flavor you have left over in your glass of milk after you finish dunking all those cookies into it.

FOR THE COOKIES

1 batch Signature Chocolate Chip dough (page 60)

FOR THE MILK

4 cups milk, cold

1 tablespoon vanilla extract

1 tablespoon brown sugar

FOR THE GARNISH

1 cup rainbow sprinkles (divided)

½ cup semisweet chocolate chips

// Preheat the oven to 350°F. Line a baking sheet with parchment paper or a silicone baking mat.

// Make the Signature Chocolate Chip dough. Use a cookie scoop to portion 10 scoops of cookie dough onto the prepared sheet and freeze for 20 minutes. Chill the remaining dough in the refrigerator.

// Bake the cookies for 13 to 15 minutes, until golden brown all over. They need to be crispier than normal for the next steps! Cool completely in the refrigerator.

// Make the milk: Pour the milk into a large bowl and add the brown sugar; stir to combine. Use your hands to break 7 of the completely cooled cookies into the cold milk mixture. Place the entire bowl in the refrigerator to soak for at least 30 minutes and no more than 24 hours. Give the bowl a shake or a stir every few minutes while completing the rest of the steps.

// Make 15 heaping teaspoon-size balls out of the remaining dough. Roll in ½ cup of the sprinkles. Set aside.

// Prepare the garnish: Place the remaining 3 completely cooled cookies in a plastic bag and crush them with the back of a measuring cup or a rolling pin. Once the cookies have the consistency of crumbs, add the remaining ½ cup sprinkles to the bag and shake to mix. Lay the crumb mixture on a plate.

// Prepare shot glasses. In a small microwave-safe bowl, heat the chocolate chips in the microwave on 50% power in 30-second increments. Stir well between each increment. Repeat just until the chocolate is melted. Dip the rim of a shot glass into the melted chocolate, then immediately dip it into the crumb and sprinkle mixture. Set on a serving tray to set. Repeat with the remaining shot glasses.

// Remove the milk from the refrigerator. Pour through a sieve into a pitcher. Lightly push on the cookies in the sieve to get all of the milk out, but don't push hard enough that cookie comes through the sieve. Stir in the vanilla.

// Pour the milk into the shot glasses. Use a knife to cut a slice about halfway through each cookie dough ball. Place the slice over the rim of the shot glass.

Store in the refrigerator and serve when the party gets started! The shots are best enjoyed within 2 hours of being poured.

/////////// *Kristen's Tip* ///////////

If you don't have time to make your cookies from scratch for Cookie Milk, you can head to the grocery store and pick out your favorite boxed variety. Just make sure they are the crispy kind!

//

\ *MAKES*
25 to 30 truffles

\ *ACTIVE TIME*
40 minutes

\ *TIME 'TIL TRUFFLES*
1 hour 40 minutes

Un-Bake-A-Balls

CUSTOMIZE *Me* · GREAT MADE *GF*

These guys are super cute, very sweet, and can be literally anything you want them to be. No, they are not on Tinder (sad, I know), but they are worth having an intimate relationship with. Dress them up and take them to your next party to make everyone jealous. Have fun! Go ballistic! Enjoy your cute date!

These customizable treats are perfect for any occasion. You can make them any flavor, add sprinkles or food coloring, make them into cute little characters, or serve them on a stick. Some of my favorite flavor combinations include:

- **Cake Batter dough (page 76) and white chocolate chips**

- **Peanut Butter dough (page 72) and milk chocolate chips**

- **Signature Chocolate Chip dough (page 60) and dark chocolate chips**

- **Blondies Have More Fun dough (page 228) and butterscotch chips**

- **Brownie Batter dough (page 64) and peanut butter chips**

1 batch any cookie dough (pages 54 to 184), chilled

2 cups any kind of chocolate chips (see suggestions above)

2 tablespoons coconut oil

6 tablespoons toppings, like chopped nuts, sprinkles, or mini chips

// Use a cookie scoop to portion cookie dough, then roll it between your hands to form a smooth ball. Freeze the balls for 1 hour.

// In a small microwave-safe container, microwave the chocolate chips and coconut oil on 50% power in 30-second increments, stirring well between each increment until melted and smooth. Don't overheat! Let the chocolate mixture cool slightly, about 5 minutes, stirring occasionally.

// Dip the cookie dough into the chocolate mixture using a fork or toothpick. Let the truffles drain on a wire rack set over waxed paper. Sprinkle with the toppings while the chocolate is still wet. Let the chocolate set for 30 minutes to 1 hour. Add additional decorations if you'd like. Serve the truffles chilled.

Store the truffles in an airtight container in the refrigerator for up to 10 days.

/////////// *Kristen's Tip* ///////////

This truffle recipe can also be made into the cutest chocolate-covered cookie dough cups! Just drop a teaspoon of melted chocolate into a mini-cupcake liner. Use a brush or waxed paper to drag chocolate up the sides of the liner and freeze for 10 minutes. Then put a teaspoon of dough in the center, flatten it out a bit with your fingers, cover with more chocolate, and freeze to set.

///

You're Basically a Blogger Sprinkles

PLAN Ahead · **NATURALLY GF**

Pinterest fails. We've all had them. You see that sparkling rainbow butterfly cake in your feed and think, "I have to make that for my niece's birthday!!" Four hours, $50 in ingredients, and a small mental breakdown later all you have is an embarrassing, lopsided blob that sort of resembles a butterfly, and your niece is getting a standard grocery store cake. Say buh-bye to your pride and your bank account.

These sprinkles aren't like that. You can make them in her most favorite color (or, you know, sparkly rainbow butterfly colors), and when you wake up the next morning you'll have a guaranteed sprinkle success! Get to sprinkling, you blogger you.

2 cups confectioners' sugar, sifted

2 tablespoons meringue powder

3 tablespoons water, at room temperature, plus more if needed

Gel food coloring

// Sift the confectioners' sugar into the bowl of a stand mixer fitted with the paddle attachment. Sprinkle the meringue powder into the bowl. Add 2 tablespoons of the water and stir with the mixer on low.

// Add the remaining 1 tablespoon water. The mixture should be thick but not dry. Add water by the teaspoon if your mixture is too dry.

// Divide the mixture into bowls and add a single color of your desired food coloring to each bowl. I find that using a fork to stir in the food coloring works well.

// Transfer each colored mixture to its own piping bag fitted with the tiny tip (I use a #4 tip for this). Pipe straight lines onto the waxed paper. Pipe dots of the mixture onto the waxed paper for round sprinkles.

// Let dry for at least 10 hours or up to 3 days. These sprinkles really need to set! Use a sharp knife to chop the sprinkles into your desired length. Roll round sprinkles with your fingertips to break off any uneven edges. Top your favorite desserts, ice cream sundaes, or even your coffee for a little extra fun!

Store the sprinkles in a mason jar or other airtight container at room temperature for up to 3 months.

290

MADE TO PARTY: CUSTOMIZABLE
TREATS & SERVING SECRETS

MAKES
18 bowls

ACTIVE TIME
25 minutes

TIME 'TIL TRUFFLES
2 hours 45 minutes

Cookie Bowls

KRISTEN'S
Fav

The word "bowl" brings back bad memories. I was traumatized by the bowl cut that began my seven-year awkward phase. I know everyone "says" they have an awkward phase, but mine truly was a disaster (see photo).

Looking back, I can laugh about it. I had an uncanny resemblance to Minkus from *Boy Meets World*. Yes, the little nerdy BOY. Glasses, shorts, blonde bowl cut, that was all me. I was Minkus, reincarnated into a food-loving, sometimes girly tomboy. No one knows what my mom was thinking.

In order to forget about the bowls that still give me nightmares, I made my own—meet the cookie bowl. A much less awkward, much cuter bowl that is much more likely to get invited to the party. Grab some ice cream, some cookie dough, some toppings of your choice, and let's all forget about Minkus.

2¼ cups heat-treated all-purpose flour (instructions on page 31)

1 teaspoon cornstarch

½ teaspoon baking soda

½ teaspoon salt

1½ sticks (12 tablespoons) unsalted butter, at room temperature

¼ cup granulated sugar

1 cup brown sugar

⅓ cup pasteurized egg whites, at room temperature

2 teaspoons vanilla extract

½ cup semisweet chocolate chips

// Make the cookie dough, using the ingredients listed in this recipe and following the method on page 60. Remove the bowl from the stand mixer. Use a rubber spatula to fold in the chocolate chips. Stick the bowl in the refrigerator for at least 1 hour to chill.

// Preheat the oven to 350°F and flip over two standard 18-hole cupcake pans.

// Remove the dough from the refrigerator and divide into 18 even portions. Use your hands to roll each portion into a ball. Flatten each ball into a circular disk shape, about ¼ inch thick. Place the cookie dough disk on the cupcake mold and fold the edges of the dough around the sides. The cookie dough should come only halfway down the mold and it should be cupping the mold evenly on all sides and hugging it tightly. Use your fingers to close any cracks and smooth the surface of the dough. Repeat with all portions of dough, 9 portions per pan.

// Freeze the entire pans for 15 minutes. Place in the oven and bake for 15 to 20 minutes, until the edges are browned and the tops are golden brown all over. Remove from the oven and let the entire pan cool on the counter for 5 minutes and place in the freezer for about 30 minutes.

// Once completely frozen, remove the pan and bend opposite corners in opposite directions like you would with an ice tray. The cookie cups will pop right off.

// Fill your bowls with ice cream, cookie dough, toppings, and whatever makes you happy!

The cookie bowls can be used immediately, stored in an airtight container for up to 3 days, or frozen for up to 1 month.

You're Basically a
Blogger Sprinkles,
page 289

Pretty in Pink Party

Ain't no party like a cookie dough party! Any occasion becomes instantly sweeter with the addition of a few sprinkles, a lot of cookie dough, some festive serving tricks, and a happy hostess. Make every get-together one to remember with these ideas for taking a simple dessert to a party-time main event.

MAKE 'EM POP!

Cookie DŌ Crispies (page 276) are fun, but you can kick the party up a notch by cutting them into special shapes or poppin' them on a stick. These fancy pops can be arranged as a display by sticking them into some floral foam. Encourage your guests to grab one and to go mingle.

SPECIALIZE YOUR STACK

My Ult-DŌ-Mate Cookie Lover's Cake (page 257) makes for a stunning centerpiece. Make it your own by customizing the dough layers. Have a spring soiree? Try Best Berry Crisp (page 127)! Planning a baby shower? One layer of Frosted Fork (page 103) and a layer of Me Want Cookie (page 100) will create a cake that's the talk of the party—perfect if you're forgoing a gender reveal.

BRILLIANT BITE-SIZE BARS

Decadent dessert bites look impressive arranged on a tiered stand. For a festive serving style, cut any sliceable treat into bite-size squares and serve them in colorful cupcake liners. Look at the fudge bites (page 240) in this picture—so easy to pick up, and easy on the eyes too!

SHOTS! SHOTS! SHOTS! SHOTS!

Cookie Milk Shots (page 285) are just the beginning! Rim shot glasses with sanding sugar, dyed chocolate, Pop Rocks, or anything that will match your party's theme. These single-serving sips are ready to add a little flair to your dessert table.

BUILD A SUNDAE BAR

Give your event an interactive twist with a build-your-own sundae bar. A bowl of cookie dough, a bowl of ice cream, all your favorite toppings, and hot fudge to top it off; what more could a guest want?! To keep ice cream cold for hours: Place ice cream in a medium bowl. Place that bowl in a much larger bowl. Fill the empty space in the larger bowl with ice and sprinkle generously with kosher salt. Pour about ½ cup of cold water over the salted ice. Set the bowl on your bar for ice cream that will stay scoop-able for hours!

A FESTIVE WINTER
WonDŌland

It's the most wonDŌful time of the year...recipes don't need to be designed for the holidays for a wintery soiree; classic flavors are instantly holiday-ready with the right garnish and presentation piece.

SPRINKLES ARE THE BOMB

Sprinkles can tie a dessert table together. Use sprinkles that complement your theme (if you can't find the right color, make them yourself; see page 289) to top bars, cover pies, or mix into your favorite dough. You can even make any bomb recipe (page 277 or 278) and fill it with sprinkles, instead of piping in the filling. Your guests are in for a festive surprise when they take their first bite, and they make a great 'gram.

HOSTESS WITH THE MOSTESS CAKE

Have a cookie lover on your hands, but need a cake and candle moment? You know I have you covered! Any dough recipe can become a cookie cake. Make sure to grease a 9" round cake pan very well. Then press the dough into the pan in a single, even layer. Bake in a preheated 350°F oven for 15 to 18 minutes, until the edges are golden brown and the center is set.

BETTER WHEN BITE-SIZE

A spoonful of dough is delightful. A fresh cookie is truly satisfying. But sometimes you just need a bite-size option for your partygoers. Shape into one-bite balls, roll in sprinkles, and serve in mini cupcake liners. They're totally adorable and the ideal size to pop in your mouth during cocktail hour.

COLORFUL CHOCOLATE COVERED COOKIE DOUGH

My Un-Bake-A-Balls (page 286) can be made in so many colors. Add food coloring to melted white chocolate, dip your dough, and cover in your favorite sprinkles. Ta da! A pop to match any party theme.

PERFECT PRESENTATION PIECES

Pack dough into charming vessels. Mini mason jars for a shabby chic get-together or shot glasses for a truly turnt-up celebration. For a to-go treat, pack up pint-size containers. Don't forget a pretty bowl of tiny spoons so your friends can dig in!

CHIC AND CLASSY CUT-OUTS

Cut-out cookies don't have to be childish. A less-is-more approach to pastel royal icing and elegant sprinkles take them from kids' table to hostess gift. Super Soft Sugar Cookie Cut-Outs (page 287) and Gingerbread Man of My Dreams (page 151) can be rolled out and cut into any shape you need. Have you tried a gingerbread football? Go for it!

Acknowledgments

This cookbook has been a very sweet dream come true. As a young girl, I got lost in cookbooks. I never dreamed I would write one of my own. Because of the help of so many talented, patient, kind, and generous humans, my dream is a reality.

I can't even begin to decide who gets the most awkwardly long hug or to whom I owe my firstborn child.

I first have to thank all of our wonderful fans, customers, and followers. Thank you for loving cookie dough as much as I do, for embracing this "no, no" no more mentality, for sharing your DŌ experiences on social media, and for indulging in your inner child. Thank you for allowing me to share my cookie dough obsession with all of you! You're the reason I do what I do.

To the entire Grand Central team including Brittany, Morgan, Albert, Ben, Tiffany, Staci, Matthew, Karen, Amanda, Leda, Yasmin, and the many others silently working behind the scenes—Thank you for believing in me and in this project from the very beginning. Your patience, guidance, and understanding with all my stubborn control-freak-like tendencies will forever be appreciated.

To my agent, Alison—I'm so glad I was able to trick you into taking me on as an author...even when you made it clear on our first call that you weren't taking new clients. You just got it from the start, and I knew you were the one. You saw my vision and helped me execute when I didn't have a playbook to follow. Thank you for championing my ideas, for talking me off the ledge, and for being the best sounding board a first-time author could ever have. I definitely won the agent lottery with you!!!

To Kelly, Sarah, Tara & everyone else at The Door. You're so much more than just my PR gals. You're my advisors, my emergency help (LOL looking at you, Kelly), my confidants, my best cheerleaders, and my friends. You all rock!

To Ally—my long-lost assistant and go-to girl. I have so many things to thank you for, but for this project specifically, thank you for abducting my brain and successfully translating everything I knew I wanted to say (but didn't know how to) onto an actual piece of paper. I think I would still be on the first sentence of the opening paragraph had it not been for you. Your dedication, attention to detail, and love for all things DŌ means more to me than you'll ever know.

Oh, Mandy—Mandy, Mandy, Mandy. PEOPLE...without Mandy this book would exist only as cookie crumbs in my keyboard. Seriously. I don't think either of us knew what we were getting ourselves into when we met in that coffee shop on West 3rd Street and talked about having you "help" with this cookbook project. I didn't know how badly I needed you until you came in like a boss and immediately ran the show. THANK YOU for treating this cookbook like your baby, giving it lots of love, attention, and late nights. I appreciate you never holding back your opinion, for calling me out on all my bulls*t, and for making what would be a jumbled rambling mess of recipes and stories into a thoughtful, meaningful piece of work I am truly proud of. I am beyond grateful for your help and our friendship. I will never be able to look like I'm smiling naturally without your help. I guess I'll give you my firstborn child only because I know you'll hand it right back:) I can't wait for what's next for you...

My forever OG Squad, Bri and Rikki—Thank you for buckling your seat-belts very early on and coming along on this crazy ride with me. As always, you rolled up your sleeves and got to work on this project without me even asking. Your loyalty and dedication is like no other. And our friendship is one I hold very close to my heart. I am indebted to you both for life. You'll always be my OGs. My Dream Team. My Squad. And to all of my DŌ employees past, present, and future: Doesn't matter how big or small your role was, is, or will be, I am grateful for you, and I thank you for being a part of this adventure.

If you have even glanced at this book, you can immediately recognize the talented team of magic photo ninjas that made all of my recipes come to life so beautifully on the page. Evan—you're a dream to work with. Thank you for putting so much love into making sure that every single photo captured a story and portrayed a perfect moment in time. Sarah—your eye and attention to detail made my vision for this book come alive. Thank you (and Quinn) for guiding me, pushing me, and making every single shot so special. And Erin—your ability to make each bite look extra gooey, melt-y, warm, fresh, sweet, and fun is a true talent. Thanks for allowing so many cooks in the kitchen. I think what we all accomplished together is nothing short of amazing. And I can't forget about Azra, for the small miracles you perform by making me look camera ready, well rested, and somehow like I have eyelashes. You're a true hero.

Laura—I am so lucky to be able to work with you on the design of the book. Your creativity, attention to detail, and impeccable design sense are like no other. You so gracefully navigated my insane asks and channeled my vision a million times better than I could have ever imagined.

All of my best friends truly deserve medals for being so supportive, so inspiring, and so helpful through the journey of starting a business and writing this book. Thank you for responding to manic late-night texts, holding my hand through the ups and downs, pouring me a margarita when I needed it most, and for challenging me to be the best I can be. Kate, Liz, Jen, Melissa, Emily, Caroline, Emily, Sara, Peggy, Jen, Stacy, Edana, Kristen, Meagan...and the list goes on...You get a medal, and you get a medal, and you get a medal (!!!!). I owe you all forever.

To the many (former) coworkers, random friends of friends, and complete strangers that I canvassed for feedback on every cookie dough topic known to man—whether it was trusting me enough to eat whatever I put in front of you, offering your opinion on my latest idea, or responding to an Instagram poll, your support and honesty through his journey is humbling and so helpful.

A huge shout-out to all of my recipe testers and taste testers along the way (and there are so many of you) who made sure each and every recipe and creation was more delicious than the next. I apologize for force-feeding you endless pounds of cookie dough, making you try *just* one more bite, and for making you bake the same thing over and over and over until you could whip it up in your sleep. Everyone who buys this book appreciates you! An especially large heart-shaped emoji goes to Hilari, Khatija, Mandy (again), and my mom! You made this book SO MUCH BETTER.

This book wouldn't be nearly as sparkly, colorful, and fabulous without the help of Rosie at @sweetapolita! Thank you for providing the sprinkles you see, giving me lots of glistening inspiration, and for adding a touch more sweetness to these pages (and recipes)!

Mom & Dad—I am forever thankful to you both. Mom, you inspired me to follow my heart from a very young age, to get messy in the kitchen, to be fiercely independent, and to never settle. My passion for cooking and baking comes from you. Thank you for being such a great mom, friend, and role model. Your willingness to recipe test and proofread at a moment's notice is much appreciated. I am so lucky to have your contribution to this project and to all aspects of my life! Dad, thank you for being my #1 fan and DŌ's best taste tester. Thank you for your endless support, listening ear, constant offer to "write me a doctor's note" so I can take a day off, and for always wanting what's best for me. I am grateful to you both for your unconditional love (especially when I was a shitty teenager). I love you!!

To my siblings—thanks for always supporting and challenging me. I wouldn't be nearly the weirdo I am today without your childhood participation. To Lauren—my wannabe twin. I'm so proud to be your little sister. Thank you for setting the best example for me to look up to, for being my voice when I truly couldn't speak for myself, and for being my best friend. You are a SAINT! Thank you to Trey for always making me laugh no matter what the situation. You give the best hugs and the best advice. Maddie—you'll always be my baby doll little sister. You know exactly how to brighten my day, how to inspire me to just be me, and how to make me feel old AF as you grow into the amazing woman you are.

To my brothers- and sister-in-law, James, Ryan, and Lindsey—thank you for your refreshing perspective. You know exactly how to see the positive in any situation, and I so appreciate you supporting me (and Chris) every step of the way. Whether it's legal advice, accounting help, or random life lessons, I know I can trust you to look out for what's best for me. I'm so lucky you are my family. Plus, ya'll make cute kids, so keep that up! Being their aunt is the best!

John and Shawn—I know whenever I need you, you will drop everything to come help out, which you have done many times in the past and will likely do many times in the future. You lead by example in teaching me the importance of always prioritizing family. I feel very lucky to be a Tomlan. Thank you!

To my everything, Chris. Thank you for never giving up. You are my rock, my soul-mate, and the absolute best friend a girl could ask for. You inspire me to work harder, think smarter, and be my true self every single day. You are heaven sent, and I feel incredibly blessed to be sharing this wild ride with you. Good thing you like cookie dough:)

Index

About the Author

KRISTEN TOMLAN is the founder and CEO of DŌ, Cookie Dough Confections, the world's first edible cookie dough confectionery. Her unique take on the formerly forbidden treat is a viral success and has inspired fans worldwide, including the likes of Reese Witherspoon, Kim Kardashian, Ryan Seacrest, and Chrissy Teigen, to eat cookie dough just the way they crave it, straight out of the mixing bowl! After starting this nostalgic nationwide trend, Kristen and her cookie dough have been featured by publications including *The New York Times*; *People* magazine; *O, The Oprah Magazine*; and *Food Network Magazine*.

Kristen, a graduate of the College of Design, Architecture, Art, and Planning (DAAP) at the University of Cincinnati, left a successful career as a design consultant when she founded DŌ in 2014. Since then, the brand has expanded to include a flagship scoop shop in New York City's Greenwich Village, partnerships with brands like Bloomingdale's and WeWork, appearances on shows like *The Chew* and *TODAY* to demo her confections, and thousands of nationwide shipments of cookie dough creations each year. She lives in Brooklyn with her husband, Chris, and their rescue pup, Nelly.